A HANDBOOK TO ASSESS AND TREAT RESISTANCE IN CHEMICAL DEPENDENCY

Michael J. Taleff, Ph.D., CAC, MAC

KENDALL/HUNT PUBLISHING COMPANY
4050 Westmark Drive   Dubuque, Iowa 52002

DEDICATION

To Stella Taleff
A most remarkable, loving, and noble human.
I have been blessed to have you as my mother.

TABLE OF CONTENTS

PREFACE   xi

CHAPTER 1: ARE YOU SURE YOU'VE "GOT" WHAT YOU'VE "GOT"   1
The Proverbial View of Resistance   4
Resistance - A Matter of Perspective   4
Tales of Being Stuck   7

CHAPTER 2: CLIENT RESISTANCE: VARIATIONS ON A THEME   11
  SECTION I: DENIAL   11
The Denial Decision Tree   11
Denial in General   12
The Traditional AODApproach to Denial   13
Denial in the Relapse Process   19
Professionals in Denial   19
Some Non-traditional Views of Denial   20
The Polar Opposite of Denial--Surrender, Acceptance, Avowal   23
True Denial   23
The Unconscious Factor in Denial   24
Some Minor Problems with the Unconscious Approach   25
The Conscious Element of Denial: Deception and Self-Deception   27
Excuse Making   27
Self-Deception   27
Motivations That Drive People to Deceive   28
Denial Lookalikes   31
The Physiological Aspects of Denial   31
Confusion   33
Ambivialence   34
Other Denial "Lookalikes"   35
A Summary of the Denial Decision Tree   38
Summary of the Decision Tree Branches   38
Chapter Summary   40

  SECTION II: ALCOHOL AND OTHER DRUG RESISTANCE:
  THROUGH THE   EYES OF MAJOR THEORISTS   41
The Content-Oriented View of Resistance   41
A Case in Point   43
The Varities of Content-Oriented Resistance   44
The Analytic Concept of Resistance   44
A few Freudian Defensive Styles   45
The Neo-Freudian Views of Resistance   47
Wilham Reich   47
George Vaillant   48
A Hierarchy of Defenses   49

Ten Major Defenses and the Association to AOD Dependency   50
The Gestalt View of Resistance   52
The Resistance Thoughts of Perls   52
Gestalt "Resistance"   53
Resistance From a Cognitive Perspective   55
Resistance According to Rational-Emotive-Behavioral Therapy   55
Resistance as a Cognitive Style   57
An Attribution Cognitive Approach to Resistance   60
Dissonance   62
Feelings Thought to Be our of Control   62
Reactance   62
Control: Not in My Hands   63
The Perferred Defense Structure of Alcoholics   64
Resistance in Relapse Dynamics   65
The Context View of Resistance   66
The Death of Resistance   67
Treatment Stratigies Using Solution Therapy   68

SECTION III: EVERYDAY RESISTANCE   70
An AOD Version of Otain's Perspective of Resistance   70
Factors That Generate Everyday Resistance   70
Category A Resistances   72
Category B Resistances   73
Intellectual Talk   73
Emotional Display   73
Symptom Preoccupation   74
Future/Past Preoccupation   74
Rhetorical Questions   75
Category C Resistances   75
Discounting   75
Limit Setting   76
Externalization   76
Second Guessing   76
Counselor Stroking   76
Seductiveness   77
Forgetting and not Understanding   77
Category D Resistances   78
Poor Appointment Keeping   78
Payment Delayed or Refusal to Pay   78
Some Last Versions of Everyday Resistance   78
The Protective Function of Resistance   78
Misconceptions About Treatment   79
Boat-Rockers   79
Developmental Resistance   80
Chapter Summary   81

CHAPTER 3: COUNSELOR RESISTANCE: WHEN WE, THE HELPERS,
    ARE RESISTANT   83
    Creating Our Own Resistance   83
    Why Would the AOD Therapist Create Resistance?   85
    Countertransference   85
    Other Reasons for Counselor Generated Resistance   87
    Just Plain Frustration   87
    Developmental Impediments   88
    "Iron Butt"   89
    Poor Training   89
    Mindlessness   90
    Poor Thinking as a Factor in Generating Resistance   91
    "My Personal Experience"   93
    Novice Anxiety   94
    Technical Terms and the Problem of Labeling   95
    Jumping Into a Session Without Preparation   96
    Pedestal Counselors   96
    The All Knowing Type   96
    The Too Busy Type Counselor   97
    The Assumtpive Manner Type   97
    Power Issues   97
    Counselor Traits That Diminish The Resistance Factor   98

CHAPTER 4: PROGRAM AND SYSTEM RESISTANCE   103
    Resistance At The Larger Level   103
    Field Resistance Thinking   103
    Group/Staff Pressured Resistance   105
    Additional Group/Staff Sourses of Resistance   107
    Suggested Anti-Group/Staff Remedies   107
    Program Resistance   108
    Resistance Generated by Literature Style   109
    Educational Induced Resistance   110
    The Clash of Different Styles of Thought   111
    The Pressure to Produce and the Resulting Resistance   112
    Nature of a Treatment Center   112
    Idols in the Mind   115
    Chapter Summary   116

CHAPTER 5: FAMILY AND GROUP STYLES OF RESISTANCE   117
    SECTION I: FAMILY RESISTANCE   117
    Insight-Oriented Family Resistances   117
    Family Process Resistance   118
    Enabling   120
    A Brief Survey of Initial Family Barriers   121

Context-Meaning Oriented Family "Resistances"   123
General AOD Family Treatment Suggestions   124
Suggested Things Not to Do   125
Suggested Things to Do   125
Section Summary   126

SECTION II: GROUP RESISTANCE   127
Types of Resistance Found In A Group Setting   127
The Group Content Resistance Orientation   127
An Assortment of Group Resistances   127
Early Group Resistance - Ambivalence   128
Silence   128
Excessive Talking   129
Flight   130
Manipulation   131
Pairing or Alliances   132
Acting Out   132
Breaches of Confidentiality   133
Power in the Group   133
Use of Chemical by a Group Member While Still in Group   133
The Context Oriented Approach To Group Resistance   134
General Group Treatment Recommendations   134
Section Summary   135

CHAPTER SIX: TECHNIQUES AND STRATEGIES   137
A Possible Resistance Avoidance Template   138
A Second Possible Resistance Template   140
Patient Matching - Content Style   142
Assessment Guide - Content Patient Matching   143
Patient Matching - Content Type   144
More Ideas To Reduce Resistance   144
Regard/Respect   145
Regard   145
Respect   145
Empathy   146
Authenticity   148
Concreteness   148
The Fine Art Of Feedback (Criticism)   149
Listening - Really Listening   151
Poor Listening Behaviors   151
Positive Listening Behaviors   152
The Biggie - Confrontation   154
Confrontation Proper   156
If You Have to Use Confrontation, Try This   157
Contextual Resistance Interventions   160

Metaphors   160
Metaphor Construction   162
Reframing   164
Solution/Brief Approaches to Treating Resistance   165
Some Basics   165
Paths That Lead to Resistance   169
Chapter Summary   170

POSTSCRIPT   171

REFERENCES   173

PREFACE

Given all the books on alcohol and other drug (AOD) treatment, one would think that an **entire** volume on the resistance factor in AOD treatment would be written by now. The concept seems like a natural idea given the endless discussion about resistant AOD clients, enabling behavior, or whole societies being in some kind of denial. Since no one has attempted such a task, this will be a first.

There are numerous journal articles and sections of books that have been written on the subject. However, there isn't a single book that exclusively addresses the broad panorama of the subject, nor brings together the wide range of existing resistance ideas in a single volume. This book provides a rich overview of those many concepts. The AOD field has never had a distinct guidebook on resistance to which it can turn, and work up new perspectives, ideas, and directions on how to engage this troublesome subject.

A first goal, therefore, is to give the reader a sweeping review of resistance as it is found in AOD treatment today. In this process, the reader is asked to constantly step back and make an effort to see the larger picture of resistance. Once this larger representation is set in place, the counselor can determine with more accuracy what it is he/she faces, and then, more effectively treat it.

This broad sweep sets the tone for the second critical goal -- that resistance is a matter of perspective. If I view it in a singular or narrow fashion I will be limited by the parameters of that view, and in turn, will treat it according to the dictates of those constrictions. If that model doesn't work -- with what am I left? The answer is -- no fresh treatment options. Then, I am stuck, as is the client.

The book is primarily for the AOD practitioner who encounters some form of this phenomenon each and every working day. It can also be used by the allied disciplines who encounter the drug and alcohol client in their work.

Writing a book tends to change a person. I am not the same person, professionally or personally, who started researching this volume years ago. I would like to think I've grown a bit. This process of growth did not come with out a price. It created profound doubt and discomfort about many of my past cherished methods and perceptions. But, that doubt allowed me to ask tough questions about the assumed resistance "facts" that permeate my field. By asking the tough questions, I find that my own counseling no longer assaults resistance. I am more flexible and engage resistance differently these days. I can differentiate it, reframe it, or sometimes just do away with the whole idea. The creativity that comes from such a perspective is sweet breath of fresh air from an often stifling field. I hope the same can happen to the reader. Perhaps you will also question yourself, your cherished theories, and techniques and subsequently grow as a result.

I am indebted to a range of people who helped with this project. This includes Brooks Slaybough, Jim Lear, plus many of my students at Penn State for their great work in helping me research this topic. Bert Nemchick made some early editing ideas. Marguerite Babcock, a fellow conspirator, also made additional edits, plus let me know that some ideas were helpful in her treatment work. Melissa Shine doubled checked the many references used in the work. Janis Van Zant my illustrator. Finally, April Neal was the first to read the entire manuscript, and made numerous suggestions to make the book more readable.

CHAPTER ONE

ARE YOU SURE YOU'VE "GOT" WHAT YOU'VE "GOT"

> There are so many vantage points.
> They change in flight.
> What matters is to leave off
> crawling in the dust.
>
> Christian

Picture this ...

You have been assigned to lead of group of twelve people who have been pressured into a drug and alcohol treatment group. They have been either court mandated into treatment, or told they will not have a job or marriage if they do not comply.

It is the first session. You open the door to the group room and take a quick glance at the assembly. They are a seething angry looking crowd. Some of the body language resembles a lynch mob with arms folded high on their chests, and you can almost see whiffs of angry smoke coming out of their ears. Others are slouched and indifferent to your presence. Some are glaring at you with daggers shooting from their eyes.

You try to introduce yourself and are met with grunts and groans. Several members even begin to voice their misgivings at having to be in this damn group. They voice their reluctance in a challenging if not intimidating manner.

You start to explain this is a drug and alcohol group and some voice from the back blares out, "Are you going to try to tell us were alcoholics? Well, I think that's bullshit." What's your assessment of the situation?

You might be fairly inaccurate if you jumped to the conclusion they were in some sort of denial If you thought it was something like reactance, you might be closer to the mark (explanation coming up). Just because something looks like denial, does not make it so. It could be merely a reflection of a biased and restricted point of view. That is what modern AOD therapists need to determine. They must constantly ask themselves tough questions that center on accountability. For example, one might ask, "Is my assessment of a situation accurate, or am I simply seeing things only from my point of view?"

If you were convinced the above situation was an AOD group exhibiting classic symptoms of denial, you would, in turn, probably choose a treatment strategy to break through the assumed resistance. That is the classic AOD approach. In this mind-set, breaking through the denial has as it's goal that the client will gain insight or come to their senses, in order to begin a recovery process. More than likely if you attempted to break through denial with this crowd, you would probably create more resistance. Why? (insert picture 1)

Because the 'breaking through' strategy would not correctly match the problem which in this case is *reactance*.

Denial usually entails some kind of avoidance, or opposition to past painful memories. To be sure this group was oppositional, but they didn't seem to be agonizing over past memories. They were angry about the coerced situation. In this case, the phenomena of reactance is more to the point. It is generally defined as an angry reaction to the threat of one's freedom. Consider how you have felt whenever anyone told you what to do, or you had no choice in a matter. You might have become oppositional and angry. Many people do that when their freedom is threatened. It looks like denial, but upon closer examination it turns out not to be the case.

Putting together a treatment plan that is based on avoidance issues (denial), when in fact, the client feels that their freedom is being threatened, would miss the treatment plan mark. It would create even more problems.

Thus, how can you be more confident of any resistance assessment you make?

That is what this book is about. Determining the real blockages to treatment and then addressing those issue(s). Egan (1994) indicated that our job is to understand the thoughts feelings and actions of our clients and not some imperfect belief.

There are a host of ideas and theories as to how and why the AOD client will resist a treatment intervention. This book will review many of these scenarios. But we have to be cautious because resistance is in no way the exclusive domain of our clients. It is also manifest in the drug and alcohol counselor.

We counselors play a major role in the development of resistance. How? Shaffer and Robbins (1995) have noted that counselors often create resistance because we become locked into a single point of view. Exclusive dependence on a "pet" theory can skew the way we view clients, and this distortion may create difficulties resulting in resistance. For example, if counselors favor the dynamic point of view they may tend to see the client in terms of hydraulics (i.e., the push and pull of conscious and unconscious factors influencing behavior). If the counselor favors a cognitive perspective, he/she will tend to see the client using irrational thinking styles.

Traditionally, the burden of responsibility for the recovery was placed squarely on the shoulders of the client. In this book, it is proposed that we take our share of responsibility by accounting for our actions as well. In this light, we must be responsible for the treatment strategies we select and use. And, that selection will be based on the perceptions we favor. If an approach isn't working, we must be able to quickly and, in an assured manner, adjust to another more fruitful strategy, rather than take days, weeks, or sometimes months to do so. In addition, AOD practitioners create resistance when our "personal issues" get in the way of a therapeutic encounter. Some call these "personal issues" countertransference or unfinished business which can, in turn, impede effective treatment (see Chapter 3).

Yet, the phenomena of client or counselor induced resistance doesn't stop with the reactant group, it is generated within the AOD field itself. As with the individual counselor, a major factor that determines field resistance is it's exclusive reliance on a single point of view to treat the complexity of alcohol and other drug problems. It's this over reliance on a single paradigm, which gets in the way of new ideas and fresh strategies.

THE PROVERBIAL VIEW OF RESISTANCE

The conventional reputation of AOD client is one of a difficult or refractive individual, or sometimes simply labeled "a pain." They have been quickly diagnosed with a label of "borderline" or tagged as "beyond help." AOD clients don't arrive at this reputation all by themselves. Frustrated and under trained AOD counselors foster this perspective. In addition, we counselors often generalize and stereotype our clients, which adds to the propensity to generate resistance. Yet, as Miller and Rollnich (1991) suggests, if we roll with the resistance and provide empathy, we obtain co-operation not resistance.

There has been a fair amount of material written on the subject of AOD resistance, but much of this material conforms to with the one-sided approach we just considered.
The traditional treatment approach to resistance has been perceived as something to be eradicated or obliterated. Freud felt this way about resistance in his early work (Breuer & Freud 893-1895, p: 282). Resistance was to be overcome by any available means "--- by which one can ordinarily exert psychical influence on another".

Resistance, and especially the potentate of resistance -- denial has been perceived as something to be broken through, lest the recovering person slip back into active use. Any form of denial or other resistance is seen to threaten one's recovery. From the traditional point of view, resistance is viewed as nothing short of pernicious, and the preferred choice of treatment is confrontation. Such a mind-set cannot help but create problems for the client and counselor.

In the last few years, there has been some softening of the hard-nosed treatment interventions that have dominated the field. Yet many AOD programs across the country remain locked in a rather rigid, dogmatic approach to treating the resistant substance abuser. Some treatments have been rather crude and abrasive. They were condoned because such "methods" were thought to be necessary to break the resistance or denial. Annis and Chan (1983) have indicated that many clients have relapsed after such abrasive encounters despite what these centers claimed was their rate of success.

RESISTANCE - A MATTER OF PERSPECTIVE

Depending on your outlook, resistance can either serve some kind of a purpose (Freud, 1926/1959), or it can be considered a natural phenomena (McMahon & Jones, 1992), or it can be seen as a concept that gets in the way of real therapy (deShazer, 1984). It all depends on the circumstances and the perception the therapist.

With that thought in mind, AOD therapists need to clearly establish what they have encountered when treatment begins to stall. Labeling a client as resistant , one who is not following a treatment plan, serves little purpose. There may be many other explanations. To slow down this inclination, the therapist needs to pause, reflect and consider alternatives. Then, with a less clouded mind, they can institute an appropriate treatment strategy that will better fit the client. In this manner, therapy can become more effective verses striking out at a client stuck in treatment because the belief system says they are in denial.

The idea that you are a slave to your opinions probably comes as no surprise to people. Yet, many professionals seem content to observe the world and it's people through those opinions. After a time, seeing the world from a certain conceptual window can easily drift into "my window is the right one." This has tremendous ramifications in the chemical dependency field. Creating such "right" windows will sooner or later generate resistance.

How many times have you read a book or attended a workshop and walked away saying to yourself "That's the answer. Now, I've got it."

Returning to your practice, you applied these new found truths to your next client. But to your chagrin, they didn't work. What often happens at this point, is that the practitioner will think to themselves, something is wrong with the client. He/she will again try to form fit the client into this new right theory. If the client remains refractive and does not adjust the result, you guessed it, is more blaming the client for being in resistance.

In such a context, the client begins to see a more rigid counselor, and the therapist begins to see more resistance coming from the client. This circular tunnel reasoning can continue for weeks, months, or in some cases, years.

Whole programs and systems can get caught up in this "My window of truth is right" mind-set. This is not to say that professionals in this field have not created many useful ideas. We have. But, once we dare think we've cornered a piece of the truth, then we will become ineffective with our clients. Why? Because we will only believe our truths and in doing so, we will miss the **living** experience of the other person.

Theories are fine. It is when they take on the texture of righteousness and are then forced onto a client population that the beginning needless resistance will seep into one's treatment work. This is an ever present problem for the drug and alcohol field.

Pause and reflect is the method used to slow down this righteous process. What else can we do to avoid it? The Institute of Medicine, (1990) has gathered evidence for a client-matching treatment approach. Matching tends to make use of the wide variety of treatment methods that are currently available and can demonstrate effectiveness for a particular client. Rather than attempt to form fit our clients into a pet theory, we need to MATCH the theories to our clients.

The theoretical framework for client-matching is straight out of George Kelly's idea of constructive alternatives (Kelly, 1963). He believed that if you can explain a concept (resistance) in another or better way, then the original definition will be suspect. Other explanations will create doubt to any one who holds tight to single theory, but it is through that doubt that new questions for more effective treatment interventions can be formulated. In this way, one can re-think an approach to a client so that is more in tune with what is really happening. It is the job of the AOD practitioner to obtain the clearest explanation of a client's behavior, and then help implement the most effective treatment.

The most significant indication that treatment is matched to a client's needs is that it works.

TALES OF BEING STUCK

When it comes to treating resistance the following examples illustrate what often occurs when professionals and AOD programs get stuck in perceptual ruts.

A client arrives at an inpatient unit. He is accompanied by a family member. He is somber and obviously angry. During the intake process, he begins to spout off that he doesn't want to be here, and if he hadn't been forced by an irate spouse or employer he would be out of this #@*% place in a minute. This attitude is then forwarded to whoever was scheduled to be the primary therapist. The attitude is immediately perceived as an affront to the program, recovery in general, and promptly labeled--DENIAL. The primary therapist who now has this individual on his caseload, will inform a colleague that a real case of denial had just been assigned to his group. The therapist states to the colleague and anyone within earshot something to the effect that, "Wait till I get that person in my group. I'll cut through his crap." The therapist would then puff himself up, rush to his office and proceed to confront this client who is in "denial."

This scenario usually produces some or all of the following:

1. The patient is confronted and gets more angry. He threatens to sue the facility and says something to the effect "I don't have to take this shit," and promptly leaves the program AMA (against medical advice). The client is then perceived as not "hurting enough" and, to be most certainly in some kind of denial.

2. The patient is so intimated or frightened at this confrontational approach that he slips into a compliance mode. In this state, the he plans to "go through the motions", stay out of trouble and avoid any other such confrontations. The perception of the staff is of a client who is cooperative, but who really is not.

3. The client digs his heels in and ends up hating the therapist, the program, self-help groups, and anything associated with treatment. More time is now spent on hating than on recovery. The perception of the staff is that this individual is resistant, while the client perceives the staff to be oppositional and non-empathic.

The obvious problem with all these scenarios is that no real therapy takes place. When approached in this traditional confrontational manner the client often ends up discharging himself, becoming compliant, or defiant. To account for these behaviors the therapist in charge will generally construe that "The client wasn't ready yet." The jest of such statements is to covertly blame the client for being in a state of resistance that was, in part, generated by the therapist.

Another perceptual scenario, such as the following has been known to occur.

A client who seems rather ambivalent upon entering treatment, is admitted to a AOD program. A good rapport is developed and treatment is progressing as expected. As the treatment begins to intensify, the client begins to feel vulnerable and her anxiety level increases as more secrets of her drugging past begin to surface. Feeling uncomfortable, she then begins to resort to some old coping styles such as isolation, silence, and withdrawal.

She resorts to these old defensive styles (withdrawal, and a reluctance to discuss her history) because her addictive past has been painful, and the thought of that past creates additional anguish. In therapy, she's beginning to experience this pain without the relief of her favorite chemicals. The treatment staff begins to interpret this change of pace as a treatment regression. The traditional response to this state of affairs is to "turn up the confrontational heat," because the silence and aloof manner is believed to be a symptom of denial.

The confrontation is applied but only serves to intensify her anxiety. In turn, she brings out more of the old coping habits. Again, no improvement is noted by the staff and more "heat" is applied. A destructive cycle has developed. A staff meeting is called to confer on the matter. The staff agrees that this individual is in denial despite the best efforts of the treatment team. A review of the issue now centers on how the client is beginning to "get over," and that a therapeutic discharge might be in order.

To an outsider, it appears that some major miscommunication has developed because no one is aware of what is really going on. No one has bothered to investigate the real issues. Rather, the client is neatly packaged into a lame concept of denial. She is threatened with discharge, or really discharged, from the treatment program for all the wrong reasons. These reasons center on the staff becoming convinced that their perception of things, is the truth of the matter. Because no other options are explored, discharge seems to be the only feasible answer to this dilemma.

One last scenario involves the counselor who is making a good, honest attempt at his work. He tries to be empathic and open minded but still gets his fair share of resistance. He begins to think "I'm working as hard as I can, but I'm still not getting anywhere." This begins to create some frustration and doubts about his competence. These feelings begin to coalesce into a perceptual pattern of "These addicts are starting to get over on me, and I can't allow that." This type of frustration when shared with other staff who are also experiencing the same type of troubles brews a major cycle of negative reinforcement. Soon a whole treatment team can begin to feel frustrated. With little in the way of alternative ideas, the result can quickly turn any AOD staff into a rigid, thwarted, uncompromising lot. This proves particularly harmful to any new clients who next walk through the door.

A prime example of this type of frustration occurred a in a program where I worked a few years ago. On a crisp autumn evening, one of those frustrated type counselors noticed a new client arriving at our facility. He stood at a window, arms folded high in his chest, watching this new arrival unloading his luggage. We both quietly watched this little drama unfold for a few minutes. Then the counselor turned toward me and declared, "Here's another "liar" (denier) coming into the program." Keep in mind that this counselor hadn't even met this individual, but labeled him long before they encountered one another. Having categorized a client as a liar even before a first meeting can only generate one thing--resistance.

Some might call this type of counselor behavior *burn-out*. Perhaps. Regardless of what it's called, the result is often the same thing, needless resistance created in a therapeutic setting, which is stuck in a perceptual rut. Quality treatment can not work well under such conditions.

Resistance can be generated not only in the clients we treat, but in the people who are supposed to be the professionals in the field at large. Determining if someone is in resistance depends on the manner in which one sees the phenomenon. The seeing is like putting on a set of eyeglasses. Those glasses will change the shape anything that passes through them. In turn, those changed perceptions will have profound influences on treatment. For our purposes, resistance can be defined as those thoughts, feelings, and actions originating in the client, counselor, system, and field that impedes or blocks the general direction of AOD treatment and recovery.

To begin this procedure, step-back and to see the big picture of resistance, the book classifies the phenomena into five major divisions. These include client-generated resistance, counselor-generated resistance, group/family-bred resistance, field-produced resistance, and some research that indicates a productive address of resistance. Each classification is a chapter that will summarize the prevailing literature on the subject. Schematically, this looks like Diagram #1.

Diagram #1

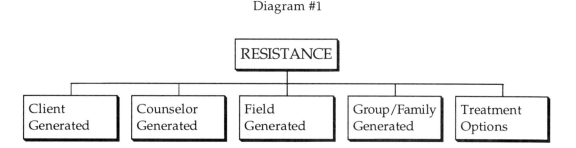

CHAPTER 2

CLIENT RESISTANCE: VARIATIONS ON A THEME

> Some people mistakenly assume that if a very
> large number of people share a value, then
> not only is it real, but it is also right.

> Christian

In this chapter, we will journey through the many definitions and explanations of client resistance. The chapter is divided into three sections to give the reader some sense of separation and clarification on the numerous viewpoints of client resistance. The first section is devoted to that particular form of resistance believed to be intrinsic to AOD treatment--denial. The second section covers the major theoretical explanations of why clients resort to resistance. Section three will cover an assortment of common forms of resistance often encountered by AOD counselors. As outlined in chapter one, you are encouraged to step back and try to examine these ideas at a distance. Hopefully, this will help you gain a wider, if not a more legible, perspective on this issue.

SECTION I - DENIAL

The subject of denial has managed to generate quite a bit of rhetoric. In all this material, it is fair to say that there is not one central overriding definition of the topic. The literature of the field clearly indicates that the subject matter of denial is redefined according to whoever is doing the defining. Such a tangle of explanations can create a high level of confusion to the AOD practitioner.

This chapter will refrain from adding another definition to the many below, because such a definition would run counter to one of the core philosophies of the book--that resistance (and denial) are a matter of perspective. It is not the purpose of this book to purport a truth, but to expose you to a multitude of ideas on this subject. The truth, if it can be attained, is to be determined by the client.

THE DENIAL DECISION TREE

To off set the confusion generated by the many definitions of denial, a decision tree has been developed to give the reader an easier understanding of this complex subject. The tree was built from the available literature on the subject. That material suggested that there are two major forms of denial that are considered to have a more "true" ring to the concept--an unconscious and a conscious type. In addition, there seems to be at least eight forms of client behaviors that look like denial but, in reality, are not. The eight lookalikes can easily be confused with the more standard definitions. If the lookalikes are confused with denial, situations like the one described at the beginning of chapter one can occur. I will build a branch for each one of these forms, so you can gain a clearer picture of the so-called true denial definitions, and those that look like denial.

The tree is intended to assist the AOD assessment process. Recall that a good approach to quality assessment is to differentiate the various types of client behavior. Such knowledge quickly and efficiently directs the tone, direction, and method of treatment. It is necessary for the counselor to ask a few general assessment questions to determine the usefulness of giving a denial label. Assessment needs to center on the following questions:

1. How do I define denial? (What is my bias?)

2. Is this client really in denial, or is it another associated event?

3. If what I am observing is denial, is it of the conscious or unconscious variety?

4. If the behavior turns out not to be an denial, what else could it be?

5. After I establish what the behavior really is, what is the best treatment approach for this individual?

An example from medicine, at this point, might help clarify the importance of a well-defined assessment. Say an individual complains of burning in his/her chest and vomiting after dinner, what would you think could be the problem? To some, it would look like a stomach or gall bladder problem. Yet, these symptoms also are leading signs of a myocardial infarction (MI). The point of this little example is that further analysis and assessment are in order, because the medical interventions of an MI and gall bladder are significantly different. The same can be said of a denial evaluation, is the individual in question, really exhibiting the qualities of denial, or is it some look alike behavior? To ascertain a more definitive answer to that question a more thoughtful analysis of a client is in order. The proposed decision tree can be helpful in this analysis.

However, before we examine the denial decision tree, a short examination of the general concept, the traditional viewpoint, and some non-traditional views of denial are in order. This will set the stage for what follows and give you an extensive overview of the subject.

DENIAL IN GENERAL

Humans seem to be perpetually keeping extensive regions of unwelcome reality out of view. That sentiment seems to have captured the traditional definition of denial. However, during my literature review on this subject, that definition is not the only one I found. I discovered that there are at least three broad themes of denial. First, denial is more involved than the simple avoidance phenomena it is often made out to be. Second, what is traditionally considered denial maybe a glib and too hasty mislabeling of client behavior. Third, any definition of denial is definitely based on the way one looks at it.

The concept "denial," and defenses in general, did not originate with the alcohol and other drug field. It originated with Sigmund Freud and psychoanalysis (Wyss, 1973), but it was Anna Freud (1966; 1946) who really developed the concept. The AOD field simply borrowed the concept and began to apply the term where it seemed to fit. You will notice the analytic shadings in most all of the definitions we will cover in this chapter. This shading is particularly evident in the writings of Wurmser (1978), Bean (1981), and Metzgar (1988). It is ironic that Bob Smith, one of founders of Alcoholics Anonymous, in his farewell address, asked the membership to stay away from all that Freudian stuff. Yet, today, we use a variation of a classic Freudian concept as the cornerstone of much that is called AOD treatment.

In a national survey of professionals across the country, Morgenstern and McGrady (1992) found that those who advocated a disease model approach to AOD, ranked a reduction of denial as the most essential aspect to recovery. Yet, the surveyed behaviorists, who do not give much credence to unconscious processes, didn't even mention denial as a factor in recovery. This is a classic demonstration of denial as a matter of perception.

Denial, however, is not the exclusive domain of addiction. Edelstein, Nathanson and Stone (1989) have found it with cancer patients, cardiac problems, holocaust survivors, homosexuality, parents' attitude toward their children, adolescence, affect blocking, and aging.

It is interesting that the word denial does not appear in the Big Book of Alcoholics Anonymous (1976). On page 31 of that book, the reference to "denial like behavior" is described as *self-deception* on the part of the alcoholic. Some might argue at this point what is the difference? There are indeed differences. Stay tuned.

The fourth edition of the *Diagnostic and Statistical Manual* (American Psychiatric Association, 1994) does not include the term in any of its symptoms of abuse or dependency. What it does state is that an individual will continue with abusive behavior despite knowledge of the harmful effects. There is no mention of self-deception or denial. In many traditional definitions of denial, there is the implication that addicts are not aware of what they are doing to themselves or to their families. This contrast, again, illustrates the different perceptions of denial used in the field.

Many practitioners in the field have assumed that most if not all AOD clients who enter treatment are suffering from some degree of denial. But, according to Lawson (1984), what may appear as denial could turn out to be a client pausing and reflecting on the whole issue of recovery. The client could be pondering what has occurred in his/her life, before committing to another way of living. Given this situation, the counselor needs to ask, "Is this client in denial or just reflecting on his/her past"? and "Are they in denial or reflecting on change?" This is an example of what we mean by Kelly's constructive alternatives (i.e., are there other explanations for a set of behaviors?). The point of an alternative explanation is to ask yourself, "Can I explain a client's behavior in another manner, perhaps in a more appropriate manner?"

THE TRADITIONAL AOD APPROACH TO DENIAL

Today, there is moderately common understanding of denial that most AOD counselors would recognize. It serves as a baseline from which those professionals assess their clients and implement treatment strategies. In addition, it holds the kernels of what will be the first two branches of true denial in the decision tree that follows. First, the reader needs to wade through a number of definitions in order to get an idea of the vast amount of material that exists on the subject. In fact, the following may be a bit of an overkill of information on the subject. But, the central idea is to clearly show that denial is a matter of perspective, and that many authors have developed many perceptions.

Jellinek (1960), the developer of the disease model of alcoholism, noted that in the *crucial phase* of the progression of alcoholism the full-blown symptoms of alcoholism would appear. Among those particular symptoms one would find denial. Bean (1981) stated that denial, as seen from the traditional prospective, is meant "...to cover a whole range of alcoholic tactics to justify, hide, or protect drinking, to block treatment, and to deny responsibility for the consequences of behavior."

The *Encyclopedia of Alcoholism* (O'Brien & Chafetz, 1982) indicates that denial is considered to be a characteristic defense mechanism of alcoholics. The Encyclopedia makes it clear that denial is a refusal to deal with the problems of life. The Encyclopedia definition also includes some of the beliefs held by those of those in denial. These include:

"I can stop any time."
"I do not have a drinking problem."
"I only drink a little."

According to the Encyclopedia these beliefs are those that distinguish the alcoholic from the social drinker. The *Psychiatric Dictionary* (1996) and Milam and Ketcham (1981) echo this refusal to admit the reality of, or the refusal to acknowledge as the primary function of denial. *The Substance Abuse Subtle Screening Inventory: Manual* (1985) describes denial much as the Encyclopedia. According to this manual, it is considered to be central place in addictions. The major focus in denial is the avoidance of recognition that there is a problem. Denial, according to this manual, is difficult to penetrate, which makes the identification of abusers difficult. This is partly due to the associated mechanisms of the minimizing and rationalization that accompanies it (see below).

The Defense Mechanisms Inventory (DMI) manual (Ihilevich & Gleser, 1993) indicates that of the five different types of defense mechanisms that it measures, the *reversal* type it most akin to denial. The authors define this reversal process as one that minimizes or fails to acknowledge assumed internal or external threats which can remove both the threatening and negative affects from one's consciousness. It is difficult to negotiate with a person using defence mechanisms because the threat and negative feelings are no longer seen by that person.

A rating scale for denial was developed by Goldsmith and Green (1988). It is a scale that has eight levels of denial ranging from level 1) *No Problem*, which is a denial of any personal or family problems, to level 8) -- *Life is Difficult*, in which life's problems are seen to be difficult, but I can deal with them. This instrument was seen to be predictive of clinical change and program completion (Newsome & Ditzler, 1993), but other research has not supported that contention (Allen, 1991).

Worden (1987) believes denial comes in two forms. The first is when the alcoholic thinks he/she can drink socially. The second is when the alcoholic insists he/she is different from real alcoholics. Along these same lines, Vaillant (1988) states that it is Alcoholics Anonymous (AA) that underscores the special ways in which alcoholics delude themselves into thinking that it is safe for them to drink. Whalen-Fitzgerald (1988) believes denial to be the hallmark of Jellineck's disease. By this she suggests that alcoholism is the only disease that tells you that you do not have a disease. It is her belief that denial is in the very nature of the disease of alcoholism. She indicates that denial dims and blunts one's self-awareness, and is the magic carpet that alcoholics lay over their tracks to hide them from scrutiny. This same sentiment is voiced by Griffin (1991).

Whalen-Fitzgerald (1988), Twerski (1990), Kearney (1996) and Wallace (1996) believe the alcoholic resorts to denial protect him/herself from the painful aspects of the addictive drinking. The first author in the above list, believes denial accomplishes this protection through three maneuvers. One maneuver entails simply turning the person off. The dynamic of "turning off" is considered to be an unconscious ability and is also considered to be the classic avoidance or evasive quality of denial. The second denial maneuver is to create blind spots which serve as the cornerstone of the alcoholics system of denial. The third is by lying at all levels of behavior.

Alcoholics are said to create blind spots so they can see nothing wrong with what they are doing, and not be held responsible for any drinking actions. In this way, the drinking can continue without any interference. These beliefs suggest that there is a denial protection factor in operation here. That factor is to protect the addiction, i.e., to maintain it so nothing comes between it and it's continued operation.

The problem, with the continued operation of denial, is that is often causes others to suffer including family and friends. In this case, it is referred to as a *garlic defense* (Cummings & Sayama, 1995). That is, those who eat garlic are not aware of the odor, but those who are around this individual are. This can sometimes be an accurate metaphor for the active addict.

Another traditional view of denial is to found in Anderson (1981), and a Hazelton publication entitled *Dealing with Denial* (1975). Here, the concept is described as a lack of awareness due to excessive AOD use. As above, it is considered to be the cardinal feature of addiction. By virtue of its presence, this denial mechanism is claimed to impair one's judgment, which results in self-delusion. In fact, the claim is made that denial is to found in not just in many chemical dependents but in **all** dependents.

Notice the "to be found in all dependents" statement. This is one of those all encompassing statements in which the unsuspecting reader is lead to believe that denial is persuasive in chemical dependency. Yet there is evidence that indicates that denial does not occur in **all** dependents (Whalen, 1978; Jacobson, 1989; Miller & Rollnick, 1991; Miller, 1991).

The traditional perspective (Anderson, 1981; Hazelden, 1985; Fox, 1967) considers denial to have many faces. A summary of these now familiar mechanisms include:

Simple denial -- insisting that alcohol is not a problem despite evidence to the contrary.

Minimizing -- making a problem appear less serious or significant than it actually is.

Blaming (Projection) -- maintaining the cause or responsibility lies outside the self and on something or someone else.

Rationalizing -- offering excuses and justifications for behavior; a "watering down" of the problem so it turns out not to be so important or serious.

Intellectualization -- dealing with addictive behavior on a level of generalization, analysis and theory to the exclusion of the emotional awareness.

Diversion -- changing the subject to avoid a topic that is too threatening.

Hostility -- becoming angry or irritable when any reference is made to drinking or chemical use.

Denial is defined by a host of other authors using this basic format but with their own spin. This list is long but, as stated, it is intended to give you a distinct feel for the traditional view of denial and see the inherent perceptual mind-sets that are often very powerful.

Here we go. Doweiko (1993), calls denial and the mechanisms of rationalization, projection, and minimization the four musketeers of addiction. Flores (1988), outlines a denial list very similar to the one above, but tranposes the essentials of denial from an individual process and applies it to a group process. Bishop (1991), Kaufman (1994), L'Abate (1992), Minkoff (1989), Miller, (1995) and Rogers, McMillin, and Hill (1988), all indicate that denial is the most striking and common feature of chemical dependency, because of it's distortion effects and persevering of the progression of the disease. Kellermann (1980), and Baekeland and Lundwall (1977) indicate that denial is the key obstacle in alcoholism because of the constant verbal contradictions exhibited by the alcoholic. Tiebout (1953) and Wallace (1978) simply describe alcoholism as the disease of denial, while Bean (1981) refers to denial as the clinical state which is called the alcoholic personality. Cohen (1985) characterizes it as an evasion of reality. Nowinski (1990) describes it in terms of stonewalling. Clark (1991) sees it as a psychological defense against the acknowledgment of a reality too painful to bear. Cermak (1986), describes it as a very active process, that requires constant energy to keep the "blinders" activated. Lehman, Myers and Corty (1989) claim that, through their research and experience that denial and the associated deceptive behaviors are part of the disease of AOD even in the most impaired psychiatric patients. Bissel (Robertson, 1988) claims there are nine types of denial, (nine were reviewed in this section) while May (1988) perceives denial as the conscious mind thoughtfully rejecting and ignoring any sign of trouble due to the ever increasing drinking. The individual doesn't recognize or even want to think about the problem associated with his drinking, and this is the essence of denial. Quite a list, but there is more.

Brower, Blow and Beresford (1989) developed a four-part denial configuration that is based on whether or not denial is directed at the chemical dependency, or directed toward other problems, both, or none. In their configuration, *complete denial* is that state that denies both the abuse and other problems. This completeness may also be indicative of character disorders.

No denial refers to clients who deny nothing and are painfully aware of their addiction and its consequences. Many of these types may have problems with suicide. The use of confrontation is contraindicated in these cases.

Partial denial - type 1 clients generally deny their chemical problems, but not the associated issues.

Partial denial - type 2 are those clients who are encouraged to focus first on their abuse, and latter in the treatment process come to see how it has affected themselves and others.

Along the same lines, is a rating scheme developed by Moore and Murphy (1961). They attempted to categorize clients according to the following five classifications.

Type 4. Clients who see no reason to change their drinking habits, and become irritated when the subject is brought up.

Type 3. Occasional and brief superficial awareness of the severity of the problem. For the most part, they also see no reason to quit.

Type 2. Awareness that drinking is harmful, but still unable to control themselves and accept external help.

Type 1. Clients who want to maintain control of their drinking, and do ask for help, but still harbor the wish that the problem really isn't theirs.

Type 0. The client who strongly wants abstinence, and is willing to ask for help whenever they are uncertain of themselves.

There's still more.

Twerski (1990) has coined a term for what he considers to be process of addictive thinking--*addictoligia*. This also encompasses the self-deception and distortion caused by denial. Addictoligia is characterized by rigid thinking. The alcoholic processes his/her world by either/or rules while thinking in extremes and with little flexibility. Beattie (1986) describes denial as, "That fog that smothers people, chokes off sensibilities and blinds them to reality." L'Abate (1992) considers denial as a defensive posture that is used to avoid the sad and painful associated with abusive AOD. Amodeo and Lidtik (1990) see denial as a set of behaviors and processes that the alcoholic uses to prevent themselves from acknowledging the realities of their drinking. Lovern (1991), typifying the traditional perspective, holds that denial is nearly an "impenetrable fortress" made of the combined forces of psychological defenses, plus the effects of the chemicals. This combined system enables the AOD dependent to literally become out of touch with reality and also have the ability to appear convincingly right. It is the addict who is sick, according to Lovern, and it is the job of the practitioner to break through that denial system.

Akin to this last perspective is the one put forth by Levin (1991), who indicates that denial is a defect in the self. The reason it is so tenacious is that the acceptance of it requires coming to terms with grievous loss. In this case, it means coming to terms with the loss of a love object, the loss of a security blanket, and the loss of a way of life. Thus, the breakdown of denial is considered a step-wise process in which only a little insight is gleaned at any one time. This makes getting through denial an extended process, and one that has many reverses and only tentative victories.

Rogers and McMillin (1988) and Berenson and Woodside-Schrier (1991) define denial as an unwillingness or inability to acknowledge the existence of one's problem. However, the latter authors extend that unwillingness to include differentiating the name of a problem versus labeling a problem. That is, *naming*, according to them is more of a generative process, like the bringing forth something. While labeling has a more enclosing quality to it. According to these authors, naming has a discovery aspect to it while labeling shuts off exploration and has a judgmental quality to it. It is easy to see how denial might be intensified, according to this idea, by the AOD counselor who labels the behavior of their clients.

McAuliffe and McAuliffe (1975) include denial as part of a *total rigid defensive system* used by the alcoholic. In this system, they refer to denial to mean any explicit rejection concerning the truth of one's chemical involvement. They note that denial is the first line of a defense that does not want to acknowledge any problems with drugs or alcohol. As part of that "denial system" they indicate some clues they believe typify denial. These include a defensiveness about anything that has to do with AOD use. In addition, they cite a series of negative attitudes or expressions that are associated with the total rigid defense system. These include such things as revulsion, rejection or demeaning venomous attacks toward anyone who questions their drinking or drugging. Further, they specify such things as despair and desperation that can be used to help the addict compile and conform to directives verses truly changing. Stalling, quibbling, anger, resentment, and "pity me" are also indications of this typical rigid defense posture.

To augment this long list of denial definitions and characterizations, Clark, (1991) adds a few of his own. These include a refusal to acknowledge the obvious, which to the outside observer looks like lying, plus a steadfast refusal to help the interviewer determine what's wrong with one's drinking.

There are still more denial ideas from the traditional camp. For example, Wallace (1985) sees denial as serving several functions. Its primary purpose is to protect the addiction, and persevere the belief that one's worth and dignity have not been damaged. This removes the threat that something might be wrong, and the abuse of the chemicals can continue in this deluded state.

Brown (1985) states that denial is a belief in controlled drinking. She however, believes that the alcoholic is selective in what he/she registers. Only the information that is in keeping with the non-alcoholic self-image is retained and allowed to be incorporated. Denial, according to Brown, is a primitive defense mechanism that requires the systematic exclusion or distortion of environmental data from entering the any part of the self.

Rogers and McMillen (1989) note the denial serves to diminish the painful anxiety situation that blinds the individual to reality. This resort to denial to avoid anxiety is also the position taken by Goleman (1985). In fact, he goes on to state that this propensity to protect the self from anxiety by dimming awareness creates a "blindspot" mechanism, which is a zone of blocked attention and self-deception. This same type of blind-spot is mentioned in the "Little Red Book" (1957).

Berenson and Woodside-Schrier (1991) consider the main reason that people refuse to name their condition is that doing so will bring them face to face with their carefully avoided emotions. These authors also address a phenomena they describe as spiritual denial. In this, the addict disavows any need for a Higher Power in their recovery program.

Recently the *National Council on Alcoholism* (1992) issued a new definition of alcoholism, and among other suggested amendments to this definition included the concept of denial. Their definition of denial is that it is a complex phenomenon determined by the many effects of psychology and physiology. They also indicated that this defination is more than the analytic defensive mechanism of disavow, and included any behavior that decreased the awareness of the fact that alcohol ingestion was a cause of a person's problems. This is in-line with the basic philosophy of this book.

From a broad perspective, Wegner (1989) indicates that if denial can redirect attention away form the source of denial, it is working. However, the denial process often just reminds the denier of the very symptoms he/she is trying to avoid. It will also remind the denier of what he/she might be, or do, if his/her denials were true. In this latter case, denial is not working. Wegner further asserts, that if the thoughts we wish to disbelieve are persistent, then we will be drawn even tighter to the denial because we have nothing else on which to depend. There seems to be no way out of this tangled web.

Denial in the Relapse Process

Denial can also be recurring. According to Gorski and Miller (1986), the denial process can reassert itself, and lead to relapse of the chemical dependent. Old alibis and rationalizations can begin again to undermine any self-awareness and progress made in recovery. Orlin and Davis (1993) speculate that the denial process that operates in relapsing is akin to ignoring or forgetting the oncoming relapse indicators. Bean (1981) notes that because of an impulse to use, the recovering individual might begin to think of self-permission statements to use again. This type of thinking causes anxiety, and it is here that the subtle denial processes will begin to allay the anxiety with a series of rationalizations. If the relapse occurs, then the individual will need to protect themselves against the guilt and shame that usually results. Denial then will serve its original purpose of protection and avoidance, and the process starts all over again.

Professionals in Denial

Implicit, in the traditional perspective, is the notion that denial has the effect of having professionals under report chemical dependency in all aspects of our field. For example, Notman, Khantzian and Koumans (1987) indicate that an accurate assessment of substance dependency is rendered difficult by the patient who is in a state of denial and by the possible countertransference impediments of the therapist. Vaillant (1988) indicates that denial can be very convincing from a client who is being interviewed, and who states that he/she does not have a problem. Bishop (1991) suggests that there is wide under reporting of alcohol related problems in hospital admissions, which is directly related to the denial process, as well as a naiveté about addictions. So, according to this under reporting belief, not only does the alcoholic have the dynamics of denial, but the professional also suffers from it.

Certainly there is under reporting of substance abuse in the field (Caton, Gralnick, Bender & Simon, 1989). However, attributing the under reporting exclusively to denial, says that professionals are actively attempting to avoid or hide the truth. This is a bit far-fetched. There is no question that some professionals are impaired and may be using denial to avoid their own set of problems. The argument presented is that professionals are marginally aware of their own difficulties and experience distress when they see it in others, therefore under report what they are actively avoiding. However, to attribute all of the under reporting issue to denial alone is to blot out other possible explanations. For example, what is called denial in the field may be due more to a lack of assessment skills and essential observational practices than to some widespread denial process that infects the field. Certainly much more research needs to be completed before we can attribute the under reporting to any cause with certainty.

All these definitions depict how the traditional school of thought perceives denial. Essentially it is seen as a very real concept, and the definitions focus on the avoidance, evasion, and the refusal to acknowledge the truth of one's drinking and drugging. The definitions usually have an unconscious or conscious tone of opposition, in or about the client. These definitions all believe denial to be a key trait or ingredient in the dynamics of addiction. It stands in the way of the recovery process, and, as such, needs to be confronted and eliminated.

But, is that the only way to conceive this phenomena?

SOME NON-TRADITIONAL VIEWS OF DENIAL

Much of the material covered so far, is easily found in most AOD books or articles. However, there are some rather different ideas of how this concept operates.

The major problem with many of the views noted above is that not all addicts demonstrate this "avoidance of the truth" behavior. Miller (1985) notes that denial is not found more often in samples of alcoholics than in nonalcoholics, and that it is not a good predictor of treatment outcome. Kaufman (1994) cautioned the field not to over label a multitude of substance abusing behaviors as denial.

Ellis, McInerney, DiGiuseppe, and Yeager (1988) refer to denial as the ability to escape quickly into an avoidance mode. They assume that alcoholics do not have a high tolerance for frustration. Thus, at the first hint of negative feelings, they feel the need to resort to drinking. According to these authors, who are using a rational-behavioral-emotive model, there may not even be any true denial working in addicts according to these authors. AOD dependents do not deny in the traditional sense because they don't feel the negative emotions, they just avoid them, and nothing is even experienced.

Overall, what is considered denial in the traditional sense is considered a faulty perception from the Rational Emotive perspective. Along these same lines, Marlett (1985) views denial as a "defensive avoidance coping pattern." This pattern can be use to ignore, justify, or even resume active use of chemicals. It is based on the addicts making irrelevant or maladaptive coping decisions induced by cognitive conflict. The client is aware of the costs of the abuse, but this awareness prompts the inappropriate behavior which in turn can be misconstrued as denial (Saunders, Wilkinson & Towers, 1996).

Kasl (1992) pointed out that much of the traditional type of denial categorizing came from the original AA alcoholic sample from which the *Big Book* was based. These were, for the most part, white upper-middle class males, who were arrogant to begin with, and exhibited these mannerisms as a part of their normal character. According to Kasl, believing that all alcoholics act in this fashion is a grave assessment mistake.

So, if one buys into, "All addicts behave in an evasive defensive manner" then problems immediately arise between the client and the therapist. This assessment will create dilemmas because this a stereotype and people do not like to categorized, even alcoholics. That position will then set up an oppositional stance between the client and counselor, which will, in turn, limit clear thinking on the part of the counselor, and therefore limit strategies and interventions.

Fingerette (1988) declares that, denial may not be the ideal way to handle any problem, but he is not at all convinced it is a symptom of a disease either. He notes that a drinker's motives are no different from anyone else's. When so-called "normals" encounter problems they are also likely to hide or deny their thoughts and feelings. Lazarus (1983) as well as Miller (1989) make this very point.

Taylor (1989) argues that there is a healthy aspect to not squarely facing reality. She maintains that in some cases self-deception is more healthy than the absolute truth. In fact, she notes that it is those who are more disposed to depression who seem to see reality as it truly is. It is the healthy minds that can cordon off negative information and create positive illusions so the individual can better cope. Of course, this does not mean that one is free to utilize denial halter shelter. It does, however, point out that some degree of self-deception seems to be health producing (Goleman, 1985).

Donovan and Marlatt (1988) indicate that addictive behaviors are characterized by a "...notable lack of awareness." A mind that is chronically intoxicated is subject to selective recall, and certain things are not seen. Often what is remembered by the client is the feeling of the intoxicated state, not the real event, which can be confused with denial (Sederer 1990). This lack of recall and awareness has always been thought to be generated by the chronic long-term ingestion of chemicals. The long-term use of chemicals distorts one's ability to accurately perceive the significance of internal or external events. It is these internal events such as core belief systems that get skewed. That skewing turns out to minimize the disadvantages and maximize the advantages of drug use, which can keep the dependent from not seeing his/her problem (Beck, Wright, Newman & Liese, 1993).

Thus, denial, according to many of the above authors, may turn out not to be some internal character trait, but a lost skill that contributes to the lack of vision and clarity. The viewpoint of denial as an innate character trait, whether it is consciously or unconsciously driven, versus a lack of a cognitive skill, is a major difference in the perception of denial, and will effect an assessment.

Miller and Rollnich (1991) tend to blame the analysts, those who believe in drives and the unconscious, for the current state of affairs in the treatment of chemical dependency. But, that may be a bit premature. There certainly are a lot of other factors that contributed to the "alcoholic in denial" theory. However, this belief in denial as the defensive style of the alcoholic has, according to these alternative view authors, set the stage for the confrontational therapeutic approach that has permeated the AOD field.

This traditional perception has historically been one in which a clients have a problem and are blamed for their "disease of denial" (Shaffer & Gambino, 1990). (That from a field that has battled so long to define alcoholism as a disease and free from blame.) Trimpey (1991), the founder of Rational Recovery (RR), states, "The term denial is probably used as often in as accusatory sense as in a descriptive one." This stance is voiced by another RR advocate, Vance Fox (1993) who indicates that denial is often a charge thrown at those who are reluctant to accept the traditional methods of recovery. He feels it less a state of mind than a tool used by manipulators. Denial, according to RR, is an indication that internal rational/irrational arguments are yet unresolved.

Miller (1989) outlined what different views of denial can do to the treatment approach a AOD counselor will take. On the one side is the confrontation-of-denial approach, and on the other is a view he calls the motivational approach. The confrontational approach advocates see denial as an alcoholic trait which requires confrontation and correction. However, the idea of confronting denial can be therapeutically destructive, because clients will often see this as psychotherapeutic persecution (Shaffer, 1990). In the motivational approach, resistance and denial are seen as an interpersonal behavior that is often influenced by the therapist's idea of things. In this case, denial is met not with confrontation, but with reflection, rolling with it, and supporting client self-efficacy. Stanton Peele (1989) embraces a perspective that if a client is told that he/she has an alcohol problem, and does not agree with that diagnosis, then that disagreement can be used as evidence that one is in denial. Peele refers to this circular logic as the "catch-22" of denial. Any denial, of a supposed alcohol problem, is considered evidence that one is in that very state. The client is expected to understand and embrace this concept because of the loss of control over the use of chemicals. Blane (1968), Hoff (1977), and Paredes (1974) agree that if a client refuses to endorse this doctrine, then it is called denial by many AOD professionals.

A similar idea is espoused by Lawson, Ellis, and Rivers (1984). They state that, "If alcoholism is a disease of denial, then the only logical diagnosis that can be made of the problem drinker is alcoholism." Because if an individual denies his alcoholism it is seen as the first stage of alcoholism. The only alternative is to accept the alcoholism diagnosis. This can quickly degenerate into a game of "Yes you are, no I'm not," and that leads right back into a catch-22 logic.

Peele and Brodsky (1991), in line with Miller and Rollnick (1991) plus Clarke and Saunders (1988), note that denial is considered to be the traditional defense to which there is one ultimate goal--breaking it. They stress that rather than confronting denial, the practitioner needs to take aim at solving problems and find solutions that work for the client. In fact, Dean and Poremba (1983) comment that there might be a healthy aspect to the client not accepting the alcoholic label. The alcoholic label still remains very much a stereotypical stigma. What might be considered denial in the traditional field may, in fact, be a healthy response from a client who is not willing to be so stigmatized.

Taleff (1994) took the solution based approach, and applied it to this concept. He speculated that chemical dependency treatment could be enhanced without a resort to denial, and how the field could use that to their advantage. Essentially, the notion is one in which the concept just gets in the way of quality assessment. It creates a negative mind-set toward all clients, and that in turn limits treatment creativity. As it is, the label, and all that it entails, places too much emphasis on pathology, and not enough energy is given to possible solutions in the recovery process.

In addition, the structure of language plays a significant part in labeling someone in denial. Note how the statement, "He/She is in denial" portrays an individual in a fixed, stuck position. The verb "to be" implies this state, and has unchangeable written all over it. That immutable way of perceiving clients entails strong measures to off-set this fixed position. That has often meant confrontation. However, not resorting to the "to be" verb changes the perception of the client. For example, "Bill seems stuck," or " Bill appears held up in his recovery process" opens new, fresh ideas in perceptions accorded to the client. These new perceptions assume that change is happening, and that the client isn't permanently fixated somehow (Walter & Peller, 1992). The function of the therapist is now to look closely at what is changing, amplify it and repeat it.

These are some of the alternatives of the denial process that are in variance to the traditional idea of denial as a trait of the alcoholic. As we have seen, these views espouse other explanations of the addict's behavior than the one of denial. We have also seen that denial is not the exclusive to alcoholics. Traditionally many counselors expect denial from the addict. When client behavior does not agree with our expectations, this behavior can easily be misperceived as in denial. Viewed this way, there is no way out for the addict, unless he/she concedes to our way of perceiving reality. Opening that reality a little more will give the practitioner more options and more treatment strategies that will match the needs of the client.

THE POLAR OPPOSITE OF DENIAL--SURRENDER, ACCEPTANCE, AVOWAL

An overall understanding of the denial concept cannot be made without considering its opposite. The traditional opposite of denial is subsumed under the terms *surrender*, *acceptance*, and *avowal*. In fact, if one were to ask the typical AOD counselor what is the final goal of treatment, he/she would probably say it is the surrender process. Surrender means to give-up or yield, especially in a voluntary manner. Further, this surrender process implies the giving up of something, especially after striving to keep it.

Acceptance and avowal have a similar interpretation. They mean to admit, to believe or to adopt a view that was quite different from a previously held view. There is also that quality of acknowledgment, which leads to acceptance and avowal, and has the implication that one reluctantly discloses something that one was trying to keep secret. Conceding a fact, declaring openly, or even confessing, all have parallel meanings for surrender, acceptance and avowal.

Fingerette (1969) took the term avowal further than these definitions, and indicated that it also means to openly spell out in an authoritative manner. In this case, one spells out or tells his/her story with weight, and possibly a sense of power. Next, he noted that avowal has an integrating quality to it. That is, whatever is avowed is synthesized deeply into the personal self. Finally, he noted a strong sense of responsibility to whatever is avowed. Taking account of what one is, but not the blame for what one is.

TRUE DENIAL

If you carefully read all the denial definitions thus far, you probably noticed a mix of views as to whether denial is of a unconscious or conscious nature. Framing it one way or the other has significant implications for assessment and treatment of the client. To clarify this predicament, I will first examine the unconscious nature of denial, then the conscious aspect, and place them appropriately on the decision tree.

THE UNCONSCIOUS FACTOR IN DENIAL

Many authors state that denial is not willful lying, but is an unconscious process (Anderson, 1981; Cermak, 1986; Whalen-Fitzgerald, 1988; Twerski, 1981, 1990; & Straussner, 1993; Walker, 1995). Denial as viewed in this form may be truly pathological (Dorpat, 1985; Vaillant, 1988). The unconscious denial process is supposed to protect the client's ego from painful feelings of the loss of control over the use of chemicals (George, 1990). The self remains safe and free from consciously experiencing distress, so the pain associated with the hopelessness of the situation is not felt. Paul (1993) notes that clients are unconsciously aligning and shaping their reality to self-serve their own perceptions and viewpoints. In this case, the inner voice is telling the client that his/her motives are pure. Therefore, when others disagree with them they can become righteous, and see those others as threats, fools, or worse These are classic definitions of repression elements of denial. Under these circumstances, chemical dependents individually are immune from the negative consequences of their usage, and can continue that use free of conscious interference. This is similar to Kernberg's (1975) idea of splitting of the ego, where one part of the self truly does not know what the other part is doing. This splitting is more in line with contemporary usage of the term denial. The original psychoanalytic meaning of denial was specific to a primitive infantile defense and a pre-oedipal psychopathology (Troise, 1995).

Moore and Murphy (1961) believe that what appears to be a willful dishonesty on the part of the alcoholic, is the unconscious at work attempting to persuade others and the self to believe in the lies. Groves (1978) noted an unconscious denial called the *self-destructive type*. This perception of denial has another striking feature that includes malice, if not self-murderous intent. These are the individuals who have been warned by their physician that they have pending cardiac problems, or other life threatening medical problems due to excessive drinking. They politely thank the doctor, leave the office, and head directly toward a bar. They seem to glory in their self-destruction, and do it with the intent of unconsciously defeating the doctor or any one else who threatens their use. These types may be rather dependent and have given up hope of ever attaining sobriety.

Why insist denial is an unconscious defense mechanism in the first place? A partial answer lies in the fact that traditionalists advocate a disease (medical) model approach to understanding chemical dependency. Simkin (1970) states, "If I am unaware of what I am doing I am not responsible for what I am doing." In a nutshell, this idea attempts to place no blame or responsibility for the onset of the disease onto the addict. On the other hand, it does place a great deal of responsibility for the recovery squarely on the shoulders of the client. Essentially, one does not cause an addiction, but one is very responsible for sobriety (Ward, 1980).

Being unconscious of what I am doing takes the morality issue out chemical dependency. It also helps make AOD field become more legitimate. This, in turn, can direct more needed money into treatment, because addiction can now to be considered a disease and not a willful act. Its biggest benefit, is that it helps a lot of recovering people come to terms with much of their painful abusing past. As a student once told me, "I wasn't accountable for what I did during my drinking. Even if I thought I was, I don't think

I could have even started my recovery. I would have been too ashamed and guilty and would have kept on drinking."

To believe that denial is other than unconscious is to maintain that the alcoholic is aware of what he is doing. This places us right back in a moral dilemma. "I didn't know how I was hurting myself and my family," is a far cry from "I knew everything, but still continued to use despite that knowledge." Thus, denial and how it is traditionally conceptualized serve some very important purposes.

Given this review, it is time to add the first branch to our decision tree.

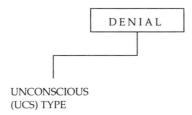

SOME MINOR PROBLEMS WITH THE UNCONSCIOUS APPROACH

After reading the section above, some counselors would close the case on unconscious perception of denial as being the tried and true answer. But, there are some problems with this approach.

First, as we noted, it is very difficult to pin-down a workable and agreed upon definition of denial as a unconscious term. There are a variety of explanations of denial, even in the ranks of the traditionalists themselves. This state of confusion is also apparent in the analytic literature. Over the years, there have been so many definitions and meanings given to denial, as it applies to analysis that, according to Willick (1985), the term had become almost meaningless. In addition, Trunnell and Holt (1974) note that much of the confusion is related to the semantic difficulty of the term. On the one hand, the dictionary describes denial as, "to declare not to be true, or refusal to grant." On the other hand, this is not how Freud intended the term. He regarded it as part of the ego-splitting, in an unconscious manner, producing an inability to accurately acknowledge what was really going on in reality. In fact, Trunnel and Holt (1974) note that many analysts intend to describe denial in the vernacular sense only to end-up defining it in the analytic sense. This could very well be the same problem that plagues the AOD explanations.

The second major problem with seeing denial as an unconscious term is that most professionals do not think the issue through. Many authors will first claim denial is an unconscious mechanism and then turn right around and describe it in terms of conscious lying. Bok (1978) in her classic book on lying, made it very clear that lying is the stated intention to deceive. Many AOD authors will describe the qualities of denial in terms of "refusal" to acknowledge that one has a disease. As soon as words like refusal are used, we have moved into the realm of lying. If I refuse to acknowledge something, that implies that I have some inkling of what I am trying to refuse. When one implies conscious awareness, that implies intent. Intention is a conscious process. For example, we noted that Cummings and Sayama (1995) indicate that denial is a garlic defense. That is, the one who has eaten the garlic is unaware of the odor, while others are. A catchy analogy to be sure, but it doesn't make sense given the authors further explanation of the denial process. They believe that clients with addiction problems come to treatment under pressure and with an explicit or implicit contract. The explicit contract is often to get a spouse or job back, while the implicit one is a desire to turn themselves into a social user. The problem with this logic is that if clients are truly unaware of their odor, how can they want to return to social AOD use? At some level, they have got to know they are out of control. And, that is not unconscious denial.

To drive a further wedge into the idea that denial is really unconscious, many AOD authors have openly stated that alcoholics are liars and that there is no unconscious action in play. Brandon (1969) indicates that the alcoholic's evasive qualities have a conscious function (not unconscious) about them. He calls it "willful disintegration" or a refusal to raise the level of one's awareness. Robertson (1988) bluntly stated, "Denial means lying--to yourself and to others." Twerski (1981) notes essentially the same thing. Abel and Sokol (1990) and Hill (1974) all agree that alcoholics lie, but Hill feels that this lying is intrinsic to their nature. He feels they lie to their friends, and they lie to themselves and even lie to other alcoholics. Pinkham (1986) flat out states, "Alcoholics defend and lie about their drinking because they don't have the ability to stop it..." Goodwin (1988) states, "Denial is a term psychiatrists apply to the lies alcoholics tell themselves and others." He further states, "Major symptoms of alcoholism, after all, are denial and rationalization--psychiatric jargon for lying." Kaufman (1994) implies that not facing one's alcohol and other drug problem is denial and lying woven together. Estes and Heinemann (1977) feel the client may be *actively* (italics mine) disagreeing with a diagnosis. Beattie (1986) states, "Persons using denial may be lying, stubbornly refusing to admit the truth of a thing...." This corresponds with Goleman (1985), who feels denial refuses to accept things as they are, however denial does not blot everything from awareness, as in real repression. In actually, the facts are rearranged to obscure the real situation. Goleman also refers to denial as being the "vital lie," where the facts of an alcohol related situation can be so brutal, that one cannot ignore them. In this case, the only resort is to alter the meaning, and just plain lie.

In conversations with AOD clients, I have had heard a few admit to using boldface lying as a method to sustain their addiction. Some admitted to the energy they felt by lying. As Gaylen (1979) notes there may even be a sense of delight, joy and even power to the lie. It is indeed a tool by which one can get his/her own way.

So denial, as defined by a host of authorities in the field, has a decidedly divided notion on whether it is really an unconscious or conscious phenomena This, as you have probability have guessed by now, reflects various perceptions on the subject. So the unconscious form of denial cannot be the final word some have tired to portray it.

Since we have alluded to the conscious element of denial, let's take a closer look at this particular denial pattern.

THE CONSCIOUS ELEMENT OF DENIAL: Deception and Self-Deception

According to the proponents of this position, denial is a conscious issue and means people know something is wrong with their behavior, and will try to consciously alter that reality. Methods to do that include lying and excuse making. If lying, (or conscious denial) has a conscious element to it, then, according to Lewis (1993), this is analogous to the problems of deception and self-deception. He notes that humans lie (deceive) to protect themselves. But, what is it that needs protection? According to Lewis, we lie to protect and spare the feelings of others: for example, saying to Aunt Maude that the argyle socks she gave you for Christmas was just what you wanted, when you really don't like argyle. We also lie to avoid punishment and to deceive ourselves. All forms of deception, or, as Sigmon and Snyder (1993) refer to it--reality negotiation, have a conscious element to them.

Excuse Making

Consider how good you and I are in giving a host of excuses for our behavior. Although our society frowns upon it, we resort to the excuse if we are connected to a negative behavior to protect the two self-assessments of, "I am good" and "I am in control" (Sigmon & Snyder, 1993). The excuse will repair any tear in our "rosy" view of ourselves, and of the view we want others to have of us (Dershowitz, 1994). Excuses seem to come to our lips more easily than boldface lies. A slight difference exists between the lie and excuse. The liar doesn't want to accept any linkage to his or her act, while the excuse has some implicit level of association. This distinction may be important when treating AOD clients, and assessing whether they accepting some level of responsibility for their behavior.

To help with this fine separation, Sigmon and Snyder (1993) outline several forms of excuse making. Some center on the "I didn't do it" type which is not far removed from a lie. Another type blames someone or something else like, "It wasn't my fault I was late. I got a flat tire." Then there are the "Yes-but" variety, and the "I didn't mean to" excuse. In the latter case, the sense of self can be persevered, because there was no real intent to harm or deceive, as in, "I didn't mean to get drunk again." Or, "I didn't mean to get fired from that job because I was drunk."

Another excuse type is the "It wasn't really me" type. In this case, the reference to the "bad" or negative act is associated to another part of the person which isn't the true self, like one's temper, behavior, impatience, or, "It was the booze talking." There are the "It wasn't so bad" or variety of excuses like, "Yes I was drinking, but I wasn't stopped by any cops when I drove home," or "It was a really bad day, and I needed a few drinks," constitute the justification excuse.

Self-Deception

What of self-deception? Is it possible to be both lair and dupe at the same time? Not so according to Baumeister (1993). It may be logically impossible but it happens. How? Self-deception can flourish in those gray areas called human beliefs and opinions. In these areas where possibilities, leaps of conclusions, and unsubstantiated truths exist, self-deception can also dwell. Essentially, we interpret the events of our lives in biased ways.

We usually take credit for our successes, but rarely for failures. We usually blame bad luck, misfortune and bias as the probable cause of those failures. In addition, there is a tendency in human thinking to believe certain things, and only see the evidence that confirms those beliefs. People will try to be objective, but this inherent disposition to see it "our way" biases their thinking.

Murphy (1975) notes that the exclusion of information is guaranteed by the building up of a picture of oneself that is to be forever enhanced and defended, so a more positive image is usually the one recalled and remembered. He also states that the way we receive and distort information is through the whole psychophysiology of the individual he calls the set. The eyes were built to see, but they are expert in not seeing. We will throw all kinds of "noise" into our information receiving channels in order to reject any unwelcome reality. In addition, the basic principle of self-deception is a delight in simplification. By engaging in this, we can escape from the reality of our inadequacies. Murphy states, "... self-deception is first and last a system of devices for enhancing and protecting our self and for defending it against injury and calamity."

Baumeister (1993) indicates that one rarely tells "whoppers" to oneself. "Instead they are more like fibs, exaggerations, selective omissions, best case scenarios, and other such distortions. Self-deception resembles propaganda rather than perjury." Perhaps, this is the situation with many AOD clients.

Motivations That Drive People to Deceive

What drives AOD dependents to consciously blot out and realign personal reality? Leonard Schierse (1990) flat out states, "Pride is behind the denial in addiction." The pride whispers, "You are in still in control of the drinking and are not like those who have lost it." This same "pride driving denial", sentiment is voiced by Kurtz (1979) and Bepko and Krestan (1985). The sense of being in control and governing one's self is one of humanity's most highly valued functions, especially in an individual-driven society like ours (Mack, 1981). This pride runs deep. Sullivan (1956) speculates that this pride is behind what he calls selective inattention which is a form of controlling the awareness of the world upon us.

The state of pride, arrogance, and vanity in humans is outlined well by that old master, Alfred Adler. In his classic *Understanding Human Nature* (1927), he denotes the characteristics of vanity as:
1. Knowing how to shift responsibility for any mistakes onto others.
2. The vain are always right and others are always wrong.
3. The vain do not allow themselves to be subordinated to the rules of society.
4. There is a desire to conquer everything and everyone.
5. There is a great deal of hostility in these people, and they take the pain of others lightly.
6. There is a tendency to deprecate others in order to make oneself feel superior.
7. They generally cannot wait until the other has finished talking in order to raise their objections.

These seven items certainly summarize what many would call the false-pride aspect of denial. However, Adler points out that behind this facade is a small sense of worth. In fact according to Halberstam (1993), vanity has more to do with ranking than with real pride. Certainly, many addicts use their false-pride to deceive themselves, but there are just as many addicts who have long since lost their sense of pride.

Bishop (1991) offers a framework of motivations behind denial, which is orientated along these Adlerian lines. He notes that from the perspective of Individual Psychology, denial is to be viewed as a safeguarding mechanism. The client will be using his own private logic based on his personal convictions and value systems to see and understand his world. In addition, this same person uses a series of basic mistakes that are aberrant conclusions about his/her life and those around him. All of this goes into preventing a people from honestly facing their disabilities, inferiorities and basic mistakes. Denial is used to preserve the addict's relationship with the chemical, and to also guard against psychological pain. It also provides a myth for the solution of problems, makes reality manageable, and provides justification for using, e.g., "I deserve it."

If you remember the list of denial features outlined by Anderson, Hazelden, and Fox in the previous section, Bishop now takes that list and specifically applies what he considers the basic Adlerian driven mistakes to each of those features. For example, in the *simple denial feature* (failing to acknowledge the problem), the basic mistake is one of, "I am always right and others don't know what they are talking about." In *minimizing*, the basic mistake is one of "People could care less what I have to say. Therefore, I only give what I have to." As for *intellectualization* and *rationalization*, Bishop indicates that these are attempts to disregard feelings. The basic mistake of the client in these cases centers on, "My feelings don't count," "It is the reasonable person who gets their way in life," "Think, don't feel." *Diversion* is the strategy of moving the focus of attention away from oneself to someone else. The basic mistake, in this case, is, "I am not responsible for negative behavior," "People are trying to make me look bad," "Therefore, don't look at me, look at them." It is these basic mistakes, according to Bishop, which need to be confronted and challenged, so the client can be retrained out of their private logic and into a more sober conducive one.

Other reasons AOD dependents are driven to use denial include the thoughts of Jellinek (1960) and Weinberg (1976), who argue that the alcoholic finds refuge in denial due to the guilt and remorse caused by the consequences of that drinking. The denial then has a tendency to deteriorate the judgment capacities of the alcoholic to the point of rejecting any responsibilities for one's action. The crux of this theory is that if one can avoid the responsibility of one's action, then one can also avoid the guilt and shame--a very useful purpose. Lewis (1993) indicates the same essential reasons (shame and guilt) for why people resort to deception. However, he notes that the problem of deception is that it does not allow people to learn from what is being deceived or denied.

Morrision (1994), Rothschild (1992), L'Abate (1992), Beattie (1986), and Flories (1988) all maintain that factors such as loss, grief, guilt, shame, remorse, pain, and fear are the major factor behind the resort to denial. As with any defense, it becomes more rigid as the emotional pain becomes stronger. As a result, this ever increasing, rigid avoidance and protection against the emotional pain gradually puts the addict more and more out of touch with reality.

Twerski (1990) states that the alcoholic resorts to denial to defend against:
1. The label of alcoholic (also Amodeo & Liftik, 1990)

2. To offset the moral degeneracy they have experienced
3. To avoid the fact that they cannot safely drink again
4. To dodge the powerlessness and lack of control that exists in the way they drink

Clark Vaughan's (1984) thoughts on denial parallel Twerski's items 1 & 2. Yet Vaughan feels that the alcoholic also turns to denial because of the addictive drinking itself and because of the social stigma attached to it. In line with the stigma idea, is Kottler's (1992) notion that people resort to resistance because they do not feel accepted. Vaughan also believes that as the progression of the AOD use increases, the addict is faced with a dilemma of facing the thought that "I am an addict, and weak willed, I must be deserving of the social stigma."

The motivation behind denial, according to Wallace (1985) and *Hazelton* (1975), is that it keeps out the reaction of society from entering the awareness of the dependent. The labels that society can and does place upon the abuser can be painful, such as weak, immoral, and crazy. The common element in such items and many more like them, is that of the stigma. Most people make attempts to avoid any labels to themselves, let alone own any stigma. Denial can be of benefit in this avoidance process. As Mueller and Ketcham, (1987) have indicated, who wants to be categorized as a derelict or a degenerate?

Paralleling this weak-willed perception is the associated idea of failure. Failure to control the substance, and failure to control the consequences of an AOD lifestyle, is often construed as total failure. This rub of failure is exacerbated by having to acknowledge to another person, as suggested by the fifth step of AA, that one is indeed has failed. This is a tough pill to swallow (no pun intended). Having to admit our weakness (Virend & Dyer, 1973) to a relative stranger, like an AOD counselor, has strong overtones of "I'm inadequate." For most individuals, this is a very difficult step to take, and from the observer perspective such difficulty can easily twisted into "That client is in denial". In this particular case, this is not self-deception but coming to terms with myself, a big, big step in recovery for many a person.

Estes and Heinemann (1977) believe alcoholics turn to denial because they are torn between two incompatible perceptions or behaviors. On the one hand is the powerful reinforcement of the positive effects of the chemicals, the energy, and euphoria. On the other hand is the negative effects caused by the abusive consequences of the addictive behavior. Denial, then, permits the alcoholic to screen off the painful side effects, or at least the connection to harmful drinking, and thereby continue the chemical use.

Forman (1988) listed several motivations behind denial. These include, the love of the chemicals to the exclusion of all other things or people. And fear, that raw frightening sensation which can cut straight to the core of a human. This fear factor is also found in Apthorp (1985) and Levin (1991) who believe the alcoholic fear is compounded by intense feelings of despair, hopelessness, and helplessness.

In summary, AOD clients seem to resort to denial, due to feelings of pride, guilt, remorse, loss, stigma/label, pain, fear, or threat. So there seems to be a conscious intent to avoid the discomfort generated by these feelings. This has aspects of suppression associated with it. Berenson and Woodside-Schrier (1991) noted that "Alcohol counselors use the term in a general sense to describe a more conscious strategy of minimizing the negative consequences of drinking."

With this section completed, it is time to add a second branch to out decision

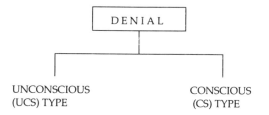

DENIAL LOOKALIKES

From here on, we begin to examine the lookalikes of denial, and their characteristics. No particular hierarchy is intended, and certainly there is rarely an individual who will neatly epitomize anyone of these divisions. Keep in mind the similarities you might find to true denial as well as the differences. Such a careful evaluation can make for a much closer fit of treatment strategies to clients.

The Physiological Aspects of Denial

There is a feeling, among many authors, that a refusal to acknowledge one's drinking and drugging is not so much caused by psychological factors but by physiological ones. For example, Forman (1988) indicates that memory loss occurs as a result of extensive chemical abuse, and this can contribute to the denial process. Mueller and Ketcham (1987) write that the judgment portion of the brain is "hit hard by alcohol," and that contributes to the denial process. Shaffer and Gambino (1990) speculate that addicts are not fully aware of their behavior because the brain's feedback channels that normally function in a sober state are impaired due to the use of chemicals.

Milhorn (1991) speculated that denial could be the result of an interplay between the brain's limbic system and cerebral cortex. He suggested that drugs acting on the limbic system produce craving, which in turn act on the cortex to produce addictive type behaviors. These addictive behaviors generally produce guilt, which will reduce the developing addictive behaviors. However, as the craving increases the guilt can no longer override them. Denial then develops to protect the mind from the internal pain that results from this growing conflict between the uncontrolled drug use and the guilt.

The Seventh Annual Report to Congress on Alcohol and Health (1990), Emerick and Aarons (1990); Zweben (1989); Gordon, Kennedy and McPeake (1988); Donovan, Walker, and Kivlahan (1987); Yankofsky, Wilson, Adler, and Verna (1986); Walker et. al., (1983); Tarter, Alterman, and Edwards (1984) and Clark (1991) have all suggested that due to the chronic ingestion of addictive substances, there is an increased inability to accurately assimilate and organize many types of information. This includes abstract reasoning abilities, learning and memory skills. These deficits are not only limited to accurately perceiving external information but to the internal cues as well. Thus, various states of cognition and emotion arousal may become clouded and confused to the practicing chemical dependent. Not able to accurately relay one's feelings to anyone outside can be easily misconstrued as denial. In reality, it is a condition called *alexithymia*, or an associated condition called *anhedonia*. It seems apparent to us what is happening to practicing addicts, but this clouded state makes it difficult for them to accurately identify what is accurately going on. This idea is in line with a similar theory of emotions reported by Goleman (1995): here the frontal lobe of the brain which moderates impulse and sustains a working memory of events is damaged by the chronic use of alcohol. Once this feedback loop is damaged, the ability to remember the consequences of a drinking bout is impaired. Simply, the alcoholic cannot recall the damage caused by his/her drinking.

Often counselors will quickly jump to a denial conclusion when clients are not behaving as they should in treatment. Confronting someone when they are really in denial is one thing, but confronting someone in a residue drug haze is something else completely. Making a distinction in assessment can make a big difference in treatment.

Muellen and Ketcham (1987) and Bean-Bayog (1988) agree that the alcoholic can remain "foggy" for months after a last drink. Neurologically this can resemble a mild dementia. Other symptoms can include disturbances in awareness and effects on memory and one's ability to abstract. The people who are just coming out of this drinking fog might certainly deny that they not have a problem, not because they are trying to hide that addiction but because they just can't remember. In addition, they may not have the ability to abstract the problem into a statement.

Foggy brain impairment is a similar response of stroke victims and other such life threatening illnesses. In a foggy situation, the addict may feel that they have become diminished in some way. The real damage of the alcohol and drug abuse has to be handled correctly. It can be misrepresented as denial, versus the physiologically induced cognitive impairment that it is.

McGrady (1987) outlines a few indicators that might help identify this type of impairment so as not to confuse it with denial.

1. The inability to remember information
2. The inability to find ones way around a treatment center
3. The inability to associate names to faces.
4. The inability to sort out relevant information from a group session or lecture
5. The inability to generate new ideas on how to solve life's problems.
6. The inability to assess the successor effectiveness of strategies or solutions to given problems
7. The inability to remember why drinking is a problem

Many years ago, I had encountered a case in which a middle-aged female had been abusing tranquilizers for years. She was in a 28-day inpatient program where I worked at the time. In the first week, she was less then responsive to most standard treatment interventions we used. In the second week, there wasn't much improvement, but certain staff began to grumble that she might be in a severe state of denial. By the third week, she hadn't improved all that much, and the grumbling staff was suggesting she be discharged because she was perceived as "getting over." I argued for her to remain in the program since she was so close to a regular discharge. In her last week, still with no real improvement, the staff was hell bent on having her discharged as soon as possible. They wanted to use her as an example to the rest of the community because no one "got over" in our program. I continued to argue for her, not really knowing the why, but sensing something of worth there. Well, the heat from the staff was getting intense at this time, when an amazing thing occurred. She cleared from the tranquilizers. I distinctly recall her walking into my office as clear as a bell, and thanking me and the program for putting up with her till she could come out of her "fog." Had I listened to the staff, we would have discharged her for being in the so-called state of denial.

As Gorden, et al., (1988) have suggested this physiological induced "resistance" may in fact be due to some cerebral dysfunction. They, in fact, suggest that AOD facilities institute active cognitive assessment retraining components into their overall programs to address this potential problem.

Blackouts also play a part in the physiological disruption of reality and therefore play a part in the denial process. The amnesia effects of a blackout can easily persuade an individual that what he/she has been accused of did not happen. If it isn't in the waking memory banks, then it is more difficult to convince someone of his/her drunken behavior.

So the physiological perspective attempts establish a physical basis for denial. Ingested chemicals can add to diminishing the awareness of a problem with those chemicals, and that is far from avoidance.

Broad treatment applications for this issue center on allowing the client time to clear under medical supervision, if not a judicious vitamin and mild exercise regime.

This lookalike represents another branch to our growing decision tree. The completed tree can be found at the end of this section.

Confusion

An interesting slant to the idea of deception in AOD dependents, is a position developed by Wallace (1978). He indicates that the position of phenomenology poses a first serious rival hypothesis to the defense conception of denial. Rather than some unconscious formulation, he believes that the alcoholic is caught in a complex epistemological problem or a massive state of confusion. This confusion idea is based on five points.

The first factor is that of an uncertain drinking history. Many alcoholics do not get falling down drunk every time they drink, nor are there negative consequences each time they drink. This intermittent quality can and does create significant confusion for alcoholics when they are attempting to come to terms with their overall drinking patterns.

A second confusion factor deals with the power of the early pleasant memories and the fun times of drinking. This friendly recollection creates confusion when it is compared to a present miserable existence of alcohol and drug abuse. Thinking of those past situations many clients can be heard to say, "Why can't I get the same good feelings now, as I used to."

A third quandary centers on the disjunctive versus the conjunctive nature of the term alcoholic. By nature, a disjunctive definition requires that all the symptoms of the problem be present in the individual. Alcoholism is just such a concept according to Wallace. It requires many symptoms before it can be given. A conjunctive category, on the other hand, only requires a partial list of symptoms to be classed in a particular category. This can cause confusion to a AOD client, because they will be perplexed by the many different classification systems of problem drinking that exist. In addition, most people prefer not to see things as conjunctive, or partial. Most prefer to see things as disjunctive, i.e., I have the problem--all of it; or I don't have the problem--none of it.

The fourth confusion item is one in which the various attributes of alcoholism are themselves complicated and problematic. That is, no one symptom of alcoholism definitely indicates the client ever has the problem, and there is the variance of a symptom over time. So this confusing situation for a client can be seen as "Am I alcoholic or just an abuser?"

The last factor in this confusion theme is that of the social comparison. Essentially, the alcoholic drinks with a great deal of other heavy drinkers and alcoholics. His/her world is colored by this environment, and the belief can easily develop that "All people drink like I do." Now, if that's not enough, drinkers are bound to find a few people who drink more and worse than they do. Thus, when faced with problematic drinking one can be confused because it seems there are others who out drink him which serves as more confusion for the client.

Treatment implications for all this confusion center on individualizing the treatment for the client. First, the whole idea of comparing self with other drinkers needs to be addressed. It is the comparison that is deluding the one who is out of control. Many clients falsely believe that they can act as they see others behave. Second, no harsh confrontation is needed here. Rather, consider the creation of a safe atmosphere that surrounds your clients in which they can examine their own behavior without the external pressure, and for themselves. (See Chapter Six.)

Given this slant on the concept of denial, we need to add another branch to our decision tree (See the end of this section). The evaluation question is directed toward determining if the client is in true denial, or if he/she just confused by one of the factors we reviewed? Please note the different treatment approaches you would use, depending on which problem the client really turns out to have.

Ambivalence

Many AOD counselors can mistakenly attribute denial like symptoms to a client who could just as well be in a state of ambivalence or reluctance, as noted by DiClemente (1991). Ambivalence and reluctance have to do with the lack of inertia and relevant knowledge in a client. When people are not informed or uncertain about change, they can be quite reluctant, as well as ambivalent. So, instead of chronic denial as the predominate issue to be addressed in AOD treatment, it might well be ambivalence or any other similar event. In fact, Gordon (1993) claims that ambivalence is a form of denial. AOD clients could really have mixed or ambivalent feelings about themselves and their problems, and not really be in a strict form of denial. They may, at one time, want very much to change, but at other times they may not. According to ambivalence theory (Miller & Rollnick, 1991; Saunders, Wilkinson & Towers, 1996), to fluctuate in the levels of one's motivation is a common human experience, not denial.

Egan (1994) indicates that there are a variety of behaviors to be seen in reluctant clients. Some behaviors include keeping a low profile and talking only about things that are safe. At times, clients set unrealistic goals and then use those unclear goals as an excuse not to work. They will also blame others for their problems. A few reasons behind these reluctant behaviors include fear of intensity in the therapeutic session, lack of trust, and shame.

Ambivalence is certainly on a spectrum of possible reasons why the AOD client would do what he/she does. The ambivalence symptomatology is similar to denial but certainly not the same. Knowing the difference will make the treatment that is directed toward the client that much more effective. All this gets us to another branch of our decision tree (See end of this section).

OTHER DENIAL "LOOKALIKES"

There are four additional items that resemble denial which we need to review. The first is the **systems/environmental** type. We will cover this variation more in Chapter Five. However, for our present purposes, this is the type of resistance that has it's roots in the communication, peer groups, and family factors that influence change in the client. For example, the unsupporting family member who chronically says something like, "Why do you go to counseling? It isn't going to help you. You're gonna' drink anyway," or, "Hell no, I'm not taken the beer outa' the refrigerator. I don't give a damn what your counselor says." Often these individuals have chemical problems of their own.

I worked with a young women several years age, in an outpatient setting, who was relapsing consistency. In our staff meetings, the usual accusations of denial where leveled at her for the repeated slips. Interestingly, this women always came back to the program and consistently voiced a desire to remain abstinent. After a little digging, we were finally able to ascertain the she had no support from her significant other because he was a practicing alcoholic. He was saying the things I listed above. Now knowing what the problem was, we shifted our treatment direction, and she began to respond in a more positive manner. This same type of interaction can occur with peer groups as well as certain cultures. Often the therapist will mistake the resistance as originating deep within the client and confront him/her, when in reality the client is living in a very unsupportive atmosphere. That takes us to another decision tree branch (See the end of this section).

Another denial lookalike includes that type of resistance which is based on the individual who is not able to discriminate his inner emotional states, or is emotionally illiterate (Goleman, 1995). For our decision tree purpose, we will call this the **psychological naive type**. Turock (1978) describes this person as having the inability to discriminate inner feelings or to have the vocabulary to identify feelings. This can be generated, in part, from some true developmental impairment. Adult concrete thinkers sometimes fit into this category. In this case, the clinician is able to ascertain that a particular emotion is evident in the client, but when inquiring about that emotional state, all we get back is "I don't know." The unknowing therapist can launch into, "You're in denial of your feelings," when what is happening is that the client cannot make sense of the emotions occurring inside. This quick attack, and labeling of a client to be in denial, can also place the client in a strong defensive position. In fact, the hard approach can have the effect of automatically sending an emotional burst of energy through the client's affective system. In this case, the client's fight or flight system is activated. When that occurs the flood of feelings will overwhelm any logic that has a chance of making sense. To many alcoholics, this attack is reminiscent of past attacks on his/her behavior, and further intensifies the defensive system of the client. This intensification of defenses observed by the therapist is often proof that the client is some state of denial.

Not much in the way of useful information has been published on this phenomena. But, I have run across it a number of times, and I have learned to be wary of thinking someone is denying their feelings when, in fact, they cannot distinguish one affective state from another. To help the discrimination process, McLachlan (1972, 1974) developed a *conceptual level* (CL) of thinking for a low CL type. These individuals tend to think in simplistic terms, or only in black and white styles. In addition, they are generally ruled by authority-oriented types of interactions. It is not a far stretch of logic to assume that such AOD types might find themselves in a quandary over differentiating their internal states, and feel belligerent about those states at the same time. This might overtly look like denial, but upon closer examination turns out to be low CL. The treatment applied to each would certainly have to be different.

Nicholi (1988) and Golemen (1995) are authors who note that tension and anxiety interfere with an individual's ability to think or express him/herself clearly. They both attest to the fact that even a simple subjective experience may be difficult to verbalize because of significant anxiety. This lack of adequately explaining oneself includes the somatic as well as the psychological realms. It would seem that this tension and anxiety component could easily be associated with the confusion type we just reviewed. Keep it in mind for those closely related patterns.

Treatment possibilities include encouraging individuals to explore the various aspects of themselves, and then apply appropriate names to the somatic sensations. With that, we need to add another branch to our decision tree (See the end of this section).

Another denial lookalike is of people, who if they had a choice, would rather not be in treatment. This is called the **disinclined/reluctant to change type** (Ritchie, 1986; Dyer & Vriend, 1988; Egan, 1994). They are the disinclined, or "I have no desire to change" type of person. DiClemente (1991) refers to this character as the type who has no investment, or a lack of energy in the change process. They seem overwhelmed by their problems, focus on low priority issues, or have just given up. They completely addicted to their chemical of choice and, most apparently, they seem to have lost all hope. Sometimes these individuals are simply not willing to make any changes in their behavior because of the strong attachment or euphoria to the chemical.

I have noted, over the years, that many a tried and true AOD counselor would scream at a client, "You're in denial," trying to break through that defense; when, in fact, the client had no intention of quitting his/her use. These individuals can hardly wait to leave your program and get drunk and/ or high.

Vriend and Dyer, (1973) have noted that the reluctant type may be acting in a nonconformist and uncooperative manner in order to be accepted in certain circles. DiClemente (1991) refers to these individuals simply as the rebellious types. A strong sense of threatened independence or fear and insecurity can often create aggression in the client in order to cover these felt vulnerabilities. Separately or in combination, these types are particularly difficult to treat, because they essentially do not want to be helped. No amount of ranting and raving is going to have much of an impact. A therapist can feel most helpless under these circumstances. Treatment options are very limited in these cases, but I recommend that you look at the solution-oriented material in Chapter Six for possible ideas. With that in mind it's time for branch number eight (Again, refer to the end of this section).

The next denial look alike in this series revolves around the **personality disorders**. Now you might think the modern AOD counselor would be able to tell the difference between true denial and cluster B (dramatic, emotional, erratic) personality types, especially the anti-social personality. Indeed, many can, but there are counselors who have trouble separating the two. For those who do, this branch of the decision tree is offered.

Schuckit (1973) was one of the earliest clinicians to distinguish the difference between the so-called alcoholic personality and antisocial. Antisocials can certainly exhibit very similar characteristics to some types of alcoholics. But, the antisocial is ingrained and pervasive throughout the personality, while true denial is specific to discussions about drinking or drugs. Nace (1990) indicates that characteristics of the antisocial personality disorder are the most commonly reported features in substance abusing patients. In fact, a Type III Alcoholic has recently been established, which includes the prevalence of AOD dependency and antisocial traits (Blum, 1991).

According to the DSM-IV (1994) the anti-social has no regard for the truth, indicated by repeated lying, use of alibis, or "conning" others. If you didn't know better, this sounds an awful lot like denial. There are a other personality disorders that can also mimic denial, such as narcissism and passive-aggression and the ever infamous borderline (cluster B types again). These personality disorders were in place long before the addiction took hold and can be easily mis-labeled as the defense posture of the addict.

Fong (1995) notes that there are a few signs that could indicate a possible personality disorder. For example, counseling may come to a sudden stop after some initial success, or the client seems unaware of the effect of his/her behavior toward others. In addition, the client is unresponsive to treatment, and often enters into an intense conflicted relationship with the program and staff. All these behaviors are similar to the traditional concept of denial. Knowing the distinction can make a world of difference in the way therapy is dispensed and the effectiveness of the intervention. Thus, we come to our next branch (See the end of this section).

The last associated phenomena which looks very similar to denial is **reactance**. We began Chapter One with the an example of this. We will address the issue with more detail in the next chapter. For our present purposes, it is the client who feels threatened or losses his/her sense of freedom. The perceived threat and loss of freedom has the tendency to make people angry and belligerent. This is how many drug and alcohol clients appear to most treatment centers across the country. So, what might be happening in this case is the client is not displaying denial symptoms but is in a high state of reactance. Most counselors will, however, assume the reactance is denial, and confront this situation. That's like throwing gasoline on a fire.

With this final denial lookalike we have completed all the branches of our tree (See the end of this section).

A SUMMARY OF THE DENIAL DECISION TREE

What are we to make of all these different points of view? The first is that denial is certainly not a single dimensional defense. Second, it has a variety of possible interpretations. Third, it is critical to know what you are dealing with. That can and will focus the treatment direction. In this way, the AOD counselor will not be trying to engage something that really isn't there. Given all that, we have been building a decision tree aimed at cutting through some of this confusion.

Before we get to the final draft of our decision tree, a few caveats are in order.
1. This is not intended to be the inclusive list on the variations of denial. It is rather intended as a broad range of the ways therapists might use this schema.
2. It is certainly not intended to be viewed in a rigid manner. Flexibility, an openness for other forms of evaluation, is the cornerstone of any good assessment Thus, this format is deliberately not "tight." It is designed this way to give the practitioner the freedom to be creative in his/her assessment process.
3. There is always the possibility of a compounding of these types. Humans rarely come across so "neat and clean" as described in the different categories.
4. Think of how to alter "You're in denial," to thinking, "Now that I have a general idea of why this person is doing, how can I can address that?" Know what drives these complexes and engage that!

In summary, we divided the concept of denial into two very broad categories--the true and the lookalike sections. True denial was further divided the unconscious type, the conscious type. The lookalike category included behaviors that could and have been easily mistaken for denial but really are something else. For each, there is the basic drive of the type, or what is pushing or motivating it. Knowing this gives the practitioner an idea of what then to truly address in one's treatment approach.

Summary of the Decision Tree Branches

(TRUE DENIAL)

- **UNCONSCIOUS TYPE** -- A true compartmentalization in which the client does not know he is even in denial. Repression and splitting would fit well into this category, as well as overtones of dissociation. This unconscious type is perhaps the most pathological of the denial variations.

- **CONSCIOUS TYPE** -- better known as the simple type or avoidance type. Lying would fit here as well as selective inattention and suppression. In this category, there are the many painful emotional states that we all to run from or conceal, e.g., anxiety, guilt, shame, are good examples. Pride or threat to one's pride is another motivator to engage a denial as well as Irrational and self-defeating thoughts. This category means disguising or hiding. Another apropos definition of this category is to pretend not to recognize or notice-- ignore.

(LOOKALIKE DENIAL)

- **PHYSIOLOGICAL INDUCED TYPE** -- These are the memory voids produced by the direct results of the ingested chemical or as a result of neurological damage caused by the chronic use of said chemicals. These voids can easily be misinterpreted as denial.

- **CONFUSION TYPE** -- This is given a separate category. It could be argued that it is really a sub-division of the conscious cognitive type. However, in this case, it is not an irrational thought process. In this case, it is more a matter of mixed messages that generate puzzlement and bewilderment.

- **THE AMBIVALENT TYPE** -- This ambivalence may look like denial, but that is only because in those times the individual is less than enthusiastic about recovery. Most humans vacillate when it comes to their own motivation. There are "up and down days," so it is with recovery. There is an aspect of reluctance operating here, and that can have a denial feel to it.

- **THE SYSTEMS/ENVIRONMENTAL TYPE** -- That type of resistance that is generated by the relational interaction. It is in these types of situations or encounters that certain people seem to bring out the best and worst in us. This classification has much to do with the support and interest of others in the client.

- **THE PSYCHOLOGICAL NAIVE TYPE** -- This denial look alike turns out to be the lack of truly knowing one's inner emotional state. What may seem as an easily identifiable emotional state to the therapist is an unknown to clients. They never have been able to accurately identify exactly how they feel or even sometimes think. We see it, but they don't. When the therapist names the feeling, clients who cannot identify their inner states disagrees with us, because they are used to calling the internal state in question something else. Many a professional will then shoot back with "You're in denial." This type of approach can lead to the foundation of a good power fight in the therapy session.

- **THE RELUCTANT/DISINCLINED TYPE** -- This type is no where ready to give up mood altering chemicals. They may still very much enjoy the effect, or they may not have felt the consequences of what the chemicals are doing to them. Not hitting bottom is a factor in this case.

- **THE PERSONALITY DISORDER TYPE** -- These individuals are not really in denial, they are in fact exhibiting a profound disorder of personality. The classic personality disorders that can easily get mixed up with denial are the anti-social types, less often the narcissistic and the passive-aggressive types.

- **REACTANCE TYPE** -- Threaten to take an individual's freedom away from them, and he/she will become very hostile and belligerent. This belligerent attitude can easily be mistaken for denial. However, when reactance is confronted as denial it only fuels the threat of more loss of freedom.

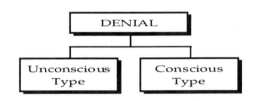

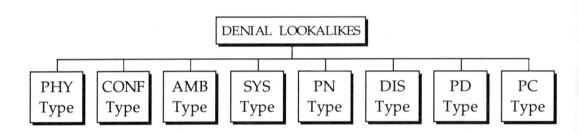

CHAPTER SUMMARY

To many AOD counselors, the term denial has been infused with messages and overtones of bad, wrong, abominable, if not an out and out evil. This mentality is often perpetuated by the field through training programs that associate denial with "a wall" to be penetrated. This chapter has tried to portray denial in terms of constructive alternatives, which can be more effectively addressed in a therapeutic setting versus the classic notion that denial is to be sternly confronted and eradicated.

Denial does not come in one simple type. It exhibits itself in a variety of styles and shades. To know that approximate style and shade can help AOD clinicians improve their assessment gathering abilities. A decision tree model has been proposed to assist the practitioner do just that. It is designed to be open and flexible and to allow the practitioner the freedom to discover what drives the so-called denial complex, and thereafter better serve the client.

SECTION II: ALCOHOL AND OTHER DRUG RESISTANCE: THROUGH THE EYES OF MAJOR THEORISTS

As we have seen, alcohol and other drug resistance behaviors, including denial, are considered a point of view, rather than a process (Schlesinger, 1982). How you perceive resistance will dictate your attitude toward it, as well as the method of treatment you will use. Furthermore, the therapist must always be aware that a client may bring a multitude of resistance characteristics to a therapy session (Dewald, 1982).

This section is designed to help the AOD practitioner navigate the many conceptual viewpoints that exist. The first step in this journey is to become knowledgeable of the two major forms that exist on the phenomena--the *content* and *contextual* orientations (See diagram 2-1).

Diagram 2-1

Resistance

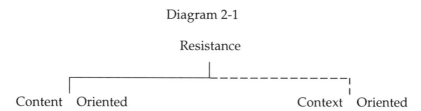

Content   Oriented   Context   Oriented

The content orientation refers to the school of thought familiar to most of us, and has, by far, the greater literature base. Many believe it to be a universal phenomena (Strean, 1993). In this view, resistance is perceived as having some type of form, theme, meaning, or drive associated with it. As with denial, resistant behavior can be attributed to anxiety, threat, fear or types of irrational thinking processes. The principle advocates of the content view are the analytic, Gestalt, and cognitive schools of thought, and these views are extensive.

The context viewpoint, on the other hand, is one in which the perception of things is not limited to the thing itself. This theory has as it's proponents such as the disciplines of brief-solution or construction therapies. The underlying theme in these perspectives is that resistance does not exist. According to this view, resistance is considered is a non-entity. The advocates of this view regard resistance as something that gets in the way of treatment. It is an issue that changes depending on the language used between a counselor and a client.

THE CONTENT-ORIENTED VIEW OF RESISTANCE

This form of resistance has advanced a variety of definitions. For example, The Clinician's Thesaurus (1991) lists 140 different terms for resistance and negative behaviors. A small sample of those terms include: guarded, evasive, stiff, uncooperative, intractable, unyielding, rigid, inflexible, and unmotivated. Many of these same descriptions are cited by Seligman and Gaaserud (1994) and Davanloo (1986). You may notice that in all these synonyms, there is an implicit oppositional ring associated to them. The client is assumed to be consciously or unconsciously fighting against the recovery process. This is the general flavor of the content oriented resistance explanations. Davidson (1976) suggests that no matter how one views resistance there is a vaguely sinful demeanor to it, which, in turn, indicates that something is wrong with the client.

From a purely definitive perspective (American Heritage Dictionary), to resist is to strive to work against, fight off or actively oppose. Additional dictionary synonyms include the act of opposition, to prevail against, to withstand or defy. Other points of views to be examined define resistance in terms of protection, a coping style, or even something normal appropriate and to be expected (Ellis, 1985; McMahon & Jones, 1992). There is even a tendency these days to name resistance by other designations like "barrier" (Blau, 1988), or difficult (Kottler, 1992). Lazarus and Fay (1982) speculate that resistance may be a function of the state of the art in psychotherapy today. They indicate that we experience resistance in our clients, we really don't understand it, and therefore we are constantly mistreating it, only to create more resistance which we can't understand.

Of course resistance can be anything that the counselor thinks it is. This is the heart of the book. Just because a client has not achieved a positive outcome in therapy or is noncompliant, is not a solid enough reason to label such behavior as resistance (Lazarus & Fay, 1982). How does one then answer the question, what is resistance? The answer is connected your point of view.

There are subcategorizes under the content perspective which include the dynamic/analytic, the cognitive realm (with a scattering of Gestalt), attribution, and preferred defensive style. Most of the well-developed content theories of resistance can be found in these particular viewpoints. In addition, there are a few authors who have taken a crack at defining the dynamics of AOD resistance. Fisher, for example, (1983), sees, "Resistance as a blocking the natural process of change and or the interpersonal blocking in the development of therapeutic relationships." Zweben (1989) states that, "Resistance is simply all those forces within, that resist change; and it is the subject of therapeutic work and not an obstacle to it." Finally, Flores (1988) feels that two simple definitions capture the flavor of resistance. He states, "Resistance is a force that prevents the freeing of unconscious material." He further states, "Resistance is the avoidance of feelings and the denial of emotion." According to Romig and Gruneke (1991) resistance is an assorted matter, and has many forms, rather than a singular definition. It is, at best, a hypothetical construct (Marshall, 1972). Yet, the field is making headway in measuring the term, trying to give it substance (American Addiction of Medicine Criteria, 1990; Mahalik, 1994).

Although these definitions are a matter of perspective, they can increase the understanding of the concept, which, in turn, avoids the ever-present problem of pigeon-holing clients into limited theoretical perspectives. Armed with a wide, encompassing view of resistance, the AOD counselor can make more accurate assessments and treatment plans.

A Case in Point

This expanded view of resistance has it's advantages. It helped me in a case about three years ago. A young man, who had just been released from a local prison, was referred to a program where I worked. Upon arrival, he made it clear that he was angry at everything and everybody. He was particularly infuriated with the legal system in which he was enmeshed. That anger, in turn, was directed at me because he saw me as an extension of that system. He was one of those individuals who, when asked a question, just growled.

The case dredged up past memories for me. There was a time when I would have just plowed into him because of his nasty attitude. The goal in those days was to make sure he knew who was boss, rather than direct him toward treatment.

I have matured a bit over the years. Rather than engage in the traditional frontal attack treatment method, I decided to give him a few days to cool down. Those days passed, but he was still angry and wanted everybody to know it. One day he walked into my relapse prevention group. He was asked to complete a written assignment. The other members of the group set about their task, but he boiled at the prospect. He began to fumble around with the paper, tapping his pencil on the table and dropping it a few times. He seemed hell bent on letting me know he was not happy.

I couldn't help but notice this behavior and, despite my best efforts, I began to get hooked into his game. I thought, "I'll ask him what's going on." So with my most neutral voice, I inquired as to whether he was going to complete the worksheet. To that, he made some inaudible sounds and gave me a quick glance of disdain. He then started to play with a styrofoam cup, as if to call more attention to his angry mood. Again, I asked him in my most professional demeanor if he intended to complete the assignment. Then it happened! He gave that styrofoam cup a brutal blow with his index finger, and it sailed across the room. This was his answer. It was a deliberate oppositional behavior, and he did it in the most passive -aggressive style he could muster. One for him, zero for me, I thought.

Needless to say I felt a twinge of rage and thought, "To hell with this nice guy stuff. It's time to rip into this "resistant bastard." I've tried to be a nice guy, and he's compromised me and my position in the group." But, just before a planned stream of obscenities was to come pouring out of my mouth, I hesitated. It happened in a flash, I thought another approach might be worth a try. So, I asked him to accompany me outside, and excused us from the group. Once outside the building, I deliberately and calmly told him that he could remain outside for as long as he wanted, or he was free to leave the group entirely.

Little did I realize what an ideal move this had been. Had I kept him in the group and confronted him as my anger wanted, we would have engaged in one hell of a power fight. He would have eventually lost face as most clients do in this type of a situation, and I would have shown him and the group just who was in charge. The sad part about such an approach would have been that both of us would have lost, because that style of confrontation would have created a lot of useless resistance.

I stood about four feet from him waiting for an answer. I waited in silence for what seemed like hours. He then began to mutter something about how frustrated he was. As he began to talk more, it became apparent that he really felt the legal system had lied to him. He was told one thing, promised something else, and none of it came true. He felt he had lost all his freedom and was "Damn well fed up with the whole thing."

I didn't say anything, but just listened with my mouth open. He wasn't really angry or resistant at me or the group. He was angry at something altogether different! This was more a case of reactance than blatant resistance. I gulped at the horror I almost committed if I had blasted this guy as my angry side wanted to do. As soon as I realized what was really going on, my frustration melted, and the professional demeanor returned. I began to acknowledge him and just continued to listen. After a time, I told him that I would have to return to the group, but he was free to stay outside. As I turned and started to walk away I heard a small but distinguished "Thanks for listening." Rather than engage in an awful power struggle, we began to communicate.

Within fifteen minutes he came back into the room and began doing the assignment with no prompting. He even managed to smile a few times that day.

I don't share this episode to pat myself on the back. I've mismanaged situations of type many times before, and even a few times after. I share it because I created options in my repertoire of skills. That day I exercised some of those options and real therapy began to occur. Yes, he was resisting but not the way I initially assumed. It turned out to be more complex. My hesitation, and discovery that something else was going on, gave me a chance to clearly see with a new perspective and finally treat this individual. Indeed, resistance can be viewed in a variety of ways.

THE VARIETIES OF CONTENT ORIENTED RESISTANCE

In this section, we will look at how the major theories of psychology perceive resistance. These include the analytic, Gestalt, cognitive, and a sampling of others. These theories are invested in the content portion of a client, so they are usually looking for problems in a client. They seek certain mechanisms that drive the resistance be is a strong feeling or irrational thought. They use their own language and concepts to describe the workings of resistance. Such approaches always give their slant on things.

The Analytic Concept of Resistance

How would the analytic oriented AOD therapist perceive resistance?

To answer that question, we return to the man who probability started all this talk about resistance--Sigmund Freud. He alluded to the process of resistance and defenses as early as 1895 (Wallerstein, 1985). Although he attached a great deal of importance to resistance, Freud, never devoted a single exclusive paper to the subject (Fine, 1973; Strean, 1990). He was however, always making modifications to this resistance theory and trying to improve it. He seemed to have trouble explaining this antithetical force (Lapanche & Pontalis, 1973). In his later work, he was able to come to a common sense conclusion. He noted that resistance was a fight against improvement, and rational insights did not seem to make an impact on it. This idea is similar to the explanations given by many drug and alcohol authors today.

Freud soon began to regard resistance as a central principle in psychoanalytic theory (General Introduction To Psychoanalysis, 1920/1965). According to Rothenburg (1988), Freud began to consider resistance as treatment's most powerful ally. He also began to examine the phenomena more closely, and delineate its functions, characteristics, and etiology.

Fundamentally, Freud felt that resistance needed to be understood and interpreted, not merely removed. He came to believe that any time a client's sense of balance was disturbed or an internal conflict arouse, anxiety resulted. If the ego could not handle the anxiety, a resistance or defense mechanism would. The resistance may not have been the best way to cope with the disturbed balance or conflict, but it was the ego's solution to the problem (Rosenthal, 1987).

Now, it doesn't take much intelligence to figure out that conflict can lead to anxiety, and that anxiety can entice an ego to resort to the use of defenses to offset the anxious state. But what about this balance thing, how could that lead to using defensive measures? Alexander (1961) explained that humans are in part motivated by a sense of inertia. We don't like to change. Alexander felt we tend to become unbalanced when we encounter novelty, and that can lead to the use of defenses. These new and changing life conditions can generate anxiety and that sets the stage for resistance.

This is the phenomena of disequilibrium. Carkoff (1969) notes that "...digging into one's inadequacies can lead to a certain amount of disequilibrium, disorganization and crises." What results from this disequilibrium is fear, anxiety, panic or threat of one's world falling apart. The only way to retain the familiar from falling apart, is to defend it. As practitioners dig into clients, those clients may not quite be ready to "own-up" to their vulnerabilities. That combination of issues creates the overt resistance that the counselor will observe and possibility mislabel.

Caprio (1974) also notes that dependence is the tendency to protect oneself against threat, criticism, blame, or any perceived attack that threatens one's status or equilibrium. Gaylen (1979) sums it up when he states that resistance is the reaction to those things which weaken our strength, insults our pride and self-confidence, or makes us feel helpless or more vulnerable. The resultant distortion created by the resistance is one of being a "gift" to the client. It brings relief in perhaps believing, "Thank God, It's not what I thought it was. I'm really not the powerless alcoholic everyone says I am. So it's got to be the job, the kids, the stress I've been under. What relief!" Who wouldn't rather believe in that fabrication, and keep their sense of balance?

A Few Freudian Defensive Styles

Freud (Inhibitions, Symptoms, and Anxiety, 1926/1955) outlined five types of resistance. The first he called *repression*. This, as we noted, was the type of resistance that the ego used to protect itself from anxiety. Keep in mind that anxiety, according to Freud, is considered to be the prime driving force behind the resort to defenses in the first place. As we saw in previous chapters, this repression has very strong ties to the denial process. This type of resistance has appeared in a number of definitions to explain the resistance process in chemical dependency dynamics.

The second was the *transference resistance*. In this type, resistance was thought to originate from the client who wishes the therapist to be a surrogate parental figure. Freud believed we all have infantile needs to be taken care of, and this desire becomes particularly strong in any significant relationship. We become at risk, so to say, to be cared for, versus transmuting these impulses into a more reality based manner. The foundation of what was later to become the codependency movement. Transference distorts by a regression process. That is, as we fixate on the impulse we have to regress to a previous style of relating. It is this regressive style that distorts one's present sense of reality. This form of resistance also has overtones of needing to defeat or frustrate the therapist .

In more modern terms, transference is the displaced feelings of a client toward the counselor (Nicholi, 1988). Most theorists who advocate this term note that the displaced feelings are from the clients' parental figures. These feelings get transferred to the present counselor because they represent the new authority figures in the client's life. As Nicholi (ibid.) states, "That although transference reactions occur in all relationships, they occur most frequently and most intensely in relationships with authority." This has strong implications to any practicing AOD counselor who often finds themselves in that very position. If you choose to see the client through this perspective, the issue to address is the transference, and not yelp at the client, "You're in denial."

Nichoi (ibid.) notes three reactions to transference that the counselor needs to recognize. The first is that transference is an unconscious process. The client may be aware of certain feelings but may not know the source. It may be the aim of treatment at this point to help the client to acknowledge those feelings and to effectively deal with them. Second, the transference feelings will be intense and often inappropriate to the situation in which they occur. Third, these transference feelings will often have an ambivalent quality to them. There can be opposite feelings coexisting within the client at the same time. The idea is not to mistreat these emotions as if they were based on the reality of the situation. That approach may only harm the therapeutic relationship. The more appropriate treatment according to the dynamic view is to explore the source of the emotion. The analytic goal is to gain insight and then move on.

The third type of resistance outlined by Freud was what he called *epinosic gain*. In this type, there is something to be gained by keeping the resistance. One might ask, "What is to be gained by holding fast to a defense that is distorting reality?" The benefit can be attention or sympathy. For those who have never experienced these "benefits" from a parent or family, it can be cause enough to withstand the discomfort pain in order to get the attention. In the case of the AOD dependent, the attention gained from the drinking could, at times, outweigh the pain of the consequences.

Freud's fourth resistance type was called *repetition compulsion*. He felt that we get ourselves into recurring harmful situations as the result of a self-destructive drive within all of us. That self-destruction is centered on our aggressive nature, and he termed it the *death wish* which was thought to be prevalent in mankind. Many of Freud's contemporaries tended to disqualify this death wish idea. But in the case of chemical dependency, when one returns again and again to a substance that is known to be harmful to a person, it is not difficult to consider that a death wish is operating. Nevertheless, the possibility of a death wish does not hold much validity these days.

Freud's fifth type of resistance is that which is derived to offset or appease intensive guilt: a self-punishment, if you will. It comes about as the result of a strong superego or severe conscious. Even the rationalist Ellis (1973) denotes such a resistance. In this cognitive perspective, the self talk centers on, "I don't deserve to be healthy because of my real or imagined past transgressions." When people believe they are to blame for something, or are riddled with guilt, they often will go to extremes to make sure they are sufficiently punished: what fertile grounds for an addiction.

Essentially, Freud felt resistance was motivated by anxiety, inertia, secondary gain, destructive drives and powerful guilt. He saw that resistance came in diverse flavors, and therefore had to be treated differently.

THE NEO-FREUDIAN VIEWS OF RESISTANCE

To say that resistance has not been addressed by a host of post-Freudians would be an understatement. In fact, Chessick (1974) states, "No satisfactory classification of resistance exists in psychotherapeutic literature." Yet, the great analyst, Menninger, tried to define this process. He (1958) noted resistance to be, "... the forces within the patient which opposes the process of ameliorative change." He also stated, "In a way, the analysis of each patient is a kind of never ending (omnipresent) duel between the analyst and the patient's resistance."

Analytical resistance theory is complex and extensive. For our purposes, let's review a few neo-Freudian theories and draw parallels to the addiction field. We start with the idea that resistance is a form of armor.

Wilhelm Reich

Wilhelm Reich is a most interesting individual in his own right. He managed to get himself drummed out of the professional ranks of analysis in the late 1930s due to some of his eccentric ideas. Before he drifted into his eccentric zones, he managed to put together an idea of resistance, which might be useful for the AOD counselor who chooses to see resistance through analytic spectacles.

In 1933, Reich wrote his famous book *Character Analysis* (1933/1976). In the book, he devoted several sections to resistance. He acknowledged Freud's influence on his thinking, and felt his ideas were an extension of Freud's, particularly those resistance types that look like cooperation but turn out to be resistance. For example, a client might verbalize his strong desire to make a change in his life but then leave his feelings out of the therapy work. The client, in this case, would give the therapist a lot of content, but would be "affective-lame." By behaving in this manner, the client could divert the therapist away from the real issues. The material brought to the session would seem important, but it would not be, because no real emotional issues would be disclosed. The session would be all talk and no feeling, and therefore no meaning would be attached to the words.

Reich called the driving force behind this facade *character armor*. This armor was a bound up style of living that was frozen in time. Basically, client would resist treatment due to some unresolved conflicts they had at a particular stage of their life. That unresolved conflict would leave a defensive attitude or rigidity in their personality. Dewald (1982) referred to this feature as a strategic resistance, and Rosenthal (1987) refers to it as the resistive factor that is expressed in the total personality.

This character armor refers to a global quality that most always accompanies the style of contact one has with the world. In the case of the AOD dependent, a past unresolved conflict could leave a particularly defensive attitude in his/her personality. This trait would resist treatment not out of a denial feature, but from a life-long style of protection.

Reich began to view resistance in terms of patterns. The character armor was one such pattern, while each individual also had a particular style to adjust to the internal and external stressors of life. Dewald (1982) refers to these maneuvers as tactical resistance, or the avoidance of the detailed aspects of one's life.

Using these ideas one could build a case for the adult children of alcoholics (ACOA) phenomena, which often states that it is old unresolved trauma of living in an addicted family that causes present day problems for the ACOA. Also, if one is to believe in Reich's character armor idea, then a case could be made for the different armor each client brings into a session. That difference would then require a different treatment approach based on the needs and background of the client.

Another point argued by Reich, is rather than bypass resistance to uncover what's beneath it, one needs to make resistance the focus of therapy. Without this directed focus, Reich felt no real therapy work could take place. He believed that the therapist's role was to help the client realize that he/she is wearing a mask and then to show him/her how to take it off. To this Reich added, the therapist should take a more active role in the treatment process. In one respect this Reichian approach cannot be seen to be much different from what is practiced in many AOD centers today.

Reich felt that even if old material from the past did come to the surface, the therapeutic attention should remain on how the client kept feeling in the unconscious back. But if the unconscious material did come through, it was considered a positive sign that the resistance was losing its power.

Compare this with an AOD client who acknowledges that he has a problem. Reich might support a continued focus on the resistance, or mask, that holds back the awareness of having a problem. By working through the how of a resistance pattern, the client could come naturally to his own insights. The resistance would lose its power to distort one's view of things, and a clearer understanding of what is happening to the self would emerge.

George Vaillant

The dynamic resistance approach is nicely summed up by Vaillant (1988). He reviewed a large body of literature, and saw resistance as the ego's adaptive efforts to cope with stress. The individual's use of resistance, or defenses as he terms it, usually alters one's internal/external perceptions. For example, denial is viewed as this same type of distortion. Denial is perceived in terms of a psychotic defense that does the altering of reality. All defenses according to Vaillant are adept at repressing conflict and stress. All these defenses differ in how they are used for short and long term adapting.

This adaptive angle of resistance espoused by Vaillant has a "health" aspect. This same health aspect has been purported by Flores (1988). Defenses, at a certain intensity, help keep emotions within bearable limits whenever there are changes in the course of one's life. They can also serve the same function if there is a serge in one's biological impulses. These defenses essentially contribute as a respite to any change that cannot be handled immediately by the ego.

Finally, they serve to mitigate those unresolved conflicts we have with others in our lives. Vaillant considers defenses to be more than just the repression of reality. They are a part of an integrated dynamic and psychological process of humans. They are a part of the whole person. They are a method of adapting, not a deficit state. This last part needs to be kept in mind in the AOD treatment circles, verses the view that resistance is something that gets in the way of a recovery process.

Vaillant points out that if we begin to work through or breach a person's defenses, we must first have his permission. If we ask the client to remove his defenses, then we must protect him with something else. Vaillant is saying if a client takes a protective stance, we practitioners need to accept that stance as the ego's wisdom, or as the best choice the ego has made at the time. He seems to be saying, make sure you know your client, don't generalize. In addition, all defenses serve a purpose, don't mindlessly confront them.

A Hierarchy of Defenses

Vaillant (1988) also classified and categorized defenses in terms of relative psychopathology (See Table 1). A similar format has been proposed by the DSM-IV (1994). In the first category. is that defense which is considered to be the most pathological - denial. Vaillant classifies denial here because of the psychotic processes that he associates with that defense. The second classification is associated with adolescents, immature adults and personality disorders. This category includes passive-aggressive, acting out, dissociation, projection, autistic fantasy, devaluation, idealization, and splitting. To the user of these mechanisms, they would seem innocent and harmless, but are irritating to anyone close to them. Vaillant considers confrontation the treatment of choice when dealing with these types.

The third class of defenses is associated with good old fashioned neurosis which is common to most everyday life. These include intellectualization, repression, reaction formation, displacement, somatizing, and undoing. These references create more problems for the user they do for others.

When we attempt to compare these defenses with how traditional AOD treatment works, there are some differences. Traditional therapy has always thought of denial and intellectualization as rather close together. Vaillant however sees the latter as a more "advanced defense." For the counselor in the field, an argument could be made in which any client movement from denial to rationalizing could be seen as some type of "positive movement" on the part of the client. This would be hypothesized as the client's apparent movement from using a more pathological defense to a less pathological defense.

The last category of Vaillant's defensive hierarchy is what he calls the mature defenses. These include suppression, altruism, sublimation, and humor. These defenses still distort but with grace and flexibility. An example of a mature defense is taking stock of an accident or sudden loss to more fully assess the situation. At a later time, one can begin to deal with the emotional state. The mature defenses can be associated with a more successful adoption to life then the less mature modes of adoption.

Table 1

Most Pathological:
  DENIAL (psychotic type), not to be confused with the denial of disavowal.
  ACTION DEFENSES: e.g., acting out, passive-aggressive behaviors.
  NEUROTIC or MENTAL INHIBITIONS: e.g., reaction formation,   intellectualization, rationalization, displacement.

Least pathological:
  MATURE DEFENSES: e.g., sublimation, suppression, humor, and altruism.

Ten Major Defenses and the Association to AOD Dependency

Parallel to this hierarchy, is an analytical list of defenses summarized by Clark (1991). It would appear that the dynamic view has come to this. It is presented here to give the reader the perspective as envisioned by this school of thought. For those who wish to see the world of AOD resistance and treatment through this perspective and utilize it in their treatment strategies, the following are suggested:

1. Once you feel comfortable assessing the particular defense you believe the client is using, then design a treatment plan built around decreasing the intensity of the defense or defenses being utilized by the client.
2. Consider what are the underlying factors driving these defenses.
3. Develop a rapport, then attempt to get the client to gain insight into the reasons behind the resort to a certain defensive style they are presently using.
4. The more insight gained, the less the need to defend. This should theoretically lead to an improved recovery process.

The Defense	An Example
DENIAL: Rejecting or avoiding responsibility for behavior	"Who me? Why I don't have a problem with alcohol
DISPLACEMENT: Shifting blame or a response to something or someone else	"It's her fault I drink."
IDENTIFICATION: Take on the actions of an idealized person or group.	"I can't wait till I grow up and can go to bars like my uncle."
INTELLECTUALIZATION: Avoid feelings through abstract thinking	"But, I can think and manage my temper after a few lines of coke."
PROJECTION: Attributing unacceptable self-behavior or thoughts onto others.	"No, I don't have a drug problem. He does."
RATIONALIZATION: Justifying one's behavior with plausible excuses.	"Everyone does drugs."
REACTION FORMATION: Exhibiting moralistic feelings to one's own true feelings.	"Everyone in this house has to stop smoking now that I have."
REGRESSION: Reverting to an earlier level of development.	"If I don't get my daily dose of drugs, I cry like a baby."
REPRESSION: Barring intolerable thought from one's consciousness.	"I really can't ever remember a time that drinking was a problem."
UNDOING: Nullifying a past behavior by a reverse action.	"I'll just buy some flowers to make-up for last night's drinking."

There is the ever present repression of instinctual impulses that fuel all these avoidance maneuvers. According to Mahoney (1991), dynamic theory expounds an inescapable conflict, and the source of this conflict is at the unconscious level.

What does this have to do with AOD therapy? All humans, according to the analytic approach, are involved in this unconscious inescapable conflict. Some can avoid this ever-present and sometimes painful anxiety, through the use of mind altering chemicals. It's the old "try to run away from your pain through booze" theory.

However, this has been a touchy subject in the in the AOD field--trying to find the "real" problem of someone's drinking. The cure was once thought to be, "Fix the conflict, and the anxiety was will to go away". The resistance was then supposed to soon disappear, and the person would then return to normal without more destructive drinking. Depending on your perspective this sounds like a clean and even elegant idea. However, many Gamma or Type II alcoholics may have forgotten, long ago, what it was they where trying to run away from, if anything. To attempt a treatment directed at the "real cause" of their drinking might prove to be futile.

In addition, this perspective states that there had to have been some kind of predisposing factors that lead to the onset of abusive drugging or drinking. The trouble is, that research does not back up this idea (Institute of Medicine, 1990). Alcoholics may be running from something, but those "somethings" may have resulted from the drinking, not as a cause of it (Vaillent & Milofsky, 1982b).

The analysts have originated a view of resistance, perhaps the most elaborate one we may find in the literature. Opinions range from those who see it as a client only phenomena, to those who see it as being a team effort of both client and therapist. It can originate from anxiety to just about anything that interferes with the therapeutic process. That can be both its strength and its weakness. The strength, we have seen, is the variety of ways to explain the resistance process. That can lead to an almost infinite amount of speculative defenses that plague the human, which is it's weakness.

THE GESTALT VIEW OF RESISTANCE

In our review of the content oriented view of resistance in AOD treatment, the Gestalt approach has a few interesting points. The Gestalt perspective of resistance follows the development of the Gestalt school itself. This has grown from the Fritz Perls days to the more modern formulations. We will follow the same route to give the reader a rendering of Gestalt's view of resistance. This developmental route was clearly noted by Breshgold (1989), and much of the following section was taken from her fine work.

The Resistance Thoughts of Perls

Fritz Perls' (1947) ideas of resistance developed out of psychoanalytic theory, but he modified that theory to fit the Gestalt mold (1951/1979). He saw the optimal human functioning as one of harmony and balance (holism) versus the Freudian conflict type theory. The neurotic (or you can substitute AOD dependent) according to Perls, results from a loss of the feel of oneself or a loss of awareness. This loss of awareness extends not only to perceptual abilities (i.e., environmental influences) but also to the loss of inner- or self- awareness. That is not a reasonable definition of the denial process: that is, those in denial can be seen to be in a low state of awareness.

This loss of awareness comes about to protect the experience of pain or feeling bad. Perls saw that while people were avoiding or blocking the awareness of those painful feelings, they were also inventing a creative way of adapting. Granted, it wasn't the most efficient method of adapting, but it protected the self. The problem was that it had the tendency to limit awareness. By turning to all these "creative" modes, the unfortunate by-products turned out to be problems for the individual. The same might be said for AOD dependents. They have developed a "creative" way to deal with the pain and discomfort of his drinking at the expense of forming other problems.

Perls alluded to other types of avoidance in the resistance process. This included what he called "not hearing", "not understanding", and saying "yes" when you really mean no. These processes served to avoid conflict with the environment, but in that process they also created internal problems.

Translating this over to AOD dynamics, a subtle and fine aspect of the denial process can be seen. How often have practitioners heard clients say that they did not really understand an assignment or, they tuned a therapist out because they did not want to hear constructive feedback. This "tuning out" process can easily be applied to the dependent who does not want to hear people around him/her complain about the growing addiction process.

Gestalt "Resistance"

The way a person grows and learns according to the Gestalt view is through contact with the various parts of the self and the environment. It is at this contact boundary that we assimilate or reject, own or disown, or identify or alienate who and what we are. This contact boundary requires awareness, and the use of discriminatory tools. Should this boundary become problematic then disturbances of contact occur. Korb, Gorrell, and Reit (1989) have outlined five such disturbances. All five patterns are considered to be a derivative of *introjection*, which is the mechanism that takes things in whole. That is, the environment is absorbed and swallowed without reflection. These include unreflected ideas, beliefs, and attitudes. On the one hand, this is not a bad method of getting information across to another individual, but on the other hand, this direct ingestion of information takes away one's individuality and dignity, and can conflict with the basic self system. For example, many people are repeatedly told that they are not smart enough, or always wrong, or bad. This kind of information taken in without reflection can be extremely damaging. If that is not bad enough, people can take in all kinds of biases and prejudices through this introjection process. Now, blend all this into a functioning human and watch the blocks and resistant patterns begin to grow and flourish. Knowing that introjection is operating in an individual can give an observant AOD counselor some insight as to why a certain client would hold so tightly to destructive self-beliefs.

The second disturbance of contact in Gestalt terms is that of *projection*. It is not that different from the analytic perspective. Basically, it is taking an internal attitude, thought or belief and imposing or projecting it onto the world. "Why", some may ask, "would one do that?" Well, anytime there is one of these internal beliefs that does not fit with a well constructed image we have of ourselves, then somehow, we must deal with that belief. In the projection method, what is unacceptable to oneself is externalized and attributed to forces or people outside the self. One can maintain a "clean" image this way. Further, it is easy to blame others for one's own secret shortcomings. For example, look how easy it is to blame someone else for any of the seven deadly sins. Also, look how easy it is to externalize drinking by pointing out that, "Everybody is drinking, not just me." The process is almost foolproof.

The third Gestalt contact disturbance is that of *retroflection*. This disturbance is the opposite of projection. In this case instead of directing unwelcome beliefs outward they are directed inward against oneself. The chemical dependent can set the stage for a lifetime of excuses to abuse oneself (see section one). These excuses can be generated by intense anger, frustration, and shame, and those feelings are often directed inward.

Deflection is the fourth Gestalt contact disturbance. The concept was first identified by Polester & Polester (1973). It is characterized by an individual who turns away (deflects) from the contact. Behaviorally, this can be accomplished by avoiding eye contact, using stereotypical language, or generalizing a conversation. When these types of behavior occur, it is a signal that the client may be resorting to deflection. In this case, the client can maintain a safe distance from others and continue abusing chemicals without outside interference.

The last disturbance of contact is called *confluence*. Individuals who employ this disturbance do not contact the boundary, they merge with it. One's inside and outside tend to become fuzzy. It can be considered a form of suppression of the self resulting in little or no self-perception. The necessary perceptions that separate who one is from another will be compromised. In this case, there are little or no boundaries to a self. When one cannot determine the self from the non-self, one may lose the power to refuse the next drink.

This last disturbance, *confluence*, sets up an interesting argument developed by Wheeler (1991). He indicated that people need some factor of resistance. According to Wheeler, if we didn't resist certain outside forces, we would not have an identity. The way the person is interacts with the world is the method of contact. Wheeler feels this is more in line with true Gestalt theory. Reframing resistance to THE function of contact does away with the notion that resistance is a force "against" health. Essentially, clients are seen as doing the best they can in the world, and where ever they are on the boundary layer--is where they are. In this view, the metaphor of contact changes from contact versus resistance, to a type of contact.

Resistance, according to the Gestalt view, is defined as a dimension or function of the contact process. For example, contact would be seen at one end of a polarity and isolation and nonexistence would be at the other. Each of the contact functions we described above would also be seen on a polarity continuum. So resistance could be seen at one end of a polarity and confluence at the other. The same would apply for projection to retention, introjection to reflection, retroflection to encounter, and deflection to focusing.

Using these ideas, the AOD counselor could change a treatment approach from attacking resistance to determining just where clients are on their polarity and addressing that in the therapeutic process. There seems to be many Gestalt possibilities, but the one that stands out for the AOD practitioner is that would not engage, or confront a resistance; one would BALANCE the "out of sync" polarity.

RESISTANCE FROM A COGNITIVE PERSPECTIVE

In this view of resistance, you have to leap from seeing resistance as being generated by a negative feeling state (anxiety, guilt) to a distorted or irrational style of thought (Meichenbaum & Gilmore, 1982; Ellis, 1985).

As many readers already know, certain thoughts can have debilitating and paralyzing effects on behavior and feelings. For example, I can incapacitate myself quite well by repeating over and over "I can't do anything right, so why try," or, "This recovery thing is way beyond me. I just don't have what it takes to do it." Simple thoughts, to be sure, but with powerful ramifications.

This cognitive perspective of resistance can be seen to originate from a series of distorted attitudes, thoughts or schema clients have of themselves and their capabilities (Beck & Emery, 1977; Beck, Wright, Newman & Liese, 1993).

If you reframe resistance from the way many traditionalists see it, to a cognitive distortion, the focus of treatment can also be redirected. The traditional view of resistance, as we noted, entails a "willful opposition" presumption behind it. Seeing resistance as a cognitive distortion, you can direct the therapy directly at the distorted thought. For example, if a client has not completed a homework assignment, the therapist does not have to compound the problem by infusing guilt or discouragement through confrontational methods. The therapist can engage the problem by providing reason and understanding. Otherwise, one can generate *transresistance* (Meichenbaum & Gilmore, 1982). That is the all too easily transmitted resistance that passes from client to counselor and back again.

Resistance According to Rational-Emotive-Behavioral Therapy

If any theorist has taken the idea of "self-talk" to all encompassing levels, it's been Albert Ellis. He developed a cognitive approach to treating people called Rational-Emotive-Behavioral Therapy (REBT). The basic assumption here is that it is not the events of life that disturb us but our perceptions or beliefs of those events that cause the problems. It's basic tenet includes an A-B-C method of understanding personality and subsequent disturbances. **A** is the activating event in the person's life. While **B** is the belief that we attach to that event that can cause us problems at **C**, the consequence of our belief. Ellis (1967) states that, "Every human being who gets disturbed really is telling him[her]self a chain of false sentences."

How does this apply to addiction? Ellis (1985) and Ellis, McInerney, DiGiuseppee, and Yeager (1988) believes that chemical dependents have a set of thinking characteristics about themselves that contribute to the onset and maintenance of the substance abuse. Such people tend to made themselves anxious and depressed by experiencing failure, rejection or by being too self-demanding. They like others, apply an arbitrary set of "shoulds" and "musts" to themselves and their world. By doing this, they create irrational beliefs that can lead to catastrophizing any event, and over exaggerating their sense of worthlessness. The following is an adapted REBT list of characteristics believed common to alcoholic and addictive thinking.

Demandingness: Alcoholics tend to make absolutist, unyielding and rigid statements about themselves, which does not allow for errors. This is a perfect a set-up to fail and perpetuate the addictive process.

Awfulizing: Alcoholics tend to magnify and exaggerate the descriptions of themselves in negative aspects. So if they can only see the "bad" in themselves, what motivation would they have to change?

Low frustration tolerance: Alcoholics believe they cannot stand much discomfort or frustration. They refuse to allow themselves to be uncomfortable long enough to learn new coping skills.

Rating self and others: This is a constant comparison to others, the alcoholic never wins. In this case, the alcoholic is constantly seen as a second-rate person or failure.

Overgeneralizing about the future: In this situation, the alcoholic must perform well and not be allowed to fail. Moreover, everyone must approve of them. Since this can never happen, it leads to chronic failure. This type of thinking is a good example of how to maintain a destructive drinking and drugging pattern.

The REBT treatment strategy is to reframe AOD resistance into one of the irrational categories listed above. This gives the therapist a much "cleaner" point of departure from which to engage resistance verses the traditional defects of character perspective.

I have found that in relapse prevention, this cognitive reframing of resistance to irrational thoughts is rather effective. For example, if am working with individuals who does not perceive their present drinking situation to be awful and terrible, rather than try to convince them that they hasn't hit bottom yet, or are still in denial; I reframe these feelings, to how they may be over rating themselves, generalizing, or are not used to a state of moderate or high frustration. With these different ways to perceive the impasse, I can inject a series of treatment interventions directed at strategic irrational thoughts to begin the disruption or interruption of these "resistances."

Instead of the client thinking, "I'm terrible and awful," or "I have some kind of flaw in my character," we can dispute those irrational thoughts, and ask the client to consider a more rational style of thinking. This can include statements like, "I seem to have difficulty tolerating stress, but that is human, and the stress will pass." The essential idea is to get the client to see they are not a bad person for having certain thoughts. There are just human. Seen this way resistance takes on a whole different look.

In this REBT model we identify and treat resistance in terms of: 1) A self-defeating or irrational belief. 2) Which then requires disputing the irrational belief, 3) Repeat this process as necessary. 4) Encourage the client to do their own self-disputing and thereafter, institute more rational sober producing beliefs.

Resistance as a Cognitive Style

In the cognitive framework, what does resistance resist? According to Meichenbaum & Gilmore (1982) resistance opposes change, or the willingness to find and test possible alternative coping strategies. The advocates of cognition see the addict as having a deficit in self-monitoring, or a cognitive blockade.

Beck and Emery (1977); Beck, Wright, Newman and Liese, (1993) developed a cognitive therapy, and specifically applied those principles to chemical dependency. In this model, what has been traditionally seen as resistance is viewed as a variety of different cognitive styles. These styles are somewhat similar to the irrational beliefs we just examined , but with more of an emphasis on core and associated schemas of thinking.

According to Beck and Emery (1977), "In order to learn how to cope with substance abuse dependency, a person has to change what [he/he] is saying about [him/her]self." Here resistance is seen as a series or network of dysfunctional beliefs (Beck, et al, 1993). However, many AOD abusers are not aware of what they are saying to themselves, because this style is so automatic to them. In fact, this automatic mode can be related to problems of impulse control, in that individuals can be seen to be prisoners of their own beliefs (McKay & Fanning, 1991). Until these automatic beliefs become more conscious, change will not occur.

Beck and Emery (1977) outline a series of core dysfunctional beliefs that many chemical dependents repeatedly use and can easily be misconstrued as resistance use. They include:

1. **Capabilities**: When the client does not believe they have the where-with-all to begin a recovery process. Some examples include, "This treatment will never work.” “I just don't have what it takes,” or, “I'm not very good at things like this."

2. **Excuses**: Here the individual finds or creates negative, hollow reasons and explanations for reasons not to quit chemicals. Examples include: "I can't make it through the day without something to calm me down," "When I'm with my friends, I always find myself using," or, "Parties are fun and make me crazy. I can't control myself."

3. **Addictive beliefs**: In these series of thoughts, the person really believes they cannot survive without the substance. Examples include: "A cold beer would really go good about now," "Just one hit on this, and I'll be good for the rest of the day," or, "I always feel better after a few, so I better get a couple in me now."

4. **Self-blame**: This is the situation in which the client begins to put him/herself down for not living up to his expectations. Examples include: "Boy, you're are dumb for doing that," "What a stupid thing to say," or, "I must have a trunk load of character defects."

In addition, these theorists outline a series of anticipatory beliefs or expectancies that the alcoholic will often believe to be true about drinking.

1. Drinking will transform most all experiences into a positive outcome.
2. Drinking will enhance one's social and physical pleasure.

3. It will increase sexual performance and satisfaction.
4. It will increase power and aggression.
5. It will increase my social assertiveness.
6. It will decrease tension.

As soon as these or a variation of the anticipatory thoughts kick in, then the abuser needs a series of facilitating or permissive beliefs. These usually center on, "I can handle it," or, "Since I'm feeling this way, just a little will pick me right up."

Many of these thoughts are automatically sequenced and seem to come out of nowhere. In fact, I have had many clients report to me that they thought these types of thoughts were normal for them. They lived with these thoughts day after day. Many clients will report that these thoughts just happen. The sensation of "just happen" can be frightening because there doesn't seem to be any rhyme or reason to it.

A powerful characteristic of the automatic thought is that the more the person believes in them the more they will uncritically accept them. No amount of logic can make a dent in such an encrusted thought as that. We practitioners often run into these types. They can be frustrating and exasperating because no amount of perfect reasoning on our part makes a difference in the way they think. Sadly, many therapists will begin to turn to the more harsher forms of confrontation, believing that the strong-arm approach is bound to work. However, framing resistance through the "eyes" of cognitive therapy the counselor can engage a line of different treatment approaches.

A good first step to address an automatic thought is to have clients learn to distance themselves from the thought or problem. That is, label the situation which can reduce the anxiety somewhat and allow a little perspective. With a name and some distance, the client can begin to think better and gain some direction. Now, the automatic thought isn't unknown anymore, it now has a name. In addition, encourage the client to stand aside of an urge or problem and watch it as an impersonal observer. This way self-rational talking can occur more easily, and not be cluttered by a host of seemingly powerful negative thinking and emotions.

Beck and Emery (1977) list the following classic distortions (resistances) about chemical dependency, and add a treatment strategy to help offset that distortion. Burns (1980) also lists a similar series of cognitive distortions that although written for depression can easily be translated to chemical dependency. The Beck and Emery distortions include:

1. Disengaging "ideas from facts." Many AOD dependents often confuse the mere thought of anything as being a fact. For example, just thinking about having a drink is enough to actually get the person to go to a bar and order one. "I thought it, so I did it," is often hear from the client. The treatment direction is to get the client to begin to believe that thoughts are not equivalent to reality, no matter how convincing the thought may be. Just because something is thought or felt to be real does not prove that it is.

2. Arbitrary interference is probably at work when one draws a conclusion when none can be drawn, or there is no evidence to back it up. Overgeneralizing a single

event into a series of never ending defeats and magnifying that event way out of proportion (mountains out of molehills) are in this classification of cognitive distortions. The suggested treatment intervention for this series of distortions is to check out the accuracy of what the client feels to be true. If the accuracy is not there, this needs to be presented to the client. Remember to repeat as necessary.

3. Minimizing is another distortion cited by Beck and Emery. However, in this case, minimizing is referred to as the tendency to belittle one's accomplishments. For example, when a client is able to put together a few no-drinking days, they may begin discounting their ability with thoughts like "I can't do it anymore. It's too tough." So, no further sober day attempts are made. A suggested counter approach is to frame that short no drinking attempt as a limited success.

4. Another distortion is to divide everything into two opposing forces--either "all good, or all bad." This all or nothing thinking is called dichotomous thinking. While in it, you cannot win. Many believe that they must be all good, and when they are not they will define themselves as a failure. This never winning or measuring up to an internal set of impossible standards can place anyone in an eternal frame of defeat. After a few years of this, the individual will not even try at all. The trick in this situation is to get the client to move into the gray area of living, where most people reside. That is, allow oneself to make mistakes, and learn from them.

5. Over reliance on others is the attribution (distortion) of believing what is stated by authority figures is the truth. Examples include, "My counselor told me that unless I do exactly as he says, I would end up failing again." The problem with authority figures is that they DO NOT have the corner on the truth or future events. Never had it, never will.
   What sadly happens, is that the empowerment of clients is slowly sapped away by believing in outside authority figures, and not in the self, where the empowerment needs to be. If clients buy into the authority game they can find their ability to make decisions erode away.

6. *Oversocialization* or *enculturation* refers to the distortion of excessive responsiveness to peer pressure. Here, an absolute belief is created by the client in which they feel bound to the norms of a cultural to which they belong. The type of thinking the epitomizes this type is, "Everybody's doing it, so to be one of the crowd, I've got to do it too." By going after the "have to" mentality associated with this enculturation, and bringing to mind a host of other possibilities, this technique can slowly begin to replace habitually, automatic thinking with a wider range of thoughts. These newer options will have the favor of being more self-chosen, and slave driven. This referencing procedure can be helpful with the urges and cravings the recovering person will endure at times.

7. Increasing the level of low frustration tolerance is important in helping offset the urges or thoughts of, "I have to use or I'll go out of my mind." It is helpful to explain to the client that some frustration, and possibly pain will need to be endured. Stating the frustration as uncomfortable, not catastrophic, can make that discomfort more tolerable. I have said this to clients in the past, which proved helpful. They did survive the discomfort, and felt better about their ability to sustain discomfort without resorting to chemicals.

Two additional types of resistance, noted by Beck and Emery are classic. Anyone who has treated a chemical dependency problem has probably run into these. The first are the clients who come across as oppositional, hostile and angry. These clients believe they have to fight the system, program and counselor (This has overtones of reactance of which we will cover shortly). This type of client argues to win or make another look foolish. A possible approach to these individuals is to have them consider that their sense of "independence" is really causing them, not others, problems. That is, the so-called victories over others are merely hallow, short-lived, and only squander opportunities to truly grow in the therapeutic process.

The second classic resistance, pointed out by Beck and Emery, are the types who think they know more than the therapist. They think this way because they believe the therapist does not have the street experience, isn't alcoholic, not of the of the same race, poor, or the right sex or culture. Anytime this has happened to me I usually agree with them, but am quick to point out that although I do not have those experiences, I do have the experience of knowing health, and have observed many people grow through a recovery process. So, we can be mutually helpful: they can teach me the "streets," and I can teach them the recovery process.

AN ATTRIBUTION COGNITIVE APPROACH TO RESISTANCE

Kirmayer (1990) outlined a way to view resistance that has overtones of the cognitive material, but with a systematic flavor. He insists that we first, "...abandon the imprecise use of the term resistance," because of the analytic association. Seen in the analytic way, resistance is perceived as originating entirely within the client, and this analytic perspective sets up a belief that the client will not be able to change because resistance is considered to be innate. He notes that anyone who labels anything resistance implies a sense of willfulness to the client not to change. Finally, Kirmayer feels that the metaphor of resistance carries with it a weight of a moral pejorative in which the client is held responsible for their own misery. Even thought the alcohol and other drug field tries hard to avoid the moral overtones of dependency, it shows its ugly face when a client is told, "You're not getting with the program, and you're still in denial." That always implicitly transmits to the person, you ARE the one who is at fault.

Kirmayer believes that this whole traditional analytical approach implies an inability to cooperate with treatment, and change is inhibited from an active opposition to the therapeutic influence. However when asked directly, clients rarely experience themselves as actively opposing helpful interventions. Yet the traditional therapist perceives the problems in treatment as some kind of client generated resistance. How do these different perception arise?

Kirmayer explains that in the psychology of self-control there is a distinction between primary and secondary perceived control. The primary control is essentially the control of one's actions and behaviors. The secondary control refers to internal thought adjustments that lead to changes in attitudes or behaviors. When a primary control fails there can be a variety of valid reasons. This can include poor skills on the part of the client who just doesn't have the abilities to handle certain situations. To account for the discrepancy (I thought I could do it, but I didn't! Now what?) the secondary processes are employed. The secondary process is more than likely not going to view itself as ill or in need of help. A failure in any behavior is not going to present as a problem until the secondary process (explanation of the primary problem) fails as well.

The secondary process can fail in two ways. First, the client may not have the internal information, knowledge or skills needed to neutralize the impact of the overt failure. Second, the individual may have the where-with-all to account for a negative consequence, but this explanation will not be satisfactory for the subsequent difficulties any new set of circumstances may bring.

It is precisely when the faulty secondary, that the therapist will misconstrue the client as resistant. The client continues to keep on using the same old thinking patterns to account for his primary control failure. For example, if the client is not maintaining abstinence the therapist may interpret the client as readjusting to the old status quo rather than creating new change. The client however experiences his symptoms as clear evidence that he is out of control. The client's resistive symptoms may be an unintended consequence of the secondary controls failure. That control (explanation) cannot account for what is happening to the client, and it is frustrating. The client is forced to continue to use his/her old outmoded thinking styles that don't work in the first place, and a vicious circle is developed.

Another important factor in this process is that the secondary process tends to be a conservative process. The process uses a series of beliefs, attitudes, and values to account for itself and its integrity. Sometimes to produce that stable self-image one will fabricate, and rewrite a personal history to match one's values or bias. A therapist, spouse, and boss says to an individual, "You're an alcoholic. You apparently can't handle just one drink." Then a drinking buddy says, "Don't listen to those guys, of course you can drink." The conservative side of the client, then says, "You've been drinking for years and handled it just fine, so my buddy must be right." And, the conservative side wins this round of the argument.

Now most of us would believe that increasing self-awareness would increase one's responsiveness to suggestions. But according to Kirmeyer, such counseling theories are not true. As one's self-awareness increases, a decrease in responsiveness occurs. This happens because as the self-awareness increases, the conservative element is amplified. This conservative element wants to stay in the status quo. So the very self-awareness engendered by the therapeutic process can lead to a rejection of ideas that are inconsistent with an internal set of beliefs. This rejection will get labeled resistance by the unknowing AOD therapist, and soon a power fight results.

When a primary control (behavior) fails to take place as it was intended, Kirmayer indicates that there will be four cognitive responses to the failure.

Dissonance

The first response to a primary control failure is one of dissonance. Dissonance (Festinger, 1957) is a situation in which two opposing thoughts are forced on an individual and often create a great deal of frustration and anxiety. Kirmayer suggests that this state of dissonance also creates irritability for individuals because their self-standards and conservative attitude cannot account for any discrepancies. When clients think they can control the use of chemicals, and then cannot, it is a primary control failure that creates irritability. To reduce this irritability, the secondary control comes to the "rescue" and modifies the belief system. So the modified thinking might come out like, "You just blew it this time. So what! You can handle it the next go-round."

Feelings Thought to Be Out of Control

A second cognitive response referred to by Kirmayer is that of emotional exacerbation. Here the problem, any problem, is made worse by focusing more attention on it, or trying harder to control something that is not amenable to self-control. The client attributes the dysfunctional behavior to him/herself. The self is unable to resolve the problem. The resulting tension and anxiety exacerbates negative feelings. An emotional cycle is formed that only widens, what the self wants to believe, and what is really happening. The treatment approach here is to reestablish a sense of self-control through learning more effective coping mechanisms.

Reactance

The third response is how people react when their freedom is threatened by being coerced into treatment or being told they can't do certain things by a probation officer. This can and will generate anger, frustration, and tension because the sense of control is seen as being taken away. This is what is called reactance (Brehm, 1966). As we have noted, it will get confused as denial or some associated resistance (Dowd & Seibel, 1990). In this example , if the anger is generated by this loss or threatened loss of freedom, it makes sense that this reactance needs to be the focus of attention, not some mythical resistance issue. In addition, this reactance issue can also be seen as a device clients use to maintain their sense of autonomy and identity. A little reactance may be seen as healthy in adults. It is when it becomes habitual and pronounced that it may create a negative identity (Dowd &. Seibel, ibid).

The reactance generated by being forced into treatment (e.g. court orders, go to treatment, or lose your job type of motivation) has had a lot of mixed and varied opinions (IOM, 1990). The notion has often been, if clients do not come to treatment for themselves, they will not get anything out of it. As well worn practitioners, many of us know that we would not have a practice nor a program long, if it were not for some type of coercion. Of course there is pressure and manipulation to get the client into some type of treatment. The question is how does the quality AOD counselor get through the client's resistance of coming to therapy against his/her will? A first step in answering that question is asking yourself, "Is the uncooperative behavior I am dealing with some factor of denial, or reactance? "

John and Lichstein (1980), and Dowd, Milne and Wise (1991) summarized the latest research on this subject. It turns out that reactance is the motivational state of a person whose freedom has been eliminated or threatened. So the opposition seen in many AOD cases is reactance, not denial.

Let's interject a few more hints for dealing with these phenomena. If you feel reactance is playing a part in the resistance then try to give the client more choices in the therapeutic decision. I do this consistently with my DUI classes and avoid a lot of needless problems.

One of my favorite strategies is to get the class involved in changing the schedule. It gives the students a sense that they can control a bit of the system. Joining the client and giving back some sense of control may be a good first move in these situations. I have repeatedly done this with many DUI groups and have ended with many cooperative and attentive classes.

Control: Not in My Hands

The fourth response, reported by Kirmayer, is when the client believes both the behavior and cause of the behavior is thought to lie in the hands of others. In this situation, there is a sense of profound helplessness, and that creates the fertile ground of withdrawal, giving up and depression. The suggested approach here is to reframe the client's helplessness in terms of self-efficacy and power. The reframe may center on an indication of the client's wisdom, and choice in yielding their control over to others, and therefore getting what they want in the long run. This reframe may be just enough for them to loosen that tight, fatalistic grip they have developed on their present situation. Remember that it is that underlying attribute that can account for the resulting response we just reviewed.

Table 2 gives a summation of the various attributed client responses and the suggested intervention.

Table: 2

COGNITIVE RESPONSE	SUGGESTED INTERVENTION
If dissonance	Try Negative reframe
If emotional exacerbation	Try symptom prescription
If Reactance	Try paradoxical injunction
If withdrawal	Try positive reframe

THE PREFERRED DEFENSE STRUCTURE OF ALCOHOLICS

Wallace (1978) developed the idea of a *Preferred Defense Structure* of alcoholics (PDS) and its relation to denial. According to Wallace, the defensive styles of AOD dependents are set of tactics and strategies that alcoholics use to protect their ego. Wallace believes this PDS is the outcome of alcoholism and not antecedent to it. This PDS can be thought of as a collection of skills and abilities that alcoholics have developed over the years, which help them achieve their chemical using ends. Viewed in this manner, denial does not have to be construed in the terms of defense mechanisms, which Wallace feels has moral overtones. In fact, the PDS doesn't have to be seen in negative terms at all. It is just the styles, strategies and tactics that alcoholics have developed over time to cope with their drinking. The PDS can also be applied to the functioning of denial. Wallace claims that deliberate denial functions as a, "...extremely valuable adjustive and coping devise" for the alcoholic. It is something alcoholics have relied on for years; they like it and it has served them well. The therapist should not confront and totally discard this "skill", instead, Wallace feels the alcoholic should redirect it. Rather than eliminating the obsessional energy of wanting to use chemicals, which can be nearly impossible, the AOD therapist should try to discover ways to transform that energy toward a recovery process. Essentially, the idea is to try to get the alcoholic to identify with others who have similar problems, which can put a painful past into perspective, as well as gain the reinforcement of a new support group.

He outlined five different PDS styles.

The first of these he called the *all or nothing profile*. He felt that alcoholics need a fair amount of certainty in their lives. This includes people, events, and situations around them. In fact this need for certainty often drifts into extremes, and has effects on their decision making abilities. Making decisions is not based on what is realistically possible; rather, decision making, for the alcoholic, is determined by narrowed, inflexible, and simplistic patterns. Alternatives are considered to be few and consist of either yes/no, on/off, go/no go types of patterns. In this limited context, one could see how the alcoholic will act impulsively and poorly to the people, events, and situations that impinge on them. It can be assumed that the only alternatives they see for themselves when life becomes difficult is to "pick-up."

This is not so much a true resistance, but more of a pattern or habitual defensive lifestyle. As such, it does not necessarily describe the process and dynamics as much as it describes traits and characteristics. The same goes for the other styles that follow.

The next item of this defensive structure is called *conflict minimization and avoidance*. According to Wallace, the alcoholic is assumed to want to avoid interpersonal conflict at all costs. Either it's not in his/her nature, or the extended use of alcohol has eroded his/her ability to weather these types of conflicts. It is for this reason that Wallace recommends no confrontation of the client, especially the hostile variety.

The next defensive structure is called *self-centered attention*. In this case, alcoholics are assumed to be obsessed with themselves and they evaluate situations that occur around them in terms of how they would react personally to such situations. Wallace seems to think there is a screening out process attached to this particular structure, which is linked to low self worth, guilt, and shame. This is assumed to be the reason why alcoholics have a difficult time taking feedback, and not learning from such criticism.

The fourth structure is called a *preference for nonanalytical modes of thinking and perceiving*. Here Wallace believes that the alcoholic is persuaded less by cool logic, than by warm, inspirational (if not altogether emotional) appeals. The charismatic approach is preferred over the reasoned one. Wallace believes that, "The alcoholic is more drawn to the warmth of magic rather than the cold objectivity of science." So when counselors address client concerns, Wallace would argue that the alcoholic would prefer the counselor who would support and advocate for them, not necessarily experts.

The last defensive structure is entitled *obsessional focusing*. Wallace believes that alcoholics are, by nature, intense and obsessive. Once they stop drinking, they begin to focus not only their drinking, but their work, cigarette smoking, and coffee drinking. He would advocate an attempt to reduce this obsession. The goal of treatment should be to redirect it toward the ritualistic attendance of AA meetings.

Given the allure of this list of defensive styles, it has to be noted that it is not supported by extensive data. Wallace admits that these profiles are based on "his clinical experience." That means he simply created a set of spectacles from which to view and categorize alcoholics. To his credit many of these styles might apply to certain alcoholics, but as we have indicated, they would not apply to all. The practitioner has to be very cautious when they employ such profiles to all their clients.

Resistance in Relapse Dynamics

For as long as I can remember, relapse was traditionally considered to be generated by a return of the denial process. Marlett and Barrett (1994) indicate that denial and rationalization often combine to distort thinking, cause uninformed choices, and then contribute to relapse. However, this perspective implies that the client failed somehow, and further, they brought the relapse on themselves. The client was again to blame for the misfortune, and the probable driving force was good ol' denial.

Today, we know that relapse can be attributed to a number of issues versus only the term denial. For example, people may not know how to maintain their sobriety once they've taken a few steps in that direction (Chaney, 1989). Clients do not fail Taleff, 1992) they just needs to learn new strategies to maintain what they developed. In fact, telling clients that they have failed and need to start the recovery process all over again may be more damaging to them in the long run, because it tends to foster a sense of defeatism and learned helplessness.

A young man convinced me of the inaccuracy of that folklore several years ago. He told me he had managed to accumulate about three years without using heroin. He sustained a relapse, and was sorely depressed because all his so-called clean associates told him that he had to start his recovery all over again. He let me know, with a tear in his eye, that no one would give him credit for the three years he had achieved. We did, and he managed to begin another period of heroin free time.

I recently heard an old story that is a great illustration of the idea that failure is the price to pay for relapse. It's about a dog who just couldn't learn to go outside to relieve himself. His master would come home and see the mess on the floor, rub the dog's nose in it, and throw him out the window. After many years of this, when he heard the master come home, the dog would immediately rub his own nose in the mess he made, and throw himself out the window.

The point is that so-called resistance in relapse can be reframed in terms of problem-solving contexts. Individuals who cannot deal effectively with certain situations may turn to old coping mechanisms (drinking & drugging) to manage. What looks like resistance that occurs in the relapse process may be poorly developed skills to handle the sobriety aspect of living. Miller (1991) indicates that in a sample of those who were recovering and those who were not, the clients with successful recovery did much better on a battery on neuropsychological tests. Those who relapsed did poorly on tests of language, abstract reasoning, planning and cognitive flexibility. This is clearly not denial nor resistance.

In addition, the notion of relapse could have other alternative explanations. For example, relapse could be accounted for by:

1. Environmental factors, such as no support from a family after the completion of treatment process, or no family involvement at all. Or returning to a neighborhood that is immersed in gun-fire and drugs.

2. Some unresolved secondary process such as a dual disorder that wasn't accounted for (personality disorder, depression).

3. Any of the cognitive process that we reviewed from awfulizing to discounting any positives in the client's life.

4. A misinterpretation of client behavior. In this case, consider reviewing the decision tree presented in chapter three to become more aware of alternatives that might be closer to the core problem.

5. Consider that developmentally, the relapser may be a concrete thinker. These types have a very difficult time abstracting possibilities, and thinking in the future tense. Things in life for them have to be acted upon. They have a difficult time picturing in their mind's eye what may happen.

6. Then again, maybe it really is denial.

THE CONTEXT VIEW OF RESISTANCE

Every perspective we have examined thus far has been of the content type of resistance. I now want to address the context view of resistance. We shift from looking at underlying causes and pathology to examining meaning and solutions. In this perspective, resistance is considered a concept the practitioner can do without.

The Death of Resistance

For those in the AOD field, who have not run across this contextual perspective of resistance before, it may seem odd that the whole idea of resistance, according to this perspective, is done away with and buried. The chief proponent of this view is deShazer (1984). His argument derives from the solution-brief perspective of therapy. This viewpoint sees psychotherapy moving from pathology in the client to that of seeing or facilitating solutions by the client (O'Hanlon & Weiner-Davis, 1989; Berg & Miller, 1992).

The perspective on resistance is different from anything we have encountered thus far. Resistance, according to deShazer, is considered to be a hold over from the homeostasis theory in which the system wants to maintain the status quo. This has a closed loop mentality to it and is an implicitly closed system. If therapists acknowledges this view, they will find themselves in a linear causation thinking pattern in which one thing leads to another. As can be easily seen, most of the previously noted resistance models can fall into this type of category. The problem with the content models, is that the therapist may be locked into their preferred theory and ignores what is really operating in the client. Essentially content models indicate that the client does not want to change, and that behavior is being manifested through the resistance. On the other hand, the proponents of the open system are indicating that the client really does want to change, but may be stuck in solutions to their problems that are not working. In fact, deShazer goes so far as to claim that the resistance we think we are seeing is really the client's way of cooperating with the treatment. This way of dealing with his/her present set of problems is a sentiment that is also shared by Kottler (1992), and some of the Gestalists (Polster & Polster, 1976; Breshgold, 1989).

Berg and Miller (1992) point out that resistance is really a breakdown in the client-counselor relationship. AOD counselors often believe that resistance is present if a client does not accept an idea presented by the counselor. This has the overtones of a "catch-22" mind set (Peele, 1989). Thinking in this fashion the client will always be the loser, or be blamed for not completing a treatment strategy that the traditional AOD counselor feels is the right one for him/her. Anyone can easily be labeled as being in denial under these circumstances. The problem as we have seen it, is that such a inflexible viewpoint can and will limit treatment options. This can only harm the overall therapy process. So as Taleff (1994) has argued, why not do away with the denial process as deShazer did away with resistance, and open the doors to new fresh ideas in chemical dependency treatment.

O'Hanlon and Weiner-Davis (1989) indicate that they also do not believe in resistance. They see that concept as one that any therapist can give to a client who is not making change in the therapeutic process. They go on to state, "...labeling our clients can limit our ideas about possible solutions and cause us to give up using the clients as partners in the change process." deShazer (1988) echoes this view when he maintains that to frame a client as "difficult" is to begin to treat that case with the appropriate "difficult" interventions. Further, the client will begin to perceive themselves as "difficult", and a circular if not self fulfilling prophecy is established.

This perspective is not without its critics. Kottler (1992) considers this "death of resistance" to be premature and considers resistance to be quite alive. He argues his case from the very position that the solution people indicate is the problem, that resistance is in the mind of the therapist. Kottler when referring to his clients states, "...I expect a hard time,..." The solutionist would say, he will probably get it.

Perhaps the closest any brief theorists would come to the standard way many in the AOD professions see resistance is offered by Zimmerman and Dickerson (1993). They indicate that individuals are sometimes held back from seeing new ideas due to the influence of a dominant story. This is what they call a negative explanation, or an understanding of events that occur "instead of" rather than "because of" other events. The focus is on restraints, rather then causes. They feel that certain perceptions of events carry an "inevitability" from which we notice things. It is these powerful perceptions that block the possibility of seeing other options in our lives. These are the dominant stories we carry, that are problem saturated. They close off options and alternatives, and the individual is left with continuing the same old ways of living.

Treatment Strategies Using Solution Therapy

We will address these types of interventions in Chapter Six, so just a small introduction will be given at this point.

This approach to resistance dispels a few common beliefs about therapy as most of us know it (Miller & Berg, 1995; Berg & Miller, 1992; O'Hanlon & Weiner-Davis, 1989). For example, clients are believed to have all the inner resources and strengths to resolve their problems. This is a far cry from how the traditionalists claim the addict does not have the inner resources for recovery and must, therefore, rely on some sort of twelve step group or outside power for the rest of their lives.

The solution view claims it is not important to know a great deal about the client's past. In other words, it is not necessary to know the cause of something in order to resolve it. Only small change is in order. A small change will affect whole behavior. Small change is a treatment goal, not large cumbersome goals in which the client may very well fail. Focus on what has worked, i.e., solutions and not pathology, plus look for exceptions to the continuing problem and take advantage of them. Rapid change is also felt to be possible, and there is not a specific way to do treatment.

These techniques include matching the client's language and sensory modalities and redirect the language away from psychological jargon, and toward everyday talk. In addition, solution-oriented questions are to be used to engage the client. These types of questions presuppose that the client will change and not remain the same. For example, at the end of a session one might ask, "How will you be different by the time we meet next week?" In this frame, the therapist is expecting the client to make some sort of change. This mind-frame has a positive feel to it, and puts the client in a solution thinking mode. Very often in traditional therapy, the client is left with a statement like, "If you make it till next week, we will move on to the next phase of treatment. If not, we will repeat what was covered today." That has more of a negative feel to it, and conveys little confidence in the client.

Other such solution-oriented questions include, "What have you done in the past that has helped you not to drink?" When the client answers, the therapist needs to amplify this solution and repeat it. The idea is, if a strategy worked do it again. Ask the client to describe what was occurring when the symptoms were less severe and shorter in duration to find what works, and then use those ideas in therapy.

The manner in which a question is formulated can direct a client to a solution. Without mentioning the solution orientation, Chan (1993) indicated that the manner in which assessment questions are delivered can trigger or not trigger denial. It depends on how and in what context the question is asked.

One of the favored approaches I have used is the technique of looking for the "hidden customer" (Berg & Miller, 1992). A client I worked with not long ago was on probation for a past drug related offense. He made it clear that probation was the customary "pain in the ass." He also made it clear that he was not enthusiastic about the idea of stopping his use of drugs. Rather than point out to him that his drug use was at the core of all his problems, and he would need to stop using in order to have a better life, I took a different approach. I figured he was not going to be a "customer" for the cessation of drug use. If I perused that angle, we would only end up in a power struggle. I decided to try to sell him something he wanted already--get his probation officer off his back. I began to ask prepositional questions of how he could get that S. O. B. out of his hair. "What could you do by next week to keep that guy out off your back?" The first couple of responses included the usual, "I would be more sneaky about my drug use." However, he soon started to say more positive things without my prompting. One of these options included an option of cutting down on the drugs, so he would avoid going back to prison. We played around with that idea for a while, and even joked about how flipped out the P.O. would be if he, the client, stopped using chemicals. He managed to stay clean for the week, and was down right tickled when the P.O. took an urine sample and found it was clean. This clean behavior continued for the time he was with our program (3 months). I have heard he's still clean after two years.

This case illustrates that when you start small, look for solutions and believe your clients have the resources to handle their own problems, you can begin see treatment possibilities through a new lenses.

SECTION III: EVERYDAY RESISTANCE

In this section we address the more tangible side of resistance. These are the types of resistances professionals see in their daily work, but they do not easily fit into the concept of denial or fall into the major theories reviewed in section 2. Munjack and Oziel (1978) felt that in differentiating many types of resistance, a therapist could effectively bring more appropriate interventions to bear on a client. This idea dovetails with the core philosophy of this book, that in developing more alternatives or variations of resistance AOD counselors will be more confident of their assessments and treatment strategies.

As each of these everyday resistance types is reviewed, a few treatment, will be suggested.

An AOD version of Otani's Perspective of Resistance

Otani (1989) defines resistance as, "The clients opposition to change in the counseling process." She presents a clear picture of various everyday resistances in a category system which is easy to follow and understand. I have adapted and expanded this classification system to include those everyday resistances often found in alcohol and other drug treatment. Many ideas in Section 2, had a single premise running through their formulations (e.g., an underlying dynamic, a style of thinking, or a boundary impediment). However, in the following scheme resistance can be generated by three major sources: anxiety, noncompliance, and negative social influence (See figure 2b-1). Each of these perspectives is given additional import by the thinking and material of other authors in and out of the AOD field.

Factors That Generate Everyday Resistance

As indicated, Otani credits *anxiety* as a major force behind resistance. Cromier and Cromier (1975) also feel that anxiety is a prime generator of resistance. Under these circumstances, resistance is used as an avoidance mechanism (Mahoney, 1991). The ego or sense of self is threatened by anxiety and that is more than it can bare. For example, anxiety can manifest itself if it is associated by memories of a painful childhood, or by insights that threaten a personification developed for protection reasons.

It is easy to see how a person with drug and alcohol problems might fit into such a scheme. For instance, consider the heightened sense of threat and anxiety that might accompany many individuals who begin to realize that they are not in control of their lives, due to the abuse of mood altering drugs. Also consider the frightening experience of coming out of a blackout and not knowing what you did the night before, where you left the car, or where that new dent in the fender came from. Imagine the anxiety.

The next prod of resistance centers on *noncompliance*. This has behavioral overtones in which assignments given by a counselor are not completed, and treatment in general is not progressing. In this case, anxiety is not generating resistance, yet the client does not follow or comply with directions. Why? Sheldon and Levy (1981) cite three major reasons for this possibility. First, clients may not have the necessary skills or knowledge to complete the task. Consider the individual who does not complete a "first step-prep" or one of those self-administered questionnaires. We could easily attribute this behavior to low motivation or to denial. Yet, the fact could be that the client does not have the skill or ability understand the instructions. That can be an especially shameful experience for those who were asked to share a written task before a group.

Rather than jump into a confrontational mode at the sight of some unfinished assignment, it might be best to clarify the set of instructions. The first time around the client may have thought the instructions were too general, or not descriptive enough. Think about having the client repeat the instructions back to you. If you determine that there is a skill deficit, then refer or give the appropriate training to offset it.

The second cause Sheldon and Levy found for non-completion of tasks revolves around a false assumption that if the abuser completes it, negative consequences will result. This negative outcome is similar to what Cromier and Cromier (1985) describe as clients who believe that there will be a pessimistic outcome to task completion, and therefore avoid it. A suggestion for dealing with this state of affairs is to encourage the client to acknowledge the presumed negative outcome to help clarify or understand what is at the core of the uncompleted task.

Encouraging clients to complete a task can come across a bit preachy and moralistic, if you insist that they can do it if they want to. To many clients statements like "This isn't that difficult," can sometimes translate into, "It's simple, but you can't get it," or, "If you put your mind to it you can finish it", which translates into, "Obviously, you haven't put your mind to it." Rather dispensing standard sentiments like this, consider matching your comments to those of the client. That is, let him/her know you understand, and it's a human feeling to be uncertain and doubtful. In addition, you may want to start off with a less intimidating task, and then proceed to the more complicated items. Also, keep in mind some appropriate neurolinguistic techniques to help with the rapport process (see Chapter 6), or some cognitive re-structuring (Seligman, 1991) to soften the perceived threat of the task.

Cromier and Cromier (1985) suggest that there are other compelling reasons for not finishing a task. This can include any shameful or embarrassing situation that exists in a person's life with a subsequent fear of ridicule. Specific examples include the embarrassment of not having a job, or the inability to pay one's bills. In this case, the client isn't resisting, he/she is just preoccupied with other matters. A suggestion to deal with these competing elements is to reduce the intensity of these factors by focusing on them. That is, formulate plans to get the bills paid, or secure some type of emergency income to get through a difficult time. Then get on with the business of treatment.

An additional noncompliant stance taken by clients may involve secondary gain. Well, you might ask, what is to be gained from the addictive use of chemicals? What about attention seeking, or feeling "a part of something" or to cover up some deep seated inadequacies? The gain to be derived in the last example is to blame the booze for always keeping them "down and out." In this way, real inadequates are kept secret and safe, even though it is a painful way to do cope. This is called "self-handicapping" (Berglas, 1987).

A last reason for noncompliance can be due to one's family. A classic example of this type of noncompliance involved a young man I was working with, who was also part of a prison release program. We clearly established early on that one of his relapse triggers was his mother. When he would visit his home, his mother would always yell to him as he walked out of the door, "Goin' out to drink again are ya'?" As he shared this episode with the group, it was obvious how upset he became as he described the episode. He realized later that he would do exactly what she predicted, which made him even more upset and apt to drink. When family and friends are so negative a quality recovery is difficult to maintain.

On to Otani's third major motivator of resistance. This is what she calls *negative social influence*. This particular item is rarely given deliberation in many AOD staff meetings, and sadly so. This negative influence refers to the resistance that occurs when poor dynamics develop between a client and the counselor. Some of the readers may see this as resembling the dynamic concept called countertransference. Well, in some respects it does. However, one of the major differences is that in this case negative social influences are defined as interpersonal artifacts that exist between the client and the counselor. This is more of a between-the-persons dynamic than an intrapersonal issue. There may not be any unconscious factors to be projected on the part of the counselor. Yet, there is a mismatch between you and the client. It is very noticeable, and indicates you and this client do not get along.

Another aspect of this negative social influence is the overlooked difference between true resistance and opposition. Strong and Matross (1973) note that resistance may be the client's non-acceptance of the counselors influence or power, while, opposition could be the client's reaction to the content of a counseling message. It could prove beneficial to know whether a client was resisting you as a person or opposing your clinical message. If one knew the difference, then one could try to institute a different strategy of treatment to properly address the prevailing issue.

Now that we have the three broad generators of resistance in place according to this viewpoint, let us turn to a modified version of Otani's classification system of client resistive behavior. I encourage you to re-assess a present or past client through this list of commonly observed behaviors. The ongoing goal remains the accurate appraisal of the client behavior.

We will examine four broad categories of resistance with sub-divisions in each.

Category A Resistances

Category A centers on how much (or how little) the client talks. The amount of relevant information is the key ingredient in this category.

You cannot have worked in the drug and alcohol field for long and not met the well-known individual who answers all your questions with a quick "a-huh," "Yeah," "Nope," or similar response. Obviously, the logic is not to talk so that a minimal amount of information is disclosed. On the other hand, a barrage of words from the client who doesn't say much can also be included in this category. In this case, a lot of talking still discloses little information. A fancy name for all this is *minimal disclosing*.

Category B Resistances

Category B deals with the response content of a client. This may be more in line with what many AOD counselors experience in their daily work. Here the content, not the quantity as in category A, is restricted. Ehrenburg and Ehrenburg (1977) note this type of resistance as 'keeping the therapist in the dark." It is here that the traditional explanations of denial, rationalization and intellectualization can easily fit.

Sub-divisions in this category include:

Intellectual Talk

Intellectual talk is the kind of discussion that has an air of pompous philosophy about it. It is debating that has an demeaning edge to it. It probes for weakness and flaws in your thinking, if not you as a person. Some signs that give this type of interaction away are the mechanical tone in the voice of the speaker, as well as the over use of technical terms. There is often a sense of one-upsmanship about the discussion, and often makes the therapist feel as if he/she is being judged and made to look inferior.

Emotional Display

Many in the AOD field assume that any emotional display from the client is a definite sign of health. It is assumed that getting those feelings out is somehow healthy in and of itself. In fact, many programs are based implicitly on this assumption. This is what is referred to as the "emotions as pus" concept (Gaylen, 1979). For example, the idea is to bring your anger or whatever to a boiling head. The counselor or group are expected to lance this emotional boil. This cathartic effect, alone, is considered to be helpful and cleansing.

A problem with this perspective is that many of the clients, to whom this approach is directed can easily elicit the very feelings they want to cleanse. It has been postulated that if you believe in this approach to therapy, the client may end up actually rehearsing the next round of emotions rather than actually diminishing them (Travis, 1982). In addition, those individuals who have not had the experience of a catharsis can be frightened by raw feelings such as anger. Associated with these emotional exhibitions are those "crocodile tears" that try to elicit sympathy from the listener. The purpose of this and an over-emotional response is to head-off any further incursions into real issues. Thus, the continual emoting of a client, e.g., tears, grief, sorrow, may not necessarily carry the intended signal of health as many therapists think. This chronic outpouring of emotion may be a subtle form of resistance.

I once treated a young client who grieved over the lose of her child to foster parents. She would give me detailed accounts of her guilt and anguish in session after session. I would think, at the end of each of these episodes, that at last we were coming to the end of the pain, and we could then begin to integrate the loss and move on. What was actually happening was that she never could come to terms with her past because of her continued emoting. She had only learned how to discharge feelings, not to cope with them. The strong feelings just got in the way and often set her up for another bout of guilt-driven drinking. Soon, I began to question my tactic of, "Letting her get it all out." We began to focus treatment in different directions (life-skill management and development) and she ceased relapsing.

Symptom Preoccupation

This resistance refers to that type of client who becomes obsessed with certain symptoms which endlessly manifest themselves. There is very often an associated air of pessimism that surrounds this preoccupation, and they think that they are not capable enough to adequately handle the symptom. These symptoms can range from repeated urges and cravings to symptoms of depression.

The concept of learned helplessness is associated with this preoccupation. To the individual under the spell of learned helplessness everything seems to be out of control, no matter what they do. It is interesting to see how this phenomena and chemical dependency intertwine. Both have a very pessimistic outlook. This is not to say that one causes the other, but they are often found together and create problems in effecting change. The learned helplessness concept was coined by Seligman (1974; 1991). Essentially, it means that people who think they are helpless, in spite of any positive actions they bring about.

Consider chronic relapsers who have this mind-set. This explanation could account for why they haven't been able to put together any long periods of abstinence. They could really believe that no matter what they do, it will not make any difference, so they don't try.

Another client I worked with often displayed this kind of preoccupation behavior. She would become so engrossed in her depressive symptoms that she would forget all that she had learned and developed through treatment. She would constantly repeat that she never was able to do anything right in the past, and would never do anything right in the future. Her predictions came true because she ended up not being very successful in her recovery.

Future/Past Preoccupation

Much of what was described in the past sections applies here, but instead of symptoms as the focus of the obsession, it is time. These individuals chronically lament over a past indiscretion, or over a future engagement like a court date. The focus on the past may have so much shame and guilt associated with it that they cannot forgive themselves. On the other hand, the future often has air of tension and anxiety associated with it. Subsequently, they cannot focus on anything else.

Simply saying to these types that they need to take care of today's business and not the past probably won't sink in. Why not? They are so preoccupied with various time frames they cannot see anything else. Now what? Consider a series of distractions to get them to unlock from these preoccupations long enough to at least communicate with THEM, not the preoccupations. I have found activities other than therapy proper is one way to unlock these preoccupations, even for a few minutes. Then I can start talking with the person instead of a preoccupation.

Another type of preoccupation centers on the fear of failure (Munjack & Oziel, 1978). Often people will not even try to change because they are thinking, "What if I don't make it. Then what will happen?" It's that attitude and feeling of fear, which can paralyze a person into inaction. Knowing that this type of fear exists, a counselor can direct an appropriate treatment strategy for the client which is aimed at reducing the intensity of the fear. It should be noted, that all those statements about a "stiff upper lip" and "keep on trying" are not very productive with this type of resistance. These statements often just exacerbate the fear, or worse, point out to the person that they have no courage.

Rhetorical Questions

In this case, clients can invoke a very good method to keep the discussion off their issues, by letting the counselor do most of the talking. In this case, the client will begin to ask a host of questions about the counselor's own recovery process or ask seemingly important questions about addictive dynamics. If counselors take the bait, they may feel compelled and happy to answer all the questions of the client. Some counselors like to show off their knowledge, and many others just like to hear themselves talk. The problem with this maneuver is the counselor is doing all the talking, while the client is not.

Sometimes our clients know how to stroke our egos, and they can get many a therapist off and running describing a pet theory, or how they became a drug and alcohol counselor. The explanation of my life as an AOD counselor might take session after session to explain, much to the delight of the client.

Category C Resistances

Category C resistance deals with response styles. This is a type of resistance in which the client manipulates the manner of information that is disclosed. Langs (1981) also lists a host of such communicative resistances that are very similar to the category C type of resistance. His material is also included in the following.

Sub-divisions of category C include:

Discounting

This response style resistance is evident in the ever present "yes-but" response of the client. This has a close affinity to the classic concept of denial we discussed in section one, but In this case, discounting has overtones of game playing, while denial has a serious avoidance tone to it. Discounting can be frustrating to therapists because each point that is made by them is "yes-butted" by the client. The counselor can begin to think they are on a merry-go-round with this type of resistance. Each point of treatment is somehow discredited by the client which is very frustrating!

Another facet of discounting is that of communications theory (Jahn & Lichstein, 1980). Here clients select what will be attended or listened to. Anything that deviates from what is expected will be dealt a major dose of resistance. Many clients have a fixed notion of what is really wrong with them. They have constructed their own "solutions" to their perception of the problem. When a counselor doesn't listen or agree with those solutions, the client may begin to view the counselor as biased, unbelievable, or even foolish, and that leads to counseling problems.

Limit Setting

In this case, the client sets limits regarding what will not be discussed. I have had a few individuals actually spell out prior to the beginning of a session that if we began to talk about sex or drinking they would get up and leave the room. Thus, my experience has been not to talk about those subject areas right away. More often than not, after a trusting relationship has developed, the client wants to talk about those very issues. The treatment recommendation in these cases are to work on developing the relationship. You will then be seen as reliable, and the client will be more prone to discuss sensitive issues.

Externalization

This is chronic blaming of everybody and everything for one's problems. This phase is akin to one of Kulber-Ross's (1971) stages of accepting death. The client may end up taking responsibility for their actions, but first they have to get over blaming the world. Knowing this process is at work, and treating it, not some other resistance factor, will profit the overall therapy process.

Second Guessing

Through this tactic, clients begin to get a counselor to second guess themselves. Questions arise from the client that sound something like, "Is this what you're trying to say?" It is usually stated with only a slight misunderstanding of what you just said, so you feel obligated to explain even more. This strategy gets the focus off the client and somehow back on to you. The dance is about semantics, not client issues. This is a subtle maneuver, and easily gets many a novice and seasoned counselor side tracked.

Counselor Stroking

If trying to get the counselor off the track doesn't work by any of the means we just discussed, then try kissing up to the counselor's ego. It will work most every time! It sounds like, "Thanks Mike, if it hadn't been for you I would probably be dead," or, "You explain things so clearly. Nobody ever explained things to me like you do." If this is chronic--beware. I know a few counselors who love this type of stroking. Their egos love to be massaged. Trouble is the course of treatment goes no where, and it is the client who has just bamboozled the counselor.

Seductiveness

If "kissing up" doesn't work for the client to get you off the track, then some subtle sexual alluring might. This can come in a variety of behaviors that range from covert flirting to overt sexual come-ons. Generally these behaviors are easily noticed and can be addressed. It is a must that these things be addressed. Suggestions include, taking the secretiveness out of the sexual implications, by talking about these issues straight-out. In addition, it is critical that you notify your supervisor about such situations, and document, document, document.

Forgetting and not Understanding

This everyday resistance deals with the client who conveniently forgets an important homework assignment, or does not bring important papers to a session as promised. One has to be careful with a client's "forgetting." Sometimes it is a legitimate mistake, due to the damage created by the ingestion of chemicals over the years. Other times forgetting can have overtones of inconvenience to it. In this latter situation, clients may be thinking the assignment was stupid, that it does not apply to them.

In addition, Munjack and Oziel (1978) plus Cromier and Cromier (1985), both expound on the client who simply does not understand what they are suppose to do. This is not a skill deficient, but a true sense of "I don't understand." For example, you give what you consider to be a self-explanatory task for a group. Invariably, someone looks at you with a funny, squelched expression, and starts scratching and shaking their head trying to figure out what this assignment is all about. You know what's coming, because they say something like, "I don't get it." This is after you gave what you thought were very clear instructions. Frustrated, one can easily attribute this to some kind of hard addiction resistance. That may not be the case. This particular category may be a prime reason why some clients are prone to relapse. Forgetting and not understanding may not be the result of denial. They just may not understand the assignments that were given to them. Rather than own up to that short coming, they fake it and don't get much out of the sessions.

Consider some of the following questions before you jump to another resistance conclusion.
1. Was the assignment incorrect or relevant to their needs?
2. Was it too threatening?
3. Did the client think it was more work than it was worth?
4. Did the client appreciate the value behind the exercise?
5. Is the therapeutic relationship at fault?
6. Is there someone in the client's social network sabotaging the therapy?
7. Is the client receiving far too many addictive "benefits" to let go of their maladaptive behavior?

By the way, confusion may also be at the core of this type of resistance. It has the feeling of, "I am really perplexed." Many of our clients can be confused due to the after effects of chronic abuse of chemicals. If we know this, we can very easily correct the situation by giving more attention to the client and more clarification to our instructions.

Strategy recommendations for this type of an event are to:
1. Provide specific and detailed instructions.
2. Consider having the client repeat back the instructions you have just given them.
3. If the need arises, you may want to help the client with some direct reading and writing skill, "training practices."

Category D resistances

These types of resistances center around logistical management (i.e. the client violates some basic rule of the counseling agreement). Again, Langs (1981) lists a very similar classification of resistance, but he calls it gross behavioral resistances. We will use a combination both lists in this section.

Sub-divisions in category D include:

Poor Appointment Keeping

This is obvious, and requires immediate attention. Again, as with the forgetting item noted above, it is important that you not over-react. There are times when clients will forget. When this seems to be a pattern, or perhaps when something important is at stake you need to take notice, for example, if the client does not show up for a family session that has been scheduled for sometime. Rogers (1942) indicates that such tardiness occur because the counseling process is becoming painful. Then it is the pain that requires treatment attention, not some assumed resistance.

Payment Delayed or Refusal to Pay

This is a point of contention for many counselors. It may be a resistance of sorts in that clients may be trying to get back at you for something said in a session. Some clients may think the service they received is not worth the agreed upon fee, and hold back on payment due. It can also serve as one of the few ways in which clients can get back at something or someone over which they feel they have no control. There could also be some type of a reactance issue operating here. This whole issue needs to be openly addressed, and the cause determined for the proper action.

Some Last Versions of Everyday Resistances

We have covered a variety of ideas and concepts. This last section addresses a few remaining resistance types not easily categorized in the above table.

The Protective Function of Resistance

This resistance is called self-protection. Here we take on a whole new framework to the concept of resistance. In all the previous resistance classification systems, there was an impediment aspect to recovery and change. With this view, resistance is see as something that is natural or protective of our integrity. This is in line with Haley's (1987) notion that symptoms or resistances have an appropriate or adaptive aspect to them. This general view presupposes the client guards and resists rapid or substantial change.

This self-protective idea emphasizes a healthy caution to radical change in oneself (Egan, 1994). With this view in mind, a counselor should not attack resistance, but expect it, and work with it. In this framework, resistance is considered quite common, not bad, nor pathological. Snyder (1988) believes that defenses are difficult to operationalize, and finds that individuals generally process the world through self-schemas and self-theories. When they do that, they process or attribute all incoming information according to what is relevant to them. This attributing is often in the form of "how I compare to others." Most people will take credit for the positive outcomes in their lives, and blame some outside force for the bad outcomes. It turns out that people may be protecting their self-concepts for times when negative things happen. Thus, if challenged, people will assume defence-like behaviors. In fact, the protection of the wounded ego may prompt a counter-attack from clients, because they may feel rejected and belittled (Kottler, 1992). These counter-attacks, although a relatively healthy sign, may be viewed by the traditionalists as a form of resistance if not blatant denial, and sadly confronted out of existence rather than integrated in a beneficial manner for the recovery process.

Working in the field one cannot treat dependents long without hearing, "At least I'm not as bad off as so and so." Rather than immediately attack that position as "Well, you don't have to be that bad," it may do you well to remember that clients may be trying to protect what little self-esteem they have. That little insight can change the direction of an intervention from an attack orientation to one of support.

Misconceptions About Treatment

There is always a contingent of clients who believe they will be brainwashed. Usually, they have not been adequately informed about the workings of treatment. Some rather wild ideas are created by the clients regarding what they expect during treatment. I've heard clients state things like, "I thought you guys were going to attach some kind of electrical probes to me," "I thought you were going to break up my marriage," or, "I thought I would loss my job." It may sound silly for those who have been around AOD treatment programs for awhile, but anything is possible to those who have not been in treatment.

The real issue for these clients is that they just do not know what to expect, and no one tells them anything at the time of admission. This lack of understanding can often generate anxiety to the newcomer. In this case, it is obligation of the program to provide some "explanation time" to prevent this resistance before it starts.

Boat-Rockers

In line with the initial misconceptions about a program or treatment are those clients who ask an endless stream of irrelevant questions. In some cases, it may be a smoke-screen to divert attention away from the task at hand, which is getting sober. However, in many other cases the questions may be doing exactly what they are intended to do, gather information. I recently completed a DUI class in which I had one of these individuals. He was bright, full of questions, and was somewhat doubtful of the various statistics I reviewed. It was difficult not to confront him, but I stuck to my belief that he had a right to ask the questions. I dutifully answered them, one after another. About half way through the class he stopped asking questions and began to listen. In fact, I think he was the most attentive student in that hot summer classroom. After the class ended and people were filling out, he stopped for a minute and shook my hand firmly, put his hand on my shoulder, leaned over and whispered, "Damn good class". He smiled turned and walked out of the room. There certainly is no way of telling if that student really got anything out of the class, but I think he did.

If I were to have open heart surgery, I would like to know as many things about the procedure as I could. Therefore, I would ask a host of questions about what the doctor would do after he/she cut me open. Even the likes of Bernie Siegel (1989) advises patients to aim many questions toward their doctor.

Developmental Resistance

What you may have noticed, about the various resistance types we have been covering so far, is that they have been basically one dimensional. They have accounted for resistance in the present tense (i.e., how resistance manifests itself in front of the counselor as he/she and the client interact). But resistance may show itself in different ways, at different times through the therapeutic time span. That is, it may develop anew in many different sessions. For example, it is generally assumed a certain resistance cluster may be found as the therapeutic session begins. These clusters could include denial and parallels Vaillent's primitive defensive styles that were mentioned earlier. As treatment continues, the resistance style may change as therapy moves to the middle or later phases. Each level of change can also include a variety of resistances (i.e., a different resistance at a different time).

Generally the beginning phase of treatment is marked by re-establishing contact with the abstinent side of oneself, and the abstinent world. At this time, there may be lingering withdrawal symptoms that can mimic the physiological denial look alike noted in section one. In addition, coming to terms with past inebriated behaviors can elicit guilt and shame. In order to protect the self, defenses of conscious denial can be brought forth. As the client progresses into a more stabilized level of recovery the issues of relapse and or relapse prevention come into play. In these situations, one might encounter the resistance of rationalization that would indicate to the client it is now "safe" to drink. As the recovery progresses, the client may begin to overcompensate for his/her past through the defence of reaction formation. In this manner, the client is not being true to themselves. They might spend more time on others than on their own recovery which poses a danger to the whole recovery process.

It would seem that each of these stages might have a different set of therapeutic circumstances as well as a set of resistance in which to cope. It is pure speculation to say that one type of resistance is to be expected at the beginning of treatment and another set of resistances is to be expected at a later point. However, as the client progresses through certain levels of recovery, it seems possible that the next level of recovery might hold a new set of resistance surprises. The caveat to all this speculation is to expect that a new set of resistance will arise as the client moves through a recovery process. That expectation may set the counselor up for a mind-set that sees resistance lurking around every bend of treatment, and that may simply not be true.

CHAPTER SUMMARY

We have examined the concepts of true denial and the denial look alikes, and outlined a denial decision tree to help distinguish the types. We have seen that resistance can be framed from the dynamic perspective, to irrational thinking styles, to boundary issues, to attributes, and to preferred defensive postures. Some theoretical camps would even want us to do away with the concept altogether. We also covered the everyday type resistances that many AOD counselors see and reviewed some broad treatment approaches to those problems. This whole chapter was meant to survey the vast array of resistance types that have been formulated by many different schools over the years. In doing this, the reader is urged to sit back and gain a wider perspective of the many ideas of AOD resistance.

The theme remains, depending on your personal theory of resistance, that theory will color the all your assessments and interventions. Please be cautious with your assessments.

CHAPTER 3

COUNSELOR RESISTANCE:
WHEN WE, THE HELPERS, ARE RESISTANT

> Q: How many AOD counselors does it take
> to change a light-bulb?
> A: One, but all he does is yell at it.
> Sandi Marshall

CREATING OUR OWN RESISTANCE

If we alcohol and other drug practitioners are to assume that every so-called resistance, roadblock, or obstacle encountered in a session is the result of client resistance, we are sadly and naively mistaken. The therapist "...is always contributing in some meaningful way to the presence of resistance in the client" (Langs, 1981). The counselor is to be seen as a major contributor to client resistance (Mahrer, Murphy, Gagnon & Gingras, 1994). The many staff meetings that I attended usually had a diagnosis of client resistance to be urgently discussed. In those discussions, some overt or implicit blame was frequently heaped onto the client for the present state of treatment. The client was always somehow at fault.

If the state of counselor resistance was ever brought up, it usually revolved around the counselor's frustration, anger, or sadness. These emotional states were deemed to be the result of utilizing all available treatment strategies on a client with little or no change. Zweben (1989) noted the same type of problem in such meetings.

Other staff would usually empathize with the frustrated counselor, and reinforce blame for the resistance onto the client. Thereafter, plans were made to either discharge the client, or have him/her endure one of those "come before the whole staff and explain yourself" meetings. Those "meetings" were about as intimidating and degrading to the client as you can get. We did those things in the name of getting honest and sober. Many assumed it is "good" for the client, because it showed him/her who was boss. In essence, it was a power fight if ever there was one.

A prime example is in order. Not long ago, I was sitting in one of those staff meetings I just described. It was actually a staff meeting plus an in-service. As the trainer of this particular in-service, I brought along a series of good research articles. I wanted to share this information with the staff on effective treatment, and accountability measures.

We got around to discussing how we often form fit clients into our favored treatment strategies. We agreed that if the client didn't match the principles of our theory, the theory usually won out, and it was the client who turned out to be in the wrong.

I thought I made that point rather well, and was rather proud of myself. All the heads in the room were nodding in agreement. Within ten minutes a staff member, who had seemed to be in agreement, began to describe a therapeutic quandary. She had been working with a self-proclaimed secular humanist, and was miffed and angry that this individual would not recognize some kind of a Higher Power needed for his recovery.

84

"How can I force him to do a second step?" was her question. FORCE HIM! Hadn't she understood our discussion?

Apparently not. She was convinced that a Higher Power was what this individual needed. Her pet theory would force this client into a no-win situation. Either the client did it her way, or he would lose. She was right, he was wrong. I stopped dead in my tracks. After a moment of utter frustration, I just smiled to myself. I thought, "Isn't it amazing how blind we are." This poor "professional" had grown such cataracts, she couldn't visualize any other way to deal with something that was alien to her point of view. I felt sorry for the secular humanist who was going to get her professional wrath the next day. As Haley (1987) notes, she became part of the problem, but didn't even know it.

This is just one of those examples of insular the AOD field can be. It isn't that one point of view is either right of wrong, it's that we cannot often see beyond our biased views. Theories are never right or wrong, they are just theories. The real enemy is a closed mind! Once we shift over to who's right and wrong, we have slipped from treatment into morality and politics.

Sadly, many counselors drift into this role (Singer & Lalich, 1996). Their focus on being right and imposing their method of recovery onto their clients is righteously driven. It is a prime example of counselor generated resistance. I was the clinical director of a small inpatient program a few years ago. I had one of these counselors on my staff. He was right about every thing and no matter what my credentials were or what length of service I developed in the field, I was wrong about everything! We managed to exchange a few pleasantries until one day he asked me if I had any good books on love. That shocked me, because these types usually hate reading, and would rather burn books than read them. Well, I carefully selected some long-forgotten book on the subject, and he read it. A month later he approached me, and muttered how he now had realized he had put a higher premium on being right than on loving. He shook my hand and walked away.

That was a happy ending, but too many cases of these attitudes still exist. Fischer (1983) points out what many of us have known for some time,"... that there is no such thing as a resistant client, only an over eager therapist." He cites Kempler (1981) who states, "It is my impression that most obstacles that emerge during the course of therapy belong to the therapist ..." Egan (1994) noted that when a professional encounters resistance, they often become disconcerted by it. They can begin to have unexpected feelings of confusion, panic, irritation, hostility and even depressive-like symptoms. It is obvious how these feelings can distort anyone's objective perspective. Once that happens, one's effectiveness is sorely diminished.

Fremont and Anderson (1986) cite evidence that client behavior that verbally attacks the counselor can lead to counselor anger. Once that anger festers, professionalism often goes out the window. Berg and Miller (1992) indicate that, "Many professionals become surprised and angry when the client does not follow the goals already set by the therapist or by the treatment program--without the client's input." Generally goals are imposed on the client without regard to their feelings. Such a maneuver cannot but help plant the seeds of resistance from both parties.

Moreover, Lazarus (1981) states, "Whenever positive outcomes are not achieved, some therapists beg the question by attributing their failures to the client's resistance." He suggests that instead of labeling as resistance those client behaviors that do not meet with the expected progress in the therapeutic situation, we ought to consider what is really causing the problem and attend to it. This sentiment is also echoed by Flores (1988) who points out that the cause of a client's failure in treatment is too often attributed to the client alone. Disturbances in the client-therapist interaction must be taken into consideration. When we label certain behaviors as resistive then there is a tendency in AOD circles not to delve into the reason behind the resistance, or consider alternative ideas. We just confront it or attribute the problem to, "He hasn't hurt enough," or "She is one of those unconstitutional incapables."

Lazarus and Fay (1982) have stated, "The concept of resistance is probably the most elaborate rationalization that therapists employ to explain their treatment failures." They go on to state, "...resistance is generally a function of the limitations of our knowledge and methods and the constraints of our personality." Zweben (1989) shares the same idea by indicating the cause of many treatment problems is the lack of training and developmental gaps in the repertoire of many an AOD counselor. She notes the adherence to a preferred model can color a therapist's perspective, be it a mental health model or a 12-Step model.

Haley (1987) is quick to point out, the therapist who believes in a certain ideology is going to impose it on the client through words, body movement, intonation, and instruction. One significant pet ideology that many a AOD counselor fall prey to, is the expectation of resistance from the chemical dependent. As Kottler (1992) notes, "If you expect a client to be difficult, that person will probably live up to your expectations." According to Mahrer, Murphy, Gagnon, and Gingras (1994), now the question is whether the client is really resistant, or is the problem the counselor's expectation ?

WHY WOULD THE AOD THERAPIST CREATE RESISTANCE?

This section examines a number of reasons why the AOD practitioner engages in resistance. The source of this resistance is as varied as that which was found in client resistance. We will see perspectives that seem to indicate that resistance has an analytic base to those therapists who believe it is caused by thinking difficulties. As with client resistance, how you perceive all this will affect your viewpoint.

Countertransference

From this perspective, there are a number of reasons a novice, or trained AOD counselor would create resistance in the therapeutic process. Freud (1910/1957) called this type of resistance--*countertransference*. He described it as, "...a result of the patient's influence on the analyst's unconscious feelings." Nicholi (1988) indicated it as, "The tendency of the therapist to displace feelings from earlier figures into the patient." He noted that countertransference means "parallel to or complementary to, as in counterpart, and not opposite to or contrary to." Strean (1993) felt that when the therapist ceases to examine their own behavior in relation to their client, countertransference may be operating.

The *Psychiatric Dictionary* (1970) defines it in terms of the effects and interference on the therapists' understanding generated from their unconscious needs or conflicts. The dictionary indicates countertransference comes in different forms. The first is of the short-term variety. This can manifest itself by acute brief behaviors by the counselor in which they will become bored, sleepy or have a difficult time concentrating on a specific section of the therapeutic session. Then there's the paranoid type. In this case the counselor wishes not to see unwanted material in themselves, yet push for that very material from the client.

The more serious countertransference is of the long lasting or frequently occurring type that is based on some of the counselor's own deeply ingrained disturbances. Elkind (1992) talks about primary vulnerabilities as they relate to the therapist. Some faults or wounds in counselors are more intolerable than others. If activated, these unaddressed wounds can create much anxiety in the counselor. When these "...areas of primary vulnerability of patient and therapist interact in problematic ways, irreconcilable mismatches may result" (Elkind, 1992).

The analytic view (Blatt & Erlich, 1982; Imhof, Hirsh, & Terenzi, 1983; Langs, 1981; Strupp & Binder, 1984) perceives both the therapist and client as generators of resistance. Whatever is unresolved in you, the counselor, can become the focus of treatment, and can become a reaction (transference) to a client (Rosenthal, 1987). Often the strongest reactions result from clients who are most like us, and therefore give us the most trouble (Kottler, 1992).

We are often influenced and moved by the therapeutic process (Yalom, 1989). According to this viewpoint, it is rare that something that occurs in treatment will not have such an effect. It is for this reason therapists need to be aware of our resistive influence in the therapeutic hour. "We have to consider our part in any client resistance," (Kottler, 1992).

Countertransference can exhibit itself in a few other interesting ways (Yalisove, 1992). Some include distancing oneself, as in moving psychologically or physically away from the client. Reaction formation is another sign where the counselor can become overly kind, permissive, and even outright angry and hostile. Other signs include covert and overt indicators (Vannicielli, 1992). Briefly, the covert are 1) Unexpected shifts in the counselor's attitude toward the client. 2) Preoccupational thoughts or ruminations toward a particular individual. 3) Having the feeling that you are stuck, lost and tired, each time the thoughts of a certain client arises.

The overt indicators include: 1) Stereotyping your responses to a certain client even though the information you are dealing with is different, 2) Beginning to express inappropriate feeling responses to the client, 3) Being late for a session, cutting them short, changing the appointment times, or not returning phone calls. Strean (1993) notes counselor silence as another form of overt countertransference. Here therapists may be retaliating through silence because of annoyance, hatred or rejection they feel from the client. In essence, "We will resort to our own protective devices the more difficult the client is," (Kottler, 1992).

Where do these behaviors originate? The following items (Strean, 1993; Rosenthal, 1987) are not an exhaustive list, but it can give you an idea of what is creating countertransference. For instance, a counselor may have a strong or unconscious need to be liked. When attacked by an irate alcoholic, this attack can tip-off this unmet need. The result will be a counter-attack or the complete avoidance of further aggressive issues which the client may need addressed. The constant need to be liked could elicit an attack or withdrawal behaviors from the therapist which would skew the whole therapeutic process.

The next item may be the counselors need for power, control, and authority. This seems to be an issue in the AOD field. I've heard many clients approach me and ask why AOD counselors are so "tight" or rigid. I personally think counselors with control problems run their treatment groups like mini Marine boot-camps. It's usually a dead give away that the counselor has control issues yet to deal with.

Often a counselor's countertransference will manifest itself through their need to be a good parent rescuing a bad child (Imhof, Hirsch & Terenzi, 1983). We want our clients to be well and develop a solid recovery, however when this becomes a compelling drive to "fix the client," we may be involved in a countertransference. Yalom (1989) states, "The overactive therapist often infantilizes the patient, he does not guide or help unfold, he imposes himself on the other."

Strern (1993) points to the type of counterresistance that is driven by the therapist's own super ego. In these cases, a client says or does something that will elicit a strong sense of outrage from the therapist. The counselor will become moral, righteous, and lose the ability to empathize. This is especially difficult to resolve when a therapist feels so justified in their outrage.

Finally, Nicholi (1988) indicates that another source of this particular counselor resistance as being "anxiety within the therapist." This anxiety and tension can have many sources and often shows itself when a certain theme is being explored in a session that rubs against our own "blind spots." Selzer (1967) indicates that the therapist has limits to what he can hear without becoming angry or otherwise involved. According to this perspective, all of us have such limits. If we are unaware of them, they can act as the blind spots previously mentioned and create on going problems in the way we conduct AOD treatment.

All these countertransferences hint at the fact that many of the individuals who get into this field do it as "wounded healers" (Maeder, 1989). Perhaps, the very problems we attempt to rectify in ourselves motivates us to a helping field. If unattended, these personal biases will interfere with the process of counseling. It is for that reason the first "law of therapy" remains, "Know Thyself."

OTHER REASONS FOR COUNSELOR GENERATED RESISTANCE

Just Plain Frustration

We alluded to frustration, but it is important to take a minute and examine this as a major source of counselor induced resistance. One cause of the frustration centers on the clients who simply do not cooperate with what we think will be beneficial to them. It also includes the expectation that a client change at the speed of the treatment program's schedule, and then they don't. Most frustrating is giving a client your "best shot," and then they proceed to relapse. If the relapse occurs soon after the treatment, generally there is more frustration (Washton, 1989). In combination, these items tend to create a sense of inadequacy in the counselor (Kottler, 1992), threaten one's sense of competence, and sometimes generate an overwhelming sense of powerlessness.

There are a number of other things that contribute to counselor generated resistance. For example, when we compare ourselves to a perfect ideal in counseling, or to other staff, or when we personalize resistance (Cromier & Cromier, 1985; Ellis, 1985; Kottler, 1992). The operative words are comparison and personalizing. When comparing, many people have a tendency to slight their abilities and potential. Those feelings can undercut action and contribute to mediocrity if not feelings of "I can't cut it." A prime example of a personalized feeling is the one that tells you, "I was conned." This is often a real blow to the counselor's pride. When the pride is bruised, I have seen this get distorted into saying, "From now on, I'm going to be a tough, no-nonsense, counselor, so I'll never get conned." Pity the next client on this counselor's caseload.

Developmental Impediments

There is an old saying, "You can't take anyone further in development of life than you have already gone yourself." The same applies to AOD counselors and their clients. Berger (1974) states, "The growth of an organism proceeds through stages during which there is differentiation and integration at successfully more complex levels of organization. What exists at one stage becomes transformed into something related to, but also different from, what existed earlier." He goes on to say, "At each new stage, a new more complex perspective is available until finally, with the attainment of the most abstract level, a person is capable of viewing all of his previous experiences--his previous "selves"--as well as the views and selves of others, from a broadened perspective." Consider the flexibility and treatment options a counselor can utilize when they operate from this broadened perspective. On the other hand, consider the potential problems that can develop when a AOD counselor does not operate from this perspective.

A review of one developmental theorist can drive this point home. It is the work of Jane Loevinger (1977). Her work centered on accurately describing and measuring the stages of ego development. She put together a theory on development that included eight stages. We just need to review three to make our point.

According to Loevinger individuals at her *conformist level* are described as able to see only a right way and a wrong way to do things. This judgment is often based on an external standard. Such individuals place a high value on reputation, appearance and belonging. They generally have only a trite and simple understanding of their inner life. They generally do not have rich or varied methods from which to examine themselves or others.

This conformist stage has certain similarities to what Kasl (1992) describes as the literalist AOD counselor. In this classification, the literalist is one who has a particularly strong tendency to "perpetuate a robot-like adherence to beliefs, myths and dogma of a program." These people tend to be despots, who can see only one way and have little room for questioning.

The next developmental stage noted by Loevinger is called the *conscientious level*. Here the individual has begun to move beyond the stereotypical thinking of the earlier stages. They can recognize inner states more easily and more accurately. They are more aware of their choices and begin to live up to ideals they have for themselves. The world is no longer a matter of right and wrong. Moral issues take on complexity, and they are no longer judged by an single external standard. Things are more individualized. Kasl (ibid) notes that counselors at this stage tolerate differences better, and their language is less peppered with platitudes and jargon.

The last stage of Loevinger, as it relates to the AOD counselor, is the *autonomous level*. At this point, there is a stronger sense of the complexity of situations and humans. There is a deep respect for people to find their own way and make their own mistakes. These individuals cope and acknowledge conflict rather than simply blot it out. Kasl (ibid) indicates that people at this stage are motivated less by fear, than by a new found sense of curiosity and interest.

So who can take clients further in the growth process?

The following example serves as a testament to the importance of counselor development.

"Iron Butt"

I was recently teaching a class in which I got to know one student a little better than most. He relayed to me that he was once an "iron butt." The term peaked my curiosity and I asked him to define an "iron butt." He said, "Oh, you know those types who feel there's only one way to recovery." I said, "It sounds like you're not one of those "iron butts" anymore. What happened? How did you change?" He thought for a minute and said something to the effect that his clients have taught him that you can't just treat everyone the same. Then he said with conviction, "There just isn't one form of treatment for everyone, and that's why I'm back in school, to learn as much as I can." In a short sentence, he was able to articulate that he was once at a certain level of development and had begun to move on. In addition, he began to see that he had been a prisoner of a certain set of beliefs (McKay & Fanning, 1991), and that inexperienced counselors are more likely to endorse an exclusive position, while those with experience see diversity and flexibility (Beitman, Goldfried & Norcross, 1989).

Witnessing personal growth and learning like that can give an educator a soft warm feeling. This was human development in action.

Poor Training

Goodwin (1991) has noted that training has been shown to be an indicator of effective treatment programs. This seems almost too elementary to state - quality therapy is related to quality training. Without training, or training only in one area, to the exclusion of another, can be a possible source of counselor resistance (Caton, Gralnick, Bender & Simon, 1989). Consider what the state of the field would be without the training aspect, and what the competency level would be for the AOD counselors without such training. It was recorded twenty years ago (Vriend & Dyer, 1973) that "...the saddest reason for a counselor's inability to be effective with reluctant clients is that few training opportunities exist where the counselor can acquire the skills needed to deal with counselee reluctance." Those who are not well trained tend to classify and treat their clients according to the limited parameters they possess. Often these parameters are woefully inadequate to met the complexity of the clients on our caseloads. These inadequacies can lead to needless resistance.

Many counselors have a tendency to stick with a tired and true treatment method even though exposed to alternative methods. The reluctance to move beyond the status quo has a variety of motivations. A common complaint that inhibits trying new techniques is one of reluctance. "These new ideas feel uncomfortable, and make me feel funny." The thought of screwing up a new training method is enough for many practitioners to retreat immediately into old and possibly ineffective methods. Because of this reluctance many professionals easily forget the things they read, or forget the basics of a workshop attended. Their rationalizations can be just as effective a screen to new ideas, as they are for a clients who use a rationalization process. Additionally, funds for improving counselor training are often at the bottom of the priority list in many AOD programs.

Mindlessness

Mindlessness develops from the rigors of being in a job too long. Langer (1989) coined the term. It is defined as becoming trapped into a set pattern of automatic behaviors characterized by habit and repetition. Have you ever noticed the day after day drudgery that seems to set in after you have gone through the honeymoon phase of a new job. You know that, "Damn! I have to get up and go to work" feeling. After being on the job for a time, things that where once alive and bright, begin to fade into the background. Our perception of clients can fall into same trap. Soon one individual begins to look pretty much like the last one. As this drudgery continues, the counselor takes in less information from the client. So after years of doing assessments, different clients begin to blend together, and special information of each individual is missed. The rhythm of the familiar can create a certain amount of resistance (by omission) to the therapeutic situation. Kottler (1992) notes the counselor in this dilemma will feel depleted, worn out, and will probably encounter more resistance. These symptoms have a particular feel to them, something like heaviness or zombie-like behavior, peppered with daydreaming of a better time to come. When therapists no longer feels enthused about their job, they are in danger of becoming repetitive and insensitive (Bugental, 1987).

Langer (1989) uses the term mindlessness in two other ways that can lead to counselor resistance. The first is called *premature cognitive commitment*. In this situation, the counselor will form a mind-set or opinion about a client before there is any reflection, or deliberation. These mindless professionals seem to commit themselves to a predetermined notion about chemical dependency without the use of deliberation. They rely too rigidly on their own reality, which only reinforces what they believe to be true about the workings of chemical dependency. When this happens other options are closed out. Counselor resistance is often caused when options are shut down. Watzlawick (1976) notes when people are trapped in this state, and then challenged with a novel situation, they will resort to an established piece of thinking to fit the challenge. This way, the mindlessness becomes self-sealing, and doesn't allow new thoughts to form. In addition, this self-sealing process can occur through the manner in which we first take in information. If information is taken in dogmatically, then that is how we will use it in the future.

If you have been this field for any length of time, you have probably seen this dogmatic type. They were often treated in a very dogmatic fashion in their own treatment past, and now feel that approach is the preferred method to treat other people. They often see confrontation as they only way to address clients. When confrontation doesn't work, they will blame the client for not progressing in treatment. They will be the first to say those awful words, "I guess they just haven't hurt enough," and demand a client be discharged from a program.

Langer's second mindless factor involves becoming trapped in a rut by *acting from a single perspective* Here one lives by a single set of rules regardless of the context. These same set of rules are endlessly applied to one problem after another. If client behavior doesn't change, then it is the fault of the client not the single perspective. No new information is allowed into such a limited perspective, and that is where the harm and resistance begins to develop. Such single perspectives can lead to mis-readings of clients, because we believe only what we believe. A mis-reading, is a mis-reading. If it is caused by a myopic viewpoint it is time to adjust the limited perspective.

For those stuck in quagmire, consider a crash course in critical thinking to begin to get you to question and question again. That can result in a sense of renewed possibilities, increased choice potential, and the feeling is liberating ta' boot. Langer's answer to get out of these ruts is a combination of adaptation, imagination, and creativity. These qualities are also the essence of quality AOD treatment.

Poor Thinking as a Factor in Generating Resistance

Counselors are known to be prone to a wide array of judgmental and inferential errors (Spengler, Strohmer, Dixon, & Shivy (1995). These error-prone thinking habits can become fertile ground for AOD counselor resistance. To highlight these judgmental errors, material was drawn from Fearside & Holther (1959), and Halpern (1989), and applied to AOD counselors. These authors discuss philosophy, critical thinking, and cogently point out difficulties people make when they debate from counterfeit arguments and points of view.

Thinking errors begin when we take short cuts in our reasoning, called *heuristics*. For our purposes, heuristics is defined as simplifying data to the point of labeling and then treating without much thought. As AOD counselors, we are forever attempting to develop classifications about the people we encounter. On one hand, classifications help us organize our information about the world, and free us from evaluating every event anew (Satir, 1983). On the other hand, "Classification never tells us what the classification really is" (Christian, 1977). When taken to extremes, they become dysfunctional. There are many different types.

The first of these dysfunctional thinking errors involves an *hasty generalizing*. Allport (1954) calls this overgeneralization, and indicates that it may be one of the commonest tricks of the human mind. Here the counselor draws a judgment from a few available facts, and simply jumps to conclusions. Stereotyping and prejudice exist in part because of the human tendency to utilize only readily available information. An example might be to think that all alcoholics are alike, and therefore should be treated in the same manner. The availability of readily accessible information is a parallel to this type of heuristic. In this case, the counselor keys into specific diagnostic categories, or pop psychology constructs to the exclusion of other more feasible interpretations (Spengler, et. al., 1995).

The second type of generalization is the *unrepresentative type*. In this type, the counselor will only look for the evidence or symptoms that will support their hunches and personal feelings. What is particularly damaging about this type of generalizing is that evidence to the contrary is overlooked. No matter what the alcoholic or heroin addict does, they will still get locked into the counselor's personal belief system. For example, The client tells you the truth, but the counselor discounts it because he/she feels all alcoholics are "known" liars. Vos Savant (1990) calls this type of thinking the *selective approach*, or that information that is based on one's prior experience. It has the tendency reinforce a previously held belief, but at the cost of comprehending new information. It is also called *representative thinking*, in which your opinions of others will be influenced by what you think is representative of a particular group.

The third type is of the *inclusive generalizing*. In this kind of thinking, wide variances in client behavior get reduced or included down to a singular explanation. It simplifies the complex human condition by its unadorned explanations. Moreover, these simplistic explanations are notoriously inaccurate.

One last thinking problem to address is of *entrapment*. Here, the counselor makes a powerful initial investment in an assessment of a client or investment in any theory. Once that is done, there is a tendency to stay with that position because of the sizable investment we have given it. One becomes entrapped by their own position, and little if any new information is ever allowed to seep in. This heuristic includes the notion that a experience is a measure of one's competence. Many become ensnared in their experience and believe that their judgment is without error. The research has indicated that one's experience will exacerbate judgmental bias (Spengler, Strohmer & Prout, (1990). Yet, experience is often seen as critically important in the AOD field.

The capacity to lump a client into your preferred molds is amplified, day after day, by its repeated use. Mischel (1986) points out that this categorizing or stereotyping is dangerous for the therapist. In fact, he notes this categorizing has a tendency to reorganize the way we recall information. It is called *retrospective distortion*. Unwittingly, AOD therapists can convince themselves that their perceptions are correct because they have distorted the way they recall information.

Haley (1987) feels that labels and molds often crystallize a problem. These preferred molds cannot but entail premature judgments or speculation about the nature of things and people. Yalom (1989) states, "We distort others by forcing into them our own preferred biases and ideas ..." Once premature judging and speculation takes place, resistance cannot be far behind. This type of thinking sets the stage for the type of AOD therapist who feels they know everything there is to know about treatment. Bugental (1987) writes, "Beware of that therapist who announces arrival at a position which needs no further change. He has lost his artistry and becomes a technician and is probably dangerous to his clients."

This labeling paradigm operates so automatically that clinicians are not able to challenge their limitations (Neuhaus, 1993). Ellis, McInerney, DiGiuseppe & Yeager, (1988) sum this style of generalized and preferred thinking by stating, "When you believe that all alcoholics are dependent, oppositional, unmotivated, or whatever, you lead yourself into a real dead end." This kind of labeling hardly encourages emotional insight or long term change for the client.

The major resistance factor that is generated by all of these issues is loss of client subtleties that exist before you. They are erased by these kinds of thinking, and resistance can be created.

There are no simple solutions to these dilemmas. Spengler, et. al., (1995) have outlined a series of ideas to improve judgment accuracy. A modified version includes:

1. Increasing counselor openness and curiosity
2. Invoking multiple methods of theory testing
3. Use empirical data in your clinical work
4. Delay judgments, especially the snap-judgment types
5. Do not become overly attached to one interpretation of anything
6. Use cognitively complex approaches on clients.

These steps can serve as a mode for self-reflection and recognition to avoid the powerful mind-traps just reviewed.

"MY Personal Experience"

Akin to the formal thinking problems listed above, and just as strong a contributor to resistance, are the ever famous lines that reflect "My personal experience has been..." I shutter every time I hear that line, because a perfectly sound assessment is often discredited due to a counselor's personal experience which is in opposition to a solid assessment. What is even worse is this "personal experience" will take precedence over well-developed research. The very nature of our personal experience can and will be the distortion of the client as seen through our eyes. Sure, it is a guide and is often cherished by many professionals as the way to truly get a handle on a client. There are limits to such experience (Sutherland, 1994; Dawes, 1994).

Anyone's personal experience has to be skewed one way or the other, because personal preferences are built on biases. That's why we do training in this field, to challenge the bias, not only for ourselves, but for our clients.

Case in point. At facility were I was the clinical director, the executive director and I had a difference of opinion on how to treat residents. She made it quite clear that her personal experience with "druggies and alcoholics" was one in which confrontation was needed at every turn. "You can never trust them, because they are always trying to get over," was her constant lament. So any attempt on my part to introduce a different form of treatment into the program was met with scorn. We proceeded to use the old confrontation approach with the residents, and when the aftercare department reported a high relapse rate the director, she predictably attributed it to, "They obviously didn't hit bottom yet. They'll just have to hurt some more."

In this case, the executive director's personal opinion was so extreme that she managed to use all sorts of heuristics to confirm those beliefs. She just couldn't see that the confrontational approach was the culprit.

This personal experience thing can also ride rough shod over quality research. An example occurred at a workshop I conducted a while back. I was making a point about some research data I had come across. I had no sooner got that sentence out, when a hand shot-up in the audience, followed by the statement, "It has been my personal experience that...". I forget the content of our little disagreement, but the context hit me hard. I noted that this workshop participant did several things at once. First, he obviously discounted some good research in favor of his experience, so everything was instantly invalidated in favor of his experience. Second, by maintaining that his perspective was the correct one, he lost the opportunity to see clients in a fresh light. His clients would probably be neatly categorized according to his personal experience. Clients don't stand of a fair assessment with someone like this.

Novice Anxiety

In this case, we are talking about feelings of incompetence generated by anxiety, that in turn, creates resistance. Generally, it is the inexperienced counselor who will encounter this competence anxiety (Cormier & Cormier, 1991). These feelings are often created by the novice counselor's notion that they are wholly responsible for the outcome of treatment (Anderson & Stewart, 1983). As a clinical supervisor, I have seen this competence anxiety develop with every new counselor I hired.

Some interesting characteristics have emerged from these novice therapists that contribute to the resistive factor in a counseling situation. First, centers on the over concern with his/her self-image, or how they are doing in the session versus paying attention to the process of counseling. They seem so very concerned with how to do things right, that they fail to notice important client expressions or behaviors. They also spend a lot time in superficial layers of communication, such as the formal or conversational levels outlined by Bugental (1988) (see Chapter Six for additional information)..

Another novice characteristic is that of wanting to do things right, to the exclusion of spontaneity. Imagine feeling powerful emotions, and being told that you did not experience them in the right or in the correct way. This general approach can lead into the next novice characteristic which is relying too much on tricks and techniques. These devices can will only take you so far in the counseling session. Thereafter, one must begin to rely on the best technique available--you.

The last item on this novice-anxiety generating resistance is the notion many counselors have that a few simple concepts about how humans operate is sufficient to explain the complexities of addiction. I've seen much resistance generated by these concepts and the counselors who hold them. The client struggles to explain their many feelings and behaviors, and is met with simple solutions and platitudes. I've had these clients come to me, and express that the simple answer they got, made them feel as if they hadn't been listened to. It was hard to tell them, that is exactly what happened to you. Chronic simplicity is not the answer to the complexity of AOD dependents, especially in these days of growing multicultural and gender issues.

Technical Terms and the Problem of Labeling

More than a few clients are thrown off by the psycho-babble used by counselors. It can create needless resistance because 1) The client just doesn't understand it. 2) That often adds to negative feelings that are already present. Good therapists have the ability to easily translate the professional jargon into everyday speech when they need to. The less secure therapist is more likely to resort to a cliché ridden, label giving vocabulary than the secure one (Nicholi, 1988). The client is often confused enough without the addition of needless technical terms. Anyway, the steady use of these terms usually has a pejorative connotation to them.

This pejorative connotation implies that I know more that you, especially when I give you a label. Walkenstein (1975) makes a powerful case against the use of this clinical habit. It applies, most appropriately, to the drug and alcohol field. She first notes that labeling is a contradiction in terms. How does one go about labeling humans who are so boundless and multitudinous without losing something in the process. She states labels "...confine, set limits, restrict growth, restrict vision, restrict discovery." They tend to destroy the humanity of the person labeled.

The great danger of labeling is that it will rob the individual of their unique characteristics. By virtue of the diagnosis, there becomes a built-in, preconceived treatment approach to handle the client. This will and has created much resistance.

Walkinstein (ibid) put together a dialogue between a psychiatrist and a patient. I modified it to the AOD field, and suspect that something like this occurs in many treatment centers that have pre-set and preconceived ideas about therapy.

Drug and Alcohol Counselor (CO): You are my client.
Client: I am me.

CO: You were sent here because you have a problem.
CL: I am multifaceted.

CO: You are an addict, alcoholic, coke-head, abuser, junkie.
CL: I am a person.

CO: You have ACOA Symptoms.
CL: I am human.

CO: Perhaps, you are codependent.
CL: I think. I feel. I make mistakes.

CO: You are in denial.
CL: Sometimes I can't see things clearly. Many can't.

CO: You need long term structured therapy. Without it, you will die.
CL: I will die anyway.

CO: You have a dual disorder.
CL: We are what we are.

CO: How much insurance coverage do you have?

Jumping Into a Session Without Preparation

I have observed many an AOD counselor plow right into a session with a new client without so much as an explanation or reason why they were doing what they were doing. Not being able to explain the rational behind a group task or an individual session, nor having a definite plan in mind prior to a session, can be disastrous for the client.

As much as I have heard the "whats and whys" of doing a group or individual session, the client hasn't. I cannot even begin to count the times I have taken the time to explain what is about to happen in a session, had a plan in mind, shared that with the client, and then received a great deal of cooperation.

This very situation recently happened when I began a highway safety class. About a third of the way into this class a student came up to me and thanked me for explaining the class to him. He had been worried all week, and was relieved to now know the class expectations, and later, shared some very personal issues. Every client has a right to know what they are getting into, and to understand what counseling is all about (Vriend & Dyer, 1973). What is often mistaken as resistance from clients is really their demanding to know what is going to happen to them. Sadly, in this field, that right, is often met with, "Shut-up! Take the cotton out of your ears and stick it in your mouth."

Pedestal Counselors

I read John Neikirk's article several years ago entitled *Getting Off the Professional Pedestal ... Dare to be Average* (1984), and was duly impressed. I have tried to share it in every talk I have given on the subject of resistance. He noted nine different types of pedestal counselors several of which we have already discussed. So we will only address those types that we haven't heard from, and how they can generate their fair share of needless counselor resistance.

The All Knowing type

This particular counselor is that type who comes across with all those cute and catchy stories, metaphors and profound statements. These "impact stories" always seem to be right in their back pockets, and ready for quick impression making. This can have a powerful effect on the client, so much so, that the client begins to think that the counselor has ALL the answers. The subtle resistance that gets created this way is, the client may stop searching for their own answers, and rely on the all-knowing counselor to provide them. Clients stop thinking for themselves, and let others provide the correct solutions to life. You can also spot these all knowing types in a staff meeting because they are always talking about how successful they are with <u>all</u> their clients. They also like to drop a few names of the notables in the field they've met.

The Too Busy Counselor

Everyone is impressed with the busy people in this world. There is an air of importance about being busy. In order to portray this importance, some counselors really act the part. Some of the more interesting methods I seen over the years include, the always on the phone counselor. You can never seem to get to talk to this person because they seem attached to the thing. Another busy manner is the 'hurried walk down the hall' style with lose papers waving in the breeze. They make it appear that they must get to their destination or the world will collapse. Seeing that, we certainly do not want to interfere, and if we do, we are very often given the old "I'll be with you in a minute" routine. This situation can often become frustrating, creating anger and reciprocal passive-aggressive behavior in return.

The Assumptive Manner Type

These counselors parallel the self-important counselors we just saw above. But, in this situation, these folks deserve a category all by themselves. They are the people your mother warned you about. They talk as if they have all the answers, and are speaking the truth. They are the ones who are constantly coming up with the cutsy one liners like "Your resistance is the result of your dysfunctional childhood." Now it doesn't matter that they just met you five minutes ago or that you didn't come from a dysfunctional family. They have stated the "facts" in an assumptive and self-assured manner. You have been signed, sealed, and labeled. If you object, you will be labeled as being in resistance. You can't win with these people, and it is best to stay clear of them.

Whenever the therapist steps off their pedestal, they will more than likely mature a little. As long as they remain on it, they will create a lot of needless resistance.

POWER ISSUES

Power! This is an especially prevalent issue for the AOD counselor. It seems to be synonymous with the very nature of traditional AOD treatment. Needless to say, it has also been at the core of much resistance to be found in a session.

An example of this power resistance is the AOD professional who demands to be in control all the time. What often lies behind this be-in-control power stance is the counselor's mind-set that clients are denial prone, highly manipulative, and not to be trusted. Thus, power and control over such people is a requirement. In some places I've worked, the motto was 'power--the more the better.'

Some say, we are getting away from that mind-set these days, but I wonder. Recently, I had a student describe a facility in which she was completing an internship. She proceeded to describe that facility in these very power and control terms. Not too many years ago I had a supervisor describe his power mentality as, "Wait till I get done with those bastards. They won't know what hit them by the time I'm done with them." He was describing how he was going to conduct a community meeting.

Generally, talk like this gets these individuals all fired up with all kinds of strategies that will maintain control. The most savored interventions used by these people are the quick and penetrating "put-downs." These come in a variety of styles and forms. Generally, they cluster around "I told him, that if he didn't shape-up he was going to die," or, "Another stupid move like that, and out the door you go." One of my personal favorites is, "Either you get with the program or get the hell out."

Threat is behind each and everyone of these statements, and a thousand other ones like them. Now, and this is the part that gets me, how can anyone consider threatening to be treatment. Somehow it is assumed that these threats are supposed to sink-in and make clients recover!

Some of the more subtle ways this power thing is perpetrated on the client was outlined by McWhirter (1991). She notes that the balance of power can be maintained on the side of the counselor by mystifying the therapy process. This includes first, using an abundant amount of specialized jargon. Most treatment centers have such a specialized language. The client who doesn't understand it, is considered on the outside of the program. This outside position is considered to be one of little understanding, while the inside position is considered to one of near "enlightenment." Second, blame the client for not getting better (we have covered that rather well), and third, refuse to share knowledge or educate the client. In this way you keep the client dependent on you and or your program. (see next section).

No matter how you cut it, all that power does--is create resistance.

We have seen a wide a variety of conditions that can promote counselor resistance from thinking styles mind-sets to unfinished personal business. It sounds like a never-ending task to be the most efficient counselor that one can be--and it is. There simply are no hard and fast tricks to keep the counselor at his/her best, save hard work. That usually means trying out creative ideas. We are constantly asking our clients to do hard work, even if people in general are afraid of change (Hoffer, 1967). Humans don't seem to like new behavior, but with support and encouragement many of our clients may try a new thought or action. Perhaps, it is time for the professionals to do the same.

COUNSELOR TRAITS THAT DIMINISH THE RESISTANCE FACTOR

There are a host of books and journal articles that have attempted to delineate just what it is that makes for a quality therapist. For instance, Nicholi (1988) points out the therapist's attitude toward the client needs to be one of equality. He states "... the patient, as a human being, is considerably more like himself then he is different...". Clients are infinitely more complex than any brilliant formulation devised by the counselor. Daniels and Horowitz (1976) note that the effective therapists talk with the client, not at him. They also indicate that these effective counselors shy away from the habit of criticizing, condemning and judging.

Other notables who commented on this subject include: May (1989), Ellis (1985), Mahoney (1991), Kottler (1992), and Bugental (1987). All had significant things to say on this subject. Let's take a quick overview of what they had to voice.

Starting from the top down, May noted that, the quality therapist is one who has a certain level of "winsomeness." This would be the therapist's ability not only to be at ease in the company of others, and enjoy that company, but to have the ability to be empathic. The outstanding quality is the ability to counsel the client by escaping from one's own rigid prejudices.

Ellis noted thirteen practices of effective counselors. (The list below is a stream-lined version.) Effective counselors are:

1. Interested and energetic in their clients
2. Unconditionally accept the client
3. Without being rigid or grandiose, believe in their therapeutic ability
4. Are flexible, undogmatic, have a wide range of knowledge and are open to new ideas
5. Are efficient at communicating
6. Can cope and take care of their own problems
7. Are hard-working, patient and persistent
8. Are ethical and responsible
9. Act professionally and like what they are doing
10. Optimistic and can urge or push clients to change
11. Help clients not only make symptom change but profound attitudinal change
12. Monitor their prejudices
13. Possess good judgment.

Mahony puts a lot of emphasis on the caring aspect of the therapist. He notes that the therapist is more likely to experience and share genuine caring states with the client if they are cared for by others. This caring is not to be considered a commodity, but a process in a relationship that will wax and wan over time. There is according to Mahoney, "[a]...deep felt desire and commitment to help the other person..."

Kottler simply notes that, "Empathy and compassion are the keys to helping clients feel understood and nurtured. These elements are crucial to any therapeutic relationship...". He quotes Book (1991) as noting that empathy and compassion reduce our tendencies to view difficult clients as bad and evil.

Finally, Bugental indicates that the best qualities of the therapist are akin to forms of art which among his list include: (Again, the list is condensed.)

1. Therapists see themselves as a primary instruments of change, not necessarily the techniques they use.
2. They perceive therapy as open-ended, so there is no perceived end or truth to it.
3. They have a disciplined sensitivity in which there is a learning of finer and finer distinctions or nuances of the therapy medium.
4. They have a set of self-determined standards which are not too stringent, because they realize the artistic standard will be otherwise stifled, too loose, or drowned in mediocrity.

In some past reading, I came across a delightful article that expounded on the qualities of good and bad teachers (Hamachek, 1968). As any seasoned therapist knows, there is not much difference between what a counselor does and the tasks of a teacher. The list was telling, and for that reason I include it.

Good teachers (counselors) can be characterized in the following ways:
1. They seem to be more courteous and have a positive view of others.
2. They do not seem to view others as critical attacking people, with ulterior motives.
3. They have a more favorable view of the democratic classroom (therapy session).
4. They do not seem to see students (clients) as persons "you do things to", but rather as individuals capable of doing for themselves once they feel trusted, respected and valued.

A while ago I was teaching a *Foundations of Guidance and Counseling* class, and is my usual style, I asked the students to write a several page description of what constitutes a good versus the not good AOD Counselor. A bright student, who was working with a group of adolescents, took a big risk and asked that same question. The results he received where poignant, and are presented pretty much as they were written.

"[The] good counselor is one that is willing to learn things about a client. [The] bad counselor is one that knows everything and don't want to see others points of view."

female, 16

"[The] good counselor is somebody that helps you out and somebody that will go a little out of their way for you, if you deserve it. [The] bad counselor is someone who is suppose to help you but doesn't, and you very seldom see that person and if you need help they can't really help you."

male, 15

"[The] good counselor always helps you and gives you respect; help me out in my problems so I feel better about myself. [The] bad counselor would probably tell you don't do this or that but really don't care for real. He's just doing time (work)."

male, 17

"[The] good counselor is helping, understanding, and caring, who tries to get the point across through our head. [The] bad counselor doesn't care and is only there for the money..."

female, 15

"[The] good counselor does this: Helps with family problems, drug problems, anger problems, and don't give up on you."

male, 16

What constitutes the good counselor? I think these people said it rather eloquently.

I can't help but notice that the lists we just reviewed have the enduring traits of flexibility and compassion, if not a lot of hard work to keep that edge. The good counselors usually stick out. I mean it is a pleasure to be around them. All that energy, curiosity, and eagerness to learn. They can be creative yet the best are rather humble..

I am reminded of the final scenes in Camelot in which King Author, before battle, is talking to a small boy who wants to join Author in the coming fight. The boy wants more than anything to be a knight of the round table, and fight beside his beloved king. Talking to the boy, Author sees his dream of Camelot is not dead as he thought. He commands the boy to run away from the impending battle, and shouts with renewed hope "Some do shine."

Some do indeed shine.

Chapter 4

PROGRAM AND SYSTEM RESISTANCE

People are not naturally cruel,
they are cruel when they become
unhappy or when they succumb
to an ideology.

deMello

RESISTANCE AT THE LARGER LEVEL

In this chapter, we examine resistance as it applies to treatment programs and systems. It is regrettable that little attention has been given to this type of resistance. This form of resistance can generate as much needless resistance as we saw originating from the AOD counselor. As in counselor resistance, there are certain mind-sets that contribute to the phenomena of program and field resistance.

Field Resistance Thinking

Much of the discussion that follows centers on the issues of closed-mindedness and dogma as they relate to resistance. The criticisms leveled at these types of resistance are not directed toward any particular theory. It is the MANNER in which some service providers present themselves that may be the problem. This manner shows itself in the way some authors or self-appointed AOD representatives, demean and disparage treatment that is outside the widely used approaches. I recently skimmed a book in which the author lambasted anything that was not within the traditional ideas of recovery. He made it clear that to practice anything other than the twelve step approach to sobriety was a sure invitation to disaster. In this case, it is not a theory that is the problem, it is the method by which he went about presenting it to the world, that invites resistance. For example, Berg and Miller (1992) state that, "The loyalty of the treatment professionals to the theoretical dogma of their treatment model prevents them from being flexible enough to accommodate the needs of the client...". It is the same old issue we met before, but here it is applied to an entire field.

Watzlawick (1976) states, "That once a tentative explanation has taken hold of our minds, information to the contrary may produce not corrections but elaborations of an explanation. The simple reason a new treatment method is not used may be that it does not fit the preferred mold of the treatment team or a program philosophy. When something of potential benefit is deliberately withheld from a client because it does not fit a pet theory, that becomes a potential for resistance and an unethical course of action.

Coles (1989) indicates that what we all too commonly find in the AOD field, is that the programs as a whole tend to use a preferred theory as a badge of membership. He goes on to explain that as we professionals keep repeating certain selected words and phrases out loud, we indoctrinate ourselves. This confirms and reinforces the correctness of what is resolutely believed. Observe a traditional staff meeting and you may notice how the participants can and do confirm each other by the use of the same jargon and phrases.

One loses sight of human individuality in this manner. This is where resistance may begin. It particularly shows itself when a client does not fit a dominant pattern of treatment facility, and is then classified as poorly motivated or uncooperative (Pattison, 1982). Yalom (1989) states, "If they are helpful to patients at all, ideological schools -- succeed because they assuage the therapist's not the patient's anxiety. The more the therapist is able to tolerate the anxiety of not knowing, the less the need for the therapist to embrace orthodoxy." This same sentiment was researched in a paper by Kemp (1962). He noted that the more close-minded the training was for a counselor the less open that counselor would be to alternative treatment options.

I encountered a client several years age who found herself caught up in this rigid, field wide, view of things. I met her two days out of a standard 28 day inpatient program. She was very angry about being sent to the program in the first place. She made it clear that if I was going to work in the same manner as the program she just left, I would be met with resistance, and a lot of it. She felt she had been indoctrinated with platitudes, rather than treatment. She felt particularly resentful toward the self help groups she was forced to attend. I learned that she was quite proud of her independence and did not like to be bossed around. I immediately began to do things she didn't expect. For example, I didn't give her directions or tell her how to live her life, and shared no platitudes. In addition, I agreed with her observation that many people had made a mistake by not giving her credit for the positive things she had done in her life. I indicated that she probably had the where-with-all to direct her own affairs, and it was about time we found out what kind of a life that would be without chemicals. At first, she was suspicious of this approach, but soon began to develop some remarkable assignments for herself. I found her to be very cooperative and experienced very little resistance or denial. This behavior was in sharp contrast to discharge summary received from the inpatient facility. Their experience described her as angry, resentful, and full of denial.

A few weeks, with this approach, helped her change short-term recovery into a few years of some of the highest quality recovery I've ever seen. She weathered significant stresses and changes in her life, and usually did it from her own resources and spirit.

We continued the sessions, off and on. All the while she continued to grow and find herself. One day she announced that her drinking spouse had just completed a different 28 day inpatient program, and managed to get two weeks of abstinence under his belt. He promptly announced that if she did not soon begin attending 12-Step groups she would soon relapse and die.

Here was a clear example of the ever-present rigidity often see in our field. It states that if one doesn't do it the established way, you are doomed. Needless to say, this made my client quite angry, and fed a lot of old resentments she had toward people who told her what to do. After some discussion, she promptly told the spouse what he could do with his kind of recovery, and continued to do what was best for her.

I recently bumped into them at a local store, and she is pushing five years of recovery, and he is nearing his second. They continue to work their own programs, and are raising a fine family.

Group/Staff Pressured Resistance

It is important we take a minute and examine the resistance factors that can be found by the simple formation of a group. In our case, this will be a group of AOD counselors or a staff meeting. Keep in mind that the group dynamics that follow are the often the same regardless of the content. For example, all groups require certain conditions be met for one to become a member. In many cases, the group creates pressure on the members to obey those conditions (Gray & Starke, 1977). Janis (1983) coined the concept of "groupthink" to account for this pressure. A rough definition of groupthink is the way people think when they are intensely involved with a group. Sometimes, an AOD staff fits this bill. It is here that the distinct possibility of hidden resistance symptoms can exist for a member of a staff or program.

We will examine several of these symptoms. This examination is not intended as an argument against groups or AOD staffs in general. The symptoms are a signal of things gone awry or even collectively pathological (Golemann, 1985). For example, there is often direct pressure on any member who expresses strong arguments against any of a group's ideas or stereotypes. That type of in-group pressure will make subtle constraints on an individual that dissent is contrary to the expectation of the group. This is clear pressure toward uniformity (Janis, ibid). This doesn't make the dissenting individuals sycophants. Many AOD staff members know that they can speak their mind, but such dissent has limits, if not consequences.

Patterson (1966) notes when one member doesn't act or think according to the expectations of that group/staff-program, then that individual will slowly be perceived as a threat. In fact, a strong, independent personality is often viewed with suspicion by the other members of the group (Whyte, 1957). The reasons for this perceived threat center around the theme of group expectation. The group expects a certain role, be it in a recovery, religious, or political realm. The individual is, for the most part, supposed to play that role according to those expectations. That role, as long as it is played according to the group's belief, will be validated. If one fails to play the role with consistency, one becomes "outside the group" and therefore a threat. Any individual who expresses dissent jeopardizes the cozy feeling of group solidarity by challenging the group's key assumptions and ideas.

If the challenge is persistent then the perceived threat can generate a fair amount of anxiety to the other members. That, in turn, can generate what Janis calls self-appointed mindguards who take the job of protecting the group from adverse or opposing information. What one then begins to hear from the mindguards are statements and sentences like "You better return to our ways or you will relapse," "You won't be able to make it without us," or, "The group is always wiser that the single person." Better yet, "Without this group you will die."

Sometimes mindguards of the group will begin to personally demean the renegade. This occurs because of the increasing level threat from the renegade. The resort to personal demeaning occurs especially if the individual begins to really stray away from the "sacred" teachings of the group. Then statements such as "This group gives you an identity and without it you will be nothing" can and will be thrown at the dissenting individual. This is not only happens in client groups, but in professional staff meetings. Although it is meant to be "helpful," statements like this only generate fear and anxiety. The subtle, if not overt message is to be less questioning of the group norms and more obedience to the them.

So what does all this have to do with resistance? Well, it is the threat that creates the defensive atmosphere of the group. In response to those threats, the mindguards toss out labels and quips to pin on someone's character or behavior. It's at this point that the group's sense of reality over-rides what's really happening. If an individual's reality does not correspond to the group's sense of reality, then the individual gets pigeonholed and resistance sets in. AOD professionals can easily be swayed by a prevailing stereotype of a group to the point that a review of a client's specific behavior is overlooked and is transformed into the dominant line of thought. That is distortion and is the prime association of groupthink to resistance. This is how, according to Janis, groups begin to make defective decisions. The staff, in this situation, creates their own problems by not allowing a free flow of thought in the group process. The professional and the client then become caught in a web of narrowed and constrained thinking. It is this constrained approach or adherence to a single idea in a situation that requires multiple ideas, which breeds the seeds of resistance.

Another issue to be addressed in a groupthink process is the diagnosing of certain pathologies because a preponderance of staff members have had the same problems (Zwebin, 1989). There is, in this case, a tendency to see one's own problem "under every rock" so to say, be it addiction, ACOA issues or codependency. It is a variation of a theme, as identified before, in which AOD staff confirm their own ideas when they see their own unresolved issues in others. This confirmation can easily become articles of faith (Zwebin, ibid), rather than solid treatment principles. So very often the recovery course from a staff person to a client gets translated into "What worked for me will work for you," or in Janis's terminology, closed-mindedness.

Right behind this mentality is the cookie-cutter or stereotypical approach to AOD treatment. Here platitudes and slogans substitute for quality treatment, even when the pathology is substantial as in clinical depression or psychosis associated dysfunctions. Again, diversity in treatment is overshadowed by sameness. As Csikszentmihaki (1990) states, "Ritual wins over substance." This ritual creates the kernel of resistance.

All this has a doubly detrimental effect for those clients who have a culture that is different from the majority of the staff. Because of that difference, clients may be often labeled as resistant due to expressions or behaviors intrinsic to their culture. It's as if some practitioners are blind to cultural variations, and then see those differences as some form of resistance. It is only recently that a movement to recognize cultural diversity has risen in the field. With training, the culture and gender differences are treated with respect, integrated into the mode of treatment, and not labeled forms of resistance.

A last issue of groupthink that can create staff resistance are those patterns that develop over time within a staff. These in turn can influence and control the behavior of the group. These patterns or norms become treatment methods in which the staff has established loyalty (Anderson & Stewart, 1983). These loyalties, and their long term effects, tend to have an air of inflexibility to them and stifling creativity. However, some might argue that established norms have contributed a definite sense of wisdom to the AOD field.

Perhaps, but past wisdom and habits may also tend to blind us to new possibilities (Csikszentmihoyi, 1990).

Long-term habits and norms that induce staff inflexibility may be based on an internal sub-group or clique (Lawson, Ellis & Rivers, 1984). These have particular set of characteristics (Gray & Strarke, 1977). They include, comparing one's status to other staff members. Hobnobbing with these self-proclaimed staff elite can have the effect of muffling the ideas of newer staff, because the new person isn't in the "experienced" clique. This turning off of ideas from outside a clique is an invitation to rigidity, and that is a sure fire way to create resistance. For example, many years ago while working in an inpatient unit, a counselor on that staff belonged to the high status sub-group of the program. Sitting at informal gatherings, he often made it a point to evaluate, or shall I say, demean other less senior staff members. Usually that created animosity among the other therapists, and the effect was doubled because it was condoned by the clinical supervisor. The sad thing about this case was that the counselor who put-down the other staff members was incredibly incompetent, and complained endlessly of how resistant his clients were. He often made jokes at the expense of his clients in our staff meetings, and this has been noted to be particularly resistance generating, (Rothenberg, 1988). Even more sad was the utter lack of confidence his clients had in his clinical skills. They would complain (to me and others) about being in his group. However, that didn't matter because he was in the elite staff sub-group.

Additional Group/Staff Sources of Resistance

One last characteristic can contribute to needless resistance for the client are established rigid norming around recovery background of staff. Essentially, this is the unsupported idea is that if one is not recovering then it is impossible to understand the addict. Once this notion gets started in a staff it overflows to the client population and can have very strong resistant factors to the other staff who are not recovering. This has been an endless battle. The Institute of Medicine (1990) reports both the recovering and non-recovering counselors effect positive change in drug and alcohol clients. One group of counselors is not superior to the other.

Suggested Anti-Groupthink Remedies

Janis (1983) suggests two methods to offset the groupthink mentally. The first suggestion is to assign the role of critical evaluator to each member of the team/staff. The supervisor should give high priority to criticism and difference needs to be encouraged if not reinforced. Second, supervisors need to set a tone of impartiality, and think of the client's needs first and not a preferred program theory. This is to develop an atmosphere of open inquiry and exploration. These simple steps may loosen the bonds of groupthink and help a AOD staff become more creative and less resistant.

Program Resistance

When ritual wins out over the substance not only does a staff become rigid, but a whole program can do the same thing. For example, take the expectation that clients are to proceed though a program's treatment stages and levels at a certain rate. Often little effort is made to accommodate the individual client's rate of recovery. I can vividly recall many times during staff meetings that a certain client was not at a specified level of achievement and discussions ensued from the staff that implied that the client should be discharged. The rational was often centered around, "If we keep this client how will it be perceived by the others?" The underlying assumption was that if we treat a client in some different manner, that in turn, would cause chaos in the community at large. On those rare occasions when we did treat people differently nothing usually happened.

If a counselor did begin to argue for a change of treatment format, they were sometimes branded an enabler by the staff at large. It seemed when one argued for the welfare of your clients, one was then considered to be in cahoots with them. The staff determined that somehow the counselor, was not seeing the client properly or missing the denial and/or resistance. It was now up to the staff to point these the errors, even if they did not spend the time with this client. So the staff ended up offering opinions based on quick interactions, and, a "gut feeling." You, the primary therapist, who did the most of the work, and spent most of the time with the client was accused of not understanding the client, because one was too close to the individual. I always thought that was supposed to be the job of therapy, gain an unique perspective by getting close to someone. Yet by getting close one was accused of losing your perspective by those who were at a distance and knew better. I never understood that logic.

This enabling has always been one of those tactics in a program that subtly or blatantly coerces one back into the fold of the program format (groupthink). It is created when program boundaries, policy and funding practices are too rigid (Caton, Gralnick, Bender & Simon, 1989). The resistance factor gets created from this coercion due to the fact that new and creative ideas cannot be allowed into such a program. The enabling label targeted at the counselor is often an accusation meant to keep the "wayward" counselor in line.

An episode concerning this very issue happened a good many years ago, but it serves my point. I had a client in treatment that I felt needed some kind of additional therapy. I suggested a relapse prevention approach and was promptly put in my place by the supervisor and staff. They insisted that to bring up such a topic would subtly send a message to the client that we were advocating drinking. It was reasoned that to talk about relapse would some how bring about the act itself. This thinking was from a staff full of master level trained people. Now, that was nearly twenty years ago. Today most solid AOD programs wouldn't be caught dead without a relapse prevention aspect to their program. Then, it was a new idea, and considered threatening if not dangerous. Why? Because it didn't fit the mold of the treatment program. Yet this same type of thing happens with different ideas and newer, empirically based therapies. They are met with essentially the same hesitation and doubt. There is a closed-minded approach to new ideas, an almost anti-scientific flavor to anything different (Pattison, 1982).

It is as if these facilities become akin to "arrived" mass movements which are preoccupied with the preservation of facility itself. Once they do that according to Hoffer (1951) they require obedience and patience not spontaneity. By their very nature programs have a tendency to become self-protective and defended. They do so, according to Watzlawick (1990), because no system can afford to re-invent a new program everyday. Further, many a program has no good reason to abandon a proven solution, especially if it was arrived at with great difficulty as many AOD programs were. They have to maintain their identity, and in the process they must protect themselves, to a certain extent, from outside influences. In doing so, they will construct arguments that address their defense against influence. Herein lies the problem. Once they create these arguments, they start to become rigid, and orthodoxy becomes solidified (Hoffer, 1967). These programs will apply more of the same ideas over and over again. It is in this treatment atmosphere that the resulting rigidity creates resistance, not only for the client, but for any creative staff members.

Strean (1993) offers an interesting view on how this sort of thing happens. He indicates that it is a function of countertransference, that is, a hated or different theoretical position, is associated with having significant unresolved conflicts over one's own envy, and feelings of vulnerability. Strean points out that we can help our clients much more when we hate the opposition less. He advocates that counselors should try to understand other points of view, tone down their rigid championing of certain beliefs, and therapeutic practices as if they were religious rituals.

Resistance Generated by Literature Style

There is an subtle literature mind-trap that is as resistance producing as any generated by a counselor or program. It is based partly on the all-or-nothing thinking that permeates aspects of our field. Aside from pockets of genuinely open-minded writing, much of the AOD literature has an either/or rhetoric to it, and manifest itself in thinking such as "either the client is in a recovery, or they're not." "Either they accept their alcoholism, or they are in denial." "Either they go to meetings, or they set themselves up for a relapse." "Either the client does exactly as the program "canons" state, or they are resisting." "Either they're in, or they're out." Frankly, there's no way to win in an either/or mind set. If one is not drinking, then that ever present possibility of that lurking just around the corner in the form of "not drinking yet." There's an ever present "yet" around every bend. That puts one on a constant vigil which sometimes creates tension and anxiety. These stressors, in turn, can have the effect of developing defensive or resistive pattern.

What we are talking about here is the manner of holding to a theory that often creates problems, not the content of the theory. Either/or forces people to do this. That type of thinking, in turn, gets us down to the core of how field resistance gets started and is maintained. The core involves our old foes--rigidly and dogma. Such thinking presents problems, because a theory is often presented in terms of this is the one and only TRUE theory on how addiction operates and therefore MUST be treated. It is presented in the terms of this is right and everything else is wrong.

110

When something is presented in that manner, there's a certain appeal to it. It rings of the truth to which many of us would like to be privy. The emotional delivery of being right and true can stir the soul, arouse the blood, and make one a strident advocate before you know what hits you.

An audience listening to such an approach will have that glassed over look to them, and will nod in agreement with every new twist and turn of these types of presentations. The problem is the audience will suck all this stuff in without a drop of questioning, and the material becomes like tar to the person. Once attached it simply will not come off without a great deal of work. In some cases, "the newly converted" will argue vehemently for the stated position even if it can be shown to be false. Now, that's a convert, not an informed professional, and that breeds resistance.

Educational Induced Resistance

I have attended a host of workshops and seminars over the years, and often came away with a feeling I was indoctrinated with information rather than educated. Videos, audio tapes, and television on the subject of addiction often give me the same impression. The instructor of these indoctrination presentations sooner or later wants you to come over to their way of thinking--or convert. They are short on research data and long on testimonials.

I recently had a student share a training episode in which he attended a codependency workshop. The instructor, of the workshop, made it clear to my student, and others, in the class that they were all were in some state of dysfunction. He tried to make it clear that he did not come from a dysfunctional family and did not meet the criteria of the codependency. He was promptly labeled as being in denial.

This is not a knock on any movement! It is, however, a knock on how some in those movements deliver their information. They deliver it in an absolute fashion. They deliver it in a manner of, "If you do not agree with what is being said--you are in denial resulting from your dysfunction". Indoctrination does that. It does not give you a choice. Either you are with us or against us. When this happens needless resistance gets generated.

A similar tonal quality gets transmitted to the field through the generalizing quality of how resistance, especially denial, is to be envisioned and treated. For instance, you cannot read many articles about denial without the author making an of analogy that denial is some type of "barrier" that has to be breached. I recently reviewed some literature on the subject, and came across a phrase that stated "denial is a wall," so "breaking through the denial," or "cracking it or conquering it" was the treatment of choose. In these types of articles, resistance of the substance abuser is considered so "onerous" that it requires intervention of a battering ram. These breaking, cracking, and battering techniques sound more like military maneuvers than treatment. If one believes in this kind of literature, it's no wonder some counselors are creating needless resistance with their clients. They see them as opponents and the enemy. That perception will definitely create resistance.

At the proverbial bottom of this resistance posture, are the different styles in which information is processed. Kramier's book *I'm Dysfunctional, You're Dysfunctional* (1992) is a prime example of information processing. She passionately makes a series of pleas to the reader that the style of thinking in the self-help movement, which is based on folklore, testimony and a re-hashing of Christian doctrine is getting us nowhere. She advocates a more precise approach to helping oneself, but the style is based on a style of thinking that is often alien to the self-help advocates. It is based on critical thinking, and not thinking from the heart as is espoused by many leaders of the self-help movement. The fundamental difference is that one side is advocating human growth from an affective emotional side, while the other is saying it this growth needs to happen from the intellect. The result is that both are operating on different frequencies. It's no wonder each side is suspicious of each other. They cannot understand each other. There is no cross over communication, and each is bound and determined to bet that the way to improve the human condition is to either "think," or "feel" your way to it (shade of either/or thinking). This misunderstanding will induce program and field resistance.

The Clash of Different Styles of Thought

Just as there are developmental differences in the counselor and the client which can create cross purpose interaction and therefore resistance; there is developmental differences within a staff and the field which can create the same kind of resistance.

For instance, counselors can find themselves coming to cross purposes due to the "different frequency" of thinking that is exchanged across a staff table. Some, on the staff, will insist on a very simple approach to treatment, which is then to be administered to the client. Others will insist on a more academic point of view. Some will insist that the accumulated street experience is the most important thing to get across to the client. Another side will insist that research, and hard data will point the way to more effective treatment. These types of arguments always end up in that useless dilemma of "Who's right?" That, as we have seen, usually gets you no where and that just creates a lot of animosity between the staff. The spill over effect is rigidity and subsequent resistance toward a client. This resistance occurs because counselors become entrenched in a certain view, and do use any thing that doesn't agree with that position.

Additional differences of thought can also be prompted by one portion of a staff who relies on a concrete thinking style, versus a more abstract mentality used by another portion of the staff. The augments and animosity will be generated in such a scenario because one side does not understand the logic of the other side. Again it is the client who will experience the negative spill over effect of staff resistance, because counselors will get stubborn and feel compelled to defend their ideas, not only in a staff meeting but in the counseling session.

This different style of thinking is not limited to a staff or a program, it is to be found through out the drug and alcohol field. This is especially true when one has the misfortune to witness a talk show on the controversy concerning the perceived differences as to the nature of addiction. Talk about "dogs and cats fighting," just watch one of those things! One side seems to be arguing from a concrete, emotional laden position while the other is one that is a more abstract, filled with data. I have watched a few of these programs and came away with the feeling that much could be resolved if we could establish a common language in which to communicate.

Noam Chomsky in a dialogue with Bill Moyers (Docteroff, 1988) noted that "...the fighting faiths have repeatedly been seen to be false." He also indicated that we ought to be an open society, not an intolerant one, and should encourage challenge. "[When] a student comes along with a new idea that threatens established beliefs, you don't kick him out of your office. You pay attention" (Moyers, ibid). Instead of arguing on Donahue or Oprah, why don't we settle this with some good old fashion facts and figures, and sprinkle in some common sense. Do we really need to continually argue, or can we do some serious work?

The Pressure to Produce and the Resulting Resistance

In spite of all the potential resistances in therapy, many clients who come to an AOD facility wanting to change their thinking and attitude from a preoccupation of chemicals, to the desire to change. It is when they are not in this mind-set, that it is considered a failure or blight on the program. Here additional problems concerning resistance can begin. For instance, if a client begins to relapse after completing a certain program, not only will the client get blamed, but the administration can get nervous. Why? Because no new clients will come to that program if the "word" is out that it only produces "failures." The logic runs thus, agencies won't refer to a program that is considered not to produce a quality product. This is the life blood of any AOD unit, and can certainly put the whole program into jeopardy. This is where the pressure to produce and perform gets generated from the upper levels of management, and it is this pressure that will skew the thinking of a treatment staff into making mistakes and becoming more rigid.

The pressure to produce will usually have a threatening overtone to it. This threat is the core of some program resistance. Not only do practitioners feel resistance from the clients, they now feel pressure from their boss demanding more effectiveness. This perceived "double whammy" creates the negative things we have been talking about-- increased frustration which in turn produces rigidity.

This type of pressure is intensified by the irate phone calls or letters that a chief executive officer will receive, following a failure. Those calls usually threaten to disclose the poor quality of the program to others. This puts administrators into a panic. That panic then gets directed to the clinical director, and, in turn, staff are told to shape up or ship out. Threat placed on anyone is not going to resolve anything. It does one thing and one thing only--it makes matters worse.

So the pressure to perform demanded by a treatment center can and will create subtle forms of resistance though out the treatment program, and eventually onto the client.

Nature of a Treatment Center

Certain programs will begin to generate resistance from the first minute a client enters the door. This process can happen in a variety of ways. First clients, whether they like it or not, are placed in a subordinate position, that of being a client, and generally a coerced one at that. The position has the tendency to create a feeling of superiority among the staff, and a feeling of inferiority among the clients. The feeling of inferiority can and will generate a need to compensate by directing energy toward developing a sense of superiority on the part of the client (Adler, 1927/1954). The feeling is especially true of clients who's culture has been one of forced inferiority to begin with. A power struggle has developed, which, is not conducive to change. It is conducive to resistance.

The second implicit resistance factor in AOD programs is that of encountering a host of rules and regulations on one's first day in a program. Nace (1990) notes that the environment of programs especially the inpatient variety are highly structured. Time is ordered, activities are tightly scheduled and behavior is enforced by regulations. According to these programs, this approach emphasizes "a reality orientation" and is suppose to strengthen ego functions that have been worn down by the abusive use of chemicals. These rules sometimes come at a price. Certainly programs cannot run without such dictates, but something is wrong when a client is threatened with various reasons for discharge within minutes of arrival. This threatening rarely builds trust.

An additional problem that accompanies these rules, is the way treatment will get way off track by any infraction of certain rules. I have seen inpatient community meetings drag on and on because of some silly rule had been broken. However, the staff was bound and determined to find out who perpetrated the heinous crime of staying up late. Clients plus staff grumble and become diverted from the recovery process after a few of these meetings. But, to hear it from the staff who conduct these types of meetings, one would think that a client's whole life and sobriety is built on rule keeping. It is not. This over emphasis on rule keeping only takes valuable time away from the real critical issues of recovery. Rule factories do not generate innovation (Gray & Starke, 1977).

Along these same lines is the thinking of Haley (1987). He does not address AOD programs directly, but does give some negative indicators of programs that could most easily fit these AOD rule factories. This includes those clinics where the rules are too rigid, and do not allow for experimentation. He notes, if such programs place a great deal of emphasis on diagnostics, and labeling you probably will not learn a great deal about therapy. In addition, many programs exist for the purposes of social control. They do not encourage diversity and new alternatives. This social control has the task of reducing diversity and forcing conformity. It is difficult to learn about change in places like that.

Without innovation a program or an entire field will begin to crumble under it's own set of rigid rules. Many don't know it but these rigid rules are generated by a host of "shoulds," "musts," and "oughts." The repeated use of these words have been tied to the very foundation of neurotic induced behavior by the early thinkers of the human condition. Yet, many programs still seem to be purporting that a quality recovery be based on these very neurotic modes of thinking.

This situation is even true when it comes to the spiritual aspect to recovery. Imagine a client being told that they must or ought to have a Higher Power to their recovery. Clients are not asked to do this or encouraged to explore it on their own but are told they must do it, or else. The Great Ones espoused love and understanding, not demanding attitude, as the way to heaven or enlightenment.

Right in line with this over emphasis on rules is the ever present issue of coercion. Now, there is no argument that many clients have begun and continue to have a strong recovery based on coercion. But, there is also a down side to coercion, and we need to address it. This is particularly true if the foundation of a program is based on coercion.

Deitch and Zweben (1984) note that within certain therapeutic communities there are clearly stated threats as well as the tacit ones. The overt ones include a rule infraction, which will get a client discharged, and the covert ones which will get you reprimanded in front of a staff meeting (or the called into the clinical director's office for "a talk"). Coercion, it must be remembered, always involves the threat of harm, never promise or benefit. Coercion has an unequaled persuasiveness that will sway not only the simple soul but the one who prides him/herself in the strength of their intellect (Hoffer, 1951). It is this type of coercion that leads to resistance.

There is a program not far from where I once worked which would engage in an interesting method of treatment called the *defense mechanisms* or DM group. What they would do is stick a client in the middle of a group of their peers, and allow the peers to verbally attack each and every little statement the client uttered. Wild accusations would be leveled at the client in the name of breaking down their defenses and "getting honest." Sometimes these clients would end up for a day in the program where I worked. They would dread going back into this madness, because the pressure never produced any internalization of a quality recovery. All it produced was gobs of needless resistance.

One sad result of such approaches is that these groups produce great rewards for conformity (Deitch & Zweben, ibid). Expressing feelings unfortunately comes to mean only showing the "tough" feelings, like anger, while little emphasis was placed on a balanced state of emotions. In turn, what occurs is what Deitch and Zweben called positional identification. Clients begin to view the power of the counselors as something to be attained and used. This often translates into wanting to be the boss of a group, so that one can order people around. I sadly hired such a person years ago. She had a very caustic therapist in her own recovery. This therapist did exactly the same type of counseling as the caustic therapist before her. No matter how much I tried to encourage her into other methods of treatment, she would always return to that caustic approach. She would endlessly justify her behavior as "That's how I got sober" There hasn't been one shred of evidence that this caustic style of treatment is effective. If anything, it has been demonstrated that the change under these circumstances does not last (Liberman, Yalom, & Miles, 1973; Jones, Weinrott & Howard, 1981; Annis & Chan, 1983).

The third issue, implicit in any AOD treatment center, especially the for-profit centers, is the ever present insurance and money angle. Anyone's perception can be twisted and feel strong pressure when it comes to money. This is true of staff who are feeling "under the gun" to do enormous amounts of work for next to nothing salaries. On top of that feeling is the chance they could be let go if the census does not improve. A staff of counselors who are worrying about their job security will in all likelihood will not be placing a great deal of concentration on their caseload. That diminished focus on the job at hand will create subtle forms of resistance.

The last issue in this money and insurance related resistance phenomena is of the client who runs out of funding or insurance. These individuals are polity told they are finished with treatment and they can now go home. Now, clients are not dumb, and they often resent this type of treatment. Other clients can "get a whiff" of this behavior, and the resistance can spread though an inpatient community in no time.

Idols in the Mind

No less a person than Francis Bacon instructed us to destroy those idols which lurk in our mind that are identical to prejudices (Shibahara, 1989). He implored us to destroy those idols, because the prejudices they cause, can be suffocating to all people who are influenced by the them. Eliminate the idols and fresh new thinking will be allowed into a mind. Bacon mentioned several such types. We will address only three.

The first idol is that of the *theater*. This is a type in which the individual begins to depend on the word of an authority or tradition. There is a strong tendency to follow the ideas of such notables, which in turn is considered to be valid and true when addressing things in general.

No one human achievement can be taken as the final truth (Csikszentmihalyi, 1990). To hear some people talk or write about this field, it sounds as if they have indeed found THE way to recovery. That way always has an implicit attitude that it is the only way, and all others are considered to be false and useless. The problem is that many in our field believe these authorities to be accurate, and by that token they begin not to think anymore. Many counselors let the expert do the all the thinking for them, and merely mouth the platitudes of those experts. When the client does not perform as the expert has predicted, frustration will gradually develop which can lead to resistance on the part of the individual and program. Powerful and very creative counseling alternatives to treating chemical dependents will get lost this way. That's what gets sacrificed when one takes the word of authorities to be the truth--new fresh ideas.

The second idol Bacon mentions is that of the *market*. Here mass produced thinking is created by the very language a whole lot of people will use. What does mass produced thinking have to do with resistance? That type of thinking generally doesn't allow for new creative ideas to come into the conversation. Mass thinking tends to confirm itself by it's constant use. Hearing it day after day habituates, if not regiments one's thought patterns to a predominant style of thinking. In addition, that language implicitly has content and a message to deliver which tends to regiment thinking patterns. It is this very regimentation that begins to create resistance. Treatment positions become hardened and inflexible, and tolerate no outside interference.

One does not have to go far to hear this type mass thinking. It can be heard in television talk shows, certain groups, academic circles, and a host of other places. The bottom line to these interactions is that they self-confirm without critical analysis. They do not allow new ideas to be discussed. So, how does one get out of this rut? Same answer as above--ask lots of questions, and do lots of reading.

The third idol is that of the *cave*. Here someone's point of view is considered to be the last word on a subject, and as usual nothing else is see as valid. Bacon undoubtedly took this particular analogy from Plato. Consider existing a lifetime in a cave in which only shadows could be seen. Somehow one individual manages to make his way to the surface of the cave. He/she sees all the wonders of the surface, and rushes back to tell the others in the cave what has been seen. However, he/she is met with skepticism and rebuke. Cave thinking has a tendency to that, reject out right any new discoveries and new ideas. That is resistance in the making.

116

How does one get out of this ruts? There are no easy answers, but a good way to start is to ask tough questions and study, study, study. The goal of all questioning and reading is to educate oneself. However, education also includes training, self-discipline, and learning all kinds, be it from life's experience or from books. Beware of the simple answers to the very complex problems we face in this field. Expand your horizons, and maybe charge a few windmills.

CHAPTER SUMMARY

In this chapter we have examined a host of reasons why trained staff and compete programs can and will generate resistance. It originates from the very structure of programs to communication problems and personal issues. It is not limited to just the programs, but can be observed through out the AOD field. Many originators of this resistance can have the same problems as we have seen for the counselor. Chief among these is rigidly and dogma.

Chapter 5

FAMILY AND GROUP STYLES OF RESISTANCE

> Insanity in individuals is rare--
> but in groups, parties, nations
> and epochs, it is the rule.
> Nietzche

The previous chapters outlined the types of AOD resistance that are perceived to be found in the individual client or counselor. At this point, we need shift gears slightly and examine those types of resistances found in crowds of people, such as groups and family systems. In order to review the information in an orderly manner, the chapter is divided into two parts. The first section addresses resistance theory that is particular to families, and the second section reviews resistance specific to groups. General strategies to address these problems are also examined.

SECTION 1:
FAMILY RESISTANCE

There are numerous theoretical approaches for understanding family therapy, as well as numerous concepts of family oriented resistance. There is no consensus of theory or resistance that holds for all of family therapy. For instance, the whole concept of resistance is not considered relevant by a section of family therapists' (Gurman, 1984), while other authors place a great deal of relevance to the idea of resistance in the family unit (Kaufman, 1994). It looks like many of the same ideas we have seen in the other chapters also apply here. So, family resistance is a matter of perspective as are the other forms we reviewed. How one grasps family resistance will influence one's picture of reality.

As in the second chapter, there are two resistance classifications. First, there are those who believe there is something to resistance and fall into the content, insight-oriented classification. A considerable portion of this chapter is based on the content perspective of resistance, because the literature is heavy with those ideas. Content, insight oriented family treatment is that which directs its energy toward attempting to remove the implicit barriers or resistances (denial, enabling) that the family is seen to produce. Second, there are those opposed to, or do not give credence to the concept. They are part of the context meaning categories. Resistance to this camp is considered to be detrimental to treating the family. The context meaning approach to family therapy focuses more on the solution to the problem rather than on the problem itself.

Insight-Oriented Family Resistances

Family therapists in the drug and alcohol field are most familiar with this perspective. Many of the popular approaches to families with addiction problems intrinsically believe that some type of resistance is at work (e.g., denial, enabling operating within such family systems). Many believe that under the influence of these resistances, the family does not have the insight to see or correct its problems. For example Crisman (1991) notes that life in an alcoholic family is a game of denial played with mirrors. Under this circumstance, the opposite of everything is perceived to be true. Without insight, the family remains dysfunctional. The whole idea of resistance and denial is considered to be very common and, therefore, something to be anticipated (McCown & Johnson, 1993). Often these denial factors are the result of maladaptive behaviors in the family, which become so entrenched and stabilized, that the family can only be resistant to change (Baptiste, 1983).

A review of chemical dependency literature in families suggests a behavior like, "Alcoholics, like drug abusers, create a "suction" that draws everyone around them into their problematic orbit (Kaufman, 1992). In the same vein, Isaacson (1991) states, "... dysfunctional behaviors and interactions that inhibit differentiation, support the continuation of the chemical dependency." Certain interactions of the addicted family, for example, repressed anger or triangulation, create conflict or distance between two parties that is automatically displaced onto a third party or substance. This process turns out to support the dysfunctional chemical dependency system (Kaufman, 1992).

Other explanations include, those families that interact in ways that perpetuate rigid and closed behaviors (Isaacson, 1991). These patterns limit other, more healthy options, while the whole system may be reinforced by generations of this type of behavior. Boszormenyi-Nagy and Krasner (1986) would refer to this type of resistance as a factual obstacle in which lasting psychological damage has occurred. Isaacson's assumptions also include attempts to cover up secrets of the family, which may include issues of shame. The rules by which the secrets are maintained are the now familiar--don't trust, don't feel, don't think or talk (Black, 1981).

In these contexts, the AOD family counselor needs to ask, what is it that is blocking the awareness "that something is wrong"? Is it denial? Fear? Anxiety? Or, as Goleman (1985) notes, is it the collusive fog of the alcoholic family? As indicated in previous chapters, it is our job to find out what is really going on and then direct our treatment focus on that issue. According to Coleman (1985), resistance in families is more complex than it is with the individual. And, as Szasz (1992) notes, how we refer to things determines how we (the counselors and clients) will behave.

Anderson and Steward (1983) outlined at least 40 sources of general family resistance, while McCown and Johnson (1993) devoted a whole book to the subject. What follows is a broad format of these materials as well as other pertinent information. All this material has then translated into the chemical dependency viewpoint of resistance.

Family Process Resistance

This is the type of resistance that occurs within the therapeutic process itself. We will examine several of these operations, but first, a quick review of some dynamics that drive family resistance.

Whitaker (1981) regards family resistance as a conviction that a present solution is the best one available. While Satir (1972) indicates that behind many family resistances is the fear of going somewhere you have not been. Jacobson (1981) indicates that the perception of family resistance really doesn't do one much good. Rather, family change is risky and difficult. So what is called resistance really reflects the costly nature of change itself. Bepko and Krestan (1985) indicate that pride is behind the family's resistance. Surviving the chaotic lifestyle of living in an alcoholic home is laced with threat and vulnerability. The skill, and roles of family members, used to survive in such an environment sometimes creates and fosters a sense of "pride." Pride can be a tool of survival but this pride can be dysfunctional, and it needs to be replaced by more functional family interactions. In addition, the concept of family homeostasis (Jackson, 1957), or later described as alcoholic homeostasis (Lewis, 1992) are operating. Lawson, Peterson, and Lawson (1983) describe homeostasis as a process or mechanism established to resist change. Lewis (1992) refers to this as system-maintaining in which the drinking behavior of the abuser, and the responses of the others can allow the family to maintain it's balance and resist change. Drug and alcohol abuse may also be seen as a system-maintained in which the family consistently play roles that allow the abuse to continue. An effort by one individual to change their role or position threatens the family's equilibrium, and provokes the other members to resist this change and maintain the status quo. Boszormenyi-Nagy and Krasner (1986) refer to this process as habitual or customary ways of relating to one another.

Loyalty also plays a part in this process whereby certain family members deflect the real status of relationships in order to avoid dealing with the possibility of protecting the abuser, and also avoiding potential loss which may be too painful to bear. When drinking is removed from the family, it is assumed such behavior will throw the family into turmoil. Old roles are replaced by new ones, and the family may begin to feel that they are not needed, nor equipped to handle the new family arrangement. Old unresolved family behaviors, which occurred prior to the addiction, are assumed to resurface. Not knowing how to handle such "new" problems can send the family off into other pathology. So the drug and alcohol abuse serves the function of stabilizing the family into patterns in which the family can "cope" (Lewis, 1992).

The well known family roles of lost child, scapegoat, mascot, family hero (Wegscheider, 1981) or adjuster, placater, responsible one (Black, 1979) can be reframed into resistance patterns. They can be seen as resistance because these patterns become rigid and stereotyped particularly when faced with stressful situations such as drinking (Todd, 1988).

The whole issue of boundaries (interactions or styles of functioning) may be viewed as barriers to change. For example, Minuchin (1974) outlined three major patterns of boundaries in the family unit. The first is the clear boundary. Here relationships are based on mutual respect. There is differentiation and flexibility, and one can also maintain closeness in this style of interaction. The second is the enmeshed or rigid boundary. Substance abusing families show a strong propensity toward enmeshment (Madanes, Dukes & Harbin, 1980). There is no room for flexibility or differences. Unity is stressed to the point of smothering the individuals. These families do not let go of their offspring. They cling to them and tolerate all kinds of abuse including substance abuse (Ranew & Serritella, 1992). The resistance is against being different or establishing one's own identity, because it will be seen as a threat to the unity of the family. The last boundary, *diffused* or *disengaged*, is often seen in dependent families. In this case, disengagement results in an isolation of one or many family members from one another or from the outside world.

There are hard and fast rules attached to this boundary style that include no talking about alcoholism, do not confront the drinking behavior, and protect the alcoholic so things don't get any worse (Lawson, et al. 1983; Lewis, 1993). The isolation creates social withdrawal and limits the contacts with other members of the community. In the long run, all this adds to the ever increasing levels of psychological, social and emotional deprivation, and even allows the possibility of child or sexual abuse (Ranew & Serritella, 1992).

Enabling

Essentially, *enabling* is a family-process resistance that covers up or makes excuses for the abuser so that individual will not feel the full force of consequences of their behavior (Ranew & Serritella, 1992; Doweiko, 1993).

Why would family members protect or enable the substance abuser so that he/she could continue their abusive lifestyle without facing the consequences? Ellis, McInerney, DiGiuseppe, and Yeager (1988) answer that question according to Rational-Emotive-Behavioral-Therapy principles. They note three types of enabling. The first is called the *joiner*. In this case, the enabler provides the abuser with the chemicals or money needed to purchase them. They openly support the abuser. The second type of enabler is called the *messiah*. This individual clearly states that they oppose the use of chemicals and campaign to stop it. However, the method in which the messiah tries to stop the abuse often prevents and insulates the abuser from feeling the full force of their drunken behavior. They usually save the addict by getting them out of jam after jam. So, they rescue the abuser by claiming that they understand his/her problem. Another reason they rescue is because they feel the abuser "needs them" in order to survive. Obviously, the rescuing behavior has the undesired effect of continuing the addiction. Beneath this behavior is the messiah's belief that they are primarily responsible for the addicts recovery. They endow themselves with the notion that their fate with this addict is a noble cause. It's made all the more noble because they are so in love with the addict. The more times they attempt to stop the addict's use the more they "prove" their love for the dependent.

The third type of enabling is called the *silent sufferer*. These individuals do not make any attempt to change the addict, nor do they try to rescue that person. Instead, they are always "there." They just take it, and absorb the pain. By doing next to nothing, the silent sufferer helps the addict believe that everything is fine. This can aid a true denial process used by the active abuser. According to silent sufferer nothing is wrong, and that stance reinforces the belief to the dependent that everything is OK, when indeed, it isn't. Behind this suffering is an extreme fear of being alone and abandoned. Silent sufferers often believe that they are essentially worthless and do not deserve any better. I encountered a middle-aged female a few years ago who had sustained several physical beatings by her mate. She was put into more debt than she could afford, and she had seen the man with another women. Each time one of these episodes occurred, she would call me in panic and want some kind of help. Repeated entreaties to have her get out of this relationship failed. I finally asked her, out of my own frustration, why she sustained such abuse. Crying, she looked at me and said, "Because nobody else will have me".

From a rational-emotive-behavior perspective, therapy with these types of individuals should determine the specific irrational belief: be it worthlessness, grandiosity, or low frustration tolerance, and then dispute it. The therapist and the client should try to substitute a more realistic or rational belief in place of the troublesome, irrational one.

A Brief Survey of Initial Family Barriers

This section reviews a few specific types of resistances often found early in AOD family treatment. The section that immediately follows addresses suggestions on how to engage these forms of resistance.

As with the individual, the family may initially deny that a problem exists. This family impediment may have it's roots in the threat of something they know is different about them, but they are afraid to face. Boszormenyi-Nagy and Ulich (1981) notes that engaging in this behavior is the way that the family avoids responsibility for their part in the overall problem.

Along the same lines is an over-reliance on an entrenched belief that some external event or genetic/chemical imbalance is to be held responsible for the family's plight. If the event or imbalance can be undone then the family could be normal. Such examples can include, "If only the system or boss would get off his back, then he wouldn't have to drink," or, "It's in her blood. Her whole family acts that way. What do you expect?"

Another type of early resistance found in AOD family treatment includes an attempt to dictate the parameters of treatment (McCown & Johnson, 1993). One example includes the family who wants to exclude a specific family member because of embarrassment or fear. Consider the anxious spouse who finds a way to get to a first appointment in spite of domestic abuse. He/she is adamant that no one know that this session took place, and if word of it leaks out, they make it clear they will deny all association with you, and drop out of treatment.

Another initial resistance often found in family therapy deals with the total dismissal of treatment (Anderson & Stewart, 1983). A classic example includes a family member who is reluctant to be involved with therapy. These people often come off as gruff. They make it clear that if it hadn't been for some external pressure that forced them into this situation, they would have never had come in the first place. In circumstances such as this, consider the reactance issue we reviewed in chapter two, as the driving force behind this behavior. If the freedom of a family or whole family is threatened then the unit may very well act in a hostile and belligerent manner.

Broad treatment recommendations for many of these problems should include avoiding head-on arguments. To do otherwise is to invite the burden of needless resistance to an already stressed family. Attend to the tone of your voice for those subtle little bits of irritation and defensiveness that may be evident. Those defensive tones can be picked up by an all ready "resistant" family which will only fuel more barriers to effective treatment.

In these situations, try to be supportive and get the family to talk more about their fears and anxieties. Another important method to address initial resistance, is to give the family as much information as possible about what constitutes therapy and the part you will play.

Many families that come into AOD treatment are ignorant of what to expect, and such information is of great benefit to them.

In line with these recommendations, is the ever critical factor of starting treatment where the family is and not where you think they need to be. They may want to begin by talking about things other than the abusive drinking and drugging. Yet, the counselor thinks it is critical to discuss the abuse issue from the start. Starting where you think treatment needs to begin can often result in an impasse because the family isn't ready to address such issues. Nothing says you have to believe what the family is telling you, but some initial disclosures may be important to them. Not to listen, and wanting to insert your favorite pet theory is to invite resistance. Eventually you will get around to the issue of the drinking or drugging.

Families have other methods of erecting resistance. One way may be to substitute a good offense instead of a poor defense. Rather than attack the therapist overtly, the family might appeal to the therapist's ego and vanity. This way the family can sideline the treatment process, never getting to the real issues, and making it look like therapy is working. Examples include "buttering you up" by letting you know how helpful you have been, and telling you that the family is functioning so much better now that you have made a few suggestions. If taken in by this ploy, therapists may congratulate themselves too prematurely, and miss the important issues.

Right along with this type of resistance is the family who does not talk, or has one member what does all the talking. In the case of the family that does not talk, consider giving permission to the family to remain silent, or ask the family not to interrupt while you are talking. These paradoxical methods have been known to elicit just the opposite of what is stated.

In the case of the family member who does all the talking, he/she may be trying to punish the identified patient or scapegoat of the family (McGown & Johnson, 1993). Pointing this out to the family may help them notice that their methods of communication do not work very well. This could set the stage for a family task which would aim at improving their communication.

Other initial resistances include the family that fails to comply with treatment recommendations and suggestions. They might state that they did not understand the assignment, or claim that they were too busy to have completed the homework. Sometimes the family therapist doesn't know it, but they assigned a task that the family cannot possibly finish, and the unfinished task is misinterpreted as resistance. In this case, try to make the instructions very specific; have the family repeat the instructions that were given, or determine whether or not the homework was too difficult. If that is the case, simplify the assignment. Also determine if someone in the family is sabotaging the homework assignments, and direct your attention to that issue. If these explanations do not account for the family's behavior, they may be hostile to the therapist for the way that the terms of the homework is dictated. They get revenge by not completing the assignment.

Another example of initial resistance is decision avoidance (McGown & Johnson, 1993). Here the family avoids the recommendation because of stress, rather than some deeper problem. Perhaps, family chooses not to choose, which has rewarding secondary gains for them. The result can be viewed as noncompliance. When failure to follow agreed upon treatment recommendations occurs, the therapist would do well to look for the source of these secondary gains (Boszormenyi-Nagy & Krasner, 1986). One or more of the family members may have something to achieve by keeping the family as it is. They may value a poor relationship because of the feelings it produces for them. In this case, theirs is a destructive entitlement, which satisfies some deep need for making things just and right. Jacobson (1981) would indicate that failure to comply may be that the short costs for the family are more dominate then any long term benefits.

Other examples of initial resistances may include superficial cooperation, or perhaps families who are out-and-out manipulative (McCown & Johnson, 1993). These behaviors are often associated with one or more family members who act in a surly, if not aggressive manner which is meant to back you off and change the subject to a "safer" topic. Superficial cooperation and manipulative behavior can be symptoms of secondary gains in operation, power coalitions, if not actual anti-social characteristics. According to the homeostasis theory, change for an addictive family can trigger into a crises. They may not have the capacity to behave in ways outside of their customary patterns, and they may find it difficult to adjust to the need for change. This inability to cope may draw them back into old dysfunctional patterns (Lewis, 1992). Given this set of factors, the family therapist has to ask whether this is really resistance or an inadequate coping style.

Canceling an appointment is another resistance issue. There may be many sources that can contribute to this problem. Among them are the shame, guilt, and anxiety that the very nature of treatment can generate. Exposure of family drinking and associated secrets to a relative stranger (therapist) may cause many family members re-consider therapy and change their minds. In situations such as this, determine if there is room to negotiate the return and consistent attendance of family members who have left or refuse to attend. Follow up calls and letters can be very helpful. It is also important to frame treatment as an aid to the family's problems, and not a stress producer (Anderson & Stewart, 1983).

The last set of initial problems for the AOD family therapist often centers on the family's disagreement as to the nature of the real problem, the desired outcome, or goals. Recommendations include identifying a problem or goal statement on which the whole family can agree. This can also be handled by having the therapist make any disagreement a part of a broader issue, and frame it in terms of improving communication between the family members. Consider giving hints or clues to all members of the family to look closer at the way they communicate with each other. Satir (1972, 1983) notes that dysfunctional communication patterns rank as significant barriers to healthy and well functioning families. Another communication suggestion (McIntyre, 1993), may be to teach the family to talk in "I" terms, in which they learn to change hidden messages into statements of "I want, I need, or I would appreciate... " Families that have been effected by long periods of chemical abuse will have a difficult time communicating in "I" terms.

Context-Meaning Oriented Family "Resistances"

From this perspective, resistance has no meaning. In fact, using the concept is discouraged. Lankton, Lankton, and Matthew (1991) sum up this position by indicating that "Resistance" is a term rarely used except to say that it is an upside-down and backward

124

way of cooperating." They feel that family therapy is slowly abandoning the concept. What is often considered to be resistance is the family's movement into areas where they have doubt, lack the appropriate coping tools, and are fearful to proceed.

O'Hanlon and Weiner-Davis (1989) note that to treat the family in the context manner is to see the family as essentially normal. If you treat the family as normal, they have a tendency to behave more normally (Haley, 1987). Further, engaging a family as if it had all the abilities to resolve their problems, creates their feelings of empowerment In the content-oriented form of therapy, there is a tendency to believe there is a right and wrong way to do treatment. That doesn't hold in the context mode. Here there is no right or wrong. The emphasis is on the data that works, that is toward a solution orientation, not a pathology orientation.

The viewpoint presented here is all part of a problem solving approach (de Shazer, 1985, 1988; Haley, 1987; Berg & Miller, 1992). According to this view, families rarely are seeking help for their deep and underlying problems. Families are generally in emotional turmoil, uncomfortable levels of pain, and they want relief from these things. So this approach takes the family at their word and works toward attaining more immediate goals. Another way to look at this is that a certain solution the family uses to engage the drinker turns out to be the problem (Todd, 1988). In the context-orientation, it is the family's job is to find new solutions, and the problems cease to exist.

This form of therapy respects the family's fear of change, ambivalence and dysfunctional communication patterns. It does not try to impose a different reality on the family as one would in a content mode of therapy. The family's reality is respected. In this way, the therapist avoids the position of being an agent of change who ends up struggling with the family's "resistance." So there is little or no loss of face if the family wants to work on just changing a little, or if they decide to proceed with treatment in a different manner.

Paradoxical methods are often used in this general approach. For example, the therapist may encourage the family to continue doing things the old way, while at the same time suggest that they think about new behaviors. In addition, the family might be told to continue to distrust one another, while at the same time they are to imagine ways in which they could begin to trust each other. Using this method, the family has its fear of change affirmed, but the paradox has them consider new ways of trusting in a relatively non-pressured fashion. The therapist aligns themselves with the "no-change" side of the family's ambivalence, which helps create a safe atmosphere for the family. The more safely secured the family is, the better the possibility they will truly think about change. Very little resistance is to be encountered in this therapeutic frame of things.

GENERAL AOD FAMILY TREATMENT SUGGESTIONS

We first reviewed strategies for specific types of resistance. In this section, we will review what some broad based family strategies. Many such family treatment suggestions fall into the things one should do, and things one should not do. Let's start with the "don'ts", and finish on a positive note with the things one should do in family AOD treatment.

Suggested Things Not to Do

Whitaker and Keith (1981) describe the do not's as technical errors. This section will loosely follow their format, include other viewpoints, and tie it to chemical dependency.

One "do not" error is to be co-opted by a chemical dependent family. In this case, the family therapist becomes apart of the family due to a blurring of boundaries or countertransference issues. An example might include a family who is going through issues similar to those that plague the family therapist him/herself. This can include old traumas, shame and guilt issues, and seeing before one's eyes a family that looks like the one with which he/she grew up.

Sometimes the session seems "like old home week." In this case, the therapist is very glad to see the family, the conversation sounds like getting caught up with old family news more than it does about getting on with the business of therapy. The problem with this is the discussion goes nowhere, and the family gets another dysfunctional member. Therapists stand to lose their professional position if they are having difficulty resolving their own issues. This obviously can have significant resistance ramifications.

At the other end of this continuum, is behavior in which the family therapist is exceedingly professional and is very aloof from the human side of the family. Therapists, in this case, uses an abundance of technical terms and actions. The basic counseling principles of empathy, regard/respect, authenticity and concreteness may be compromised. Again, issues of countertransference, if not novice jitters, may be behind such a "professional front" and may elicit resistance.

McGown and Johnson, (1993) developed a delightful list of don'ts at the end of their book. I have summarized it, and made it applicable to chemical dependency.

- Don't beg or force a family by threatening them. This will usually make things worse and elicit more resistance.
- Rescuing is out! We all have limits, and the solid family therapist knows this.
- Avoid all those final sounding words like "always," "never," "ought," "must," "should," etc.
- Do not destabilize a family that is unstable to begin with (unless there are issues of threat and harm).
- Do not become disrespectful, nor pessimistic, even if your frustration level is high.
- Learn what treatment a previous family therapist may have attempted, which didn't work. Then, do not do the same thing.

Suggested Things to Do

McGown and Johnson (1993); and Dunst, Trivett, and Deal (1988) have put together a list of broad treatment recommendations that are intended to reduce family resistance, expedite change, and empower the family. This empowerment philosophy has as its belief in a family that has competence. It is proactive and designed to enable the family to experience their own success, improve their ability levels, and see themselves as the creators of that change. The suggestions are summarized, and applied to AOD treatment.

- Speak in the language and style of the family.
- Focus on identified behavior that can be addressed.
- Try to have only one person at a time talk.
- Respect the family members.
- A focus on the present helps avoid the problem of repeatedly bringing up the past, and throwing that in someone's face.
- Promote positive and proactive levels of communication within the family.
- Permit the family the right to decide whether they want help or not.
- Help that comes in the form which the family is accustomed will be received better than those interventions that do not.
- Structure the treatment so that immediate success is achieved. Keep treatment goals specific and attainable. This way the family will feel successful, empowered, and may begin to use their own resources and/or those of the community.
- Consider reframing the family problems so they do not get repeatedly stuck in dead-end thinking, which sabotages their ability to empower themselves with new ideas and family solutions (Constantine, Fish, & Piercy, 1984).

SECTION SUMMARY

The section was divided into two broad sections that address resistance very differently. One viewpoint was the content-approach, which sees resistances as a real with specific and actual dynamics. Such dynamics include disparaging the whole process of treatment, giving therapy process half efforts, enabling, and having various members of the family assume certain roles to protect the AOD family's secret. Resistance from this content family perspective is seen to be a very complex problem because it requires the participation of many individuals. However, the context perspective of family resistance does not see as valid issue. Here, the emphasis was to redirect the form of treatment, and not to accuse the family of being in a state of resistance. A list of do's and don'ts to treat the dependent family was reviewed. Some of those items included no threatening or rescuing, but respecting the family, focusing on present issues, and improving communication patterns.

SECTION II
GROUP RESISTANCE

TYPES OF RESISTANCE FOUND IN A GROUP SETTING

As we have seen, it is the viewpoint the professional takes toward resistance that dictates how the resistance will be perceived and subsequently treated. The situation is no different in a group setting. In groups, as well as in the family or with the individual, the professional can perceive resistance as something that is quite real and substantive or meaningless and not substantive. Following the previous section, this one is divided into the content and context sub-sections. The content perspective of resistance constitutes the bulk of ideas in group resistance theory. Many of the context ideas toward resistance are modified individual concepts, and are covered later in this section, and again in Chapter Six.

The Group Content Resistance Orientation

Edelwich and Brodsky (1992) maintain that resistance is a staple of groups, and these resistances may be expressed by some or all of the group members (Meissner, 1988). Ohlsen (1970) defines group resistance as that "...failure to cooperate in the therapeutic process, or the blocking of another client's growth within the treatment group, is resistance." Denial also plays a defensive role in the group by suppressing the unpleasant reality of one's life and not allowing it to gain a foothold in consciousness (Corey, 1990).

A review of two books on group dynamics for chemical dependency, Flores (1988), Rogers and McMillen (1989), imply that resistance is certain to be found in groups composed of addicted populations. Vannicelli (1992) goes as far as to outline at least 45 different types of resistance to be found in a chemical dependency group.

Meissner (1988) notes that in the group, emphasis shifts away from the individual and is redirected toward understanding interpersonal relationships. Group therapy is focused on developing more effective ways of relating and dealing with the various emotions found in that setting. Because of the shift, the form of resistance is somewhat different. In it's working phase the group creates certain inevitable strains that give rise to anxiety, tension and conflict. At these points a group begins to generate resistance. As with the family and individual, the group appears to have several different resistance forms.

An Assortment of Group Resistances

The following is a brief sketch of the some of the varieties of content resistance found in a group setting. There is no hierarchy here, because these content type resistances have a habit of showing up at various times through out the group process. The broad format that follows is loosely based on Edelwich and Brodsky (1992), and Vannicelli (1992), but I have integrated many other ideas and translated for chemical dependency assessment and treatment.

Early Group Resistance - Ambivalence

Yalom (1985) notes ambivalence as a condition of group behavior. He indicates that new members have many concerns that center on a preoccupation with acceptance, approval, commitment, and maintaining control. Many of these concerns are riddled with ambivalence. Such concerns can include ambivalence to commit to a group, ambivalence to self-disclose (and feel accepted thereafter), or self-examine (maintain the control and facade). Corey (1990) also notes that possible ambivalent expressions of group members that, if not properly identified, can be easily confused with some type of resistance. They include:

- Why do I have to share my personal and drinking history with this group? What is that supposed to do?
- I'll make a fool of myself in a group. I can feel the fear building inside of me.
- If I have to disclose, I'll be vulnerable and unguarded. I want to be sober, but I'm afraid.
- Will these people accept me after they have heard what I've done on cocaine. I just know they will reject me.
- I've always been in control. If I start disclosing, I'll lose that control.
- I'm afraid I might become too dependent on these people, then I won't be able to take care of myself.
- I've got to protect myself. If I get too close to these people it will hurt like hell when they begin to leave, and I'll be abandoned again.

A simple treatment recommendation for individuals early on in the group process and in a state of ambivalence is to make them--SAFE. That means developing a lot of support and taking a little time to gain a workable relationship that is based on trust and respect (see Chapter Six).

Silence

Another resistance found early in an AOD group is that of silence. It is important to differentiate the type of silence that is of the protective and defensive nature, versus the connected and pondering type of working silence (Vannicelli, 1992). We will focus on the former. Here the silence can engulf an entire group or only a single member. If not addressed in some way this silence can often turn into a test of wills in which members become resolved to maintain their silence longer than any other. Before it evolves that far, the therapist has to assess what is happening. From a content point of view silence can perceived to be a number of things. For instance, it may be the result of over-dependency on the counselor to do something during each and every second of the group (Meissner, 1988). On this point, Ohlsen (1970) notes that early in the group process the members may not be acting out of resistance, but out of inadequate structuring. The group may be over- or under-structured. Either way, the members are perplexed because adequate directions were not given, or because there is an implied sense of power in the group, or a member, who is being ignored. This sense of bewilderment simply adds to the strain of being in a group.

Another cause of silence in a group can be attributed to its hostility that is sometimes directed at the leader. The group may act this way because the leader wants the group to share and cooperate with one another when the members are not ready (Rosenthal, 1987). Such a disagreement over goals and treatment direction may create some level of resistance.

Yalom (1985) notes that a particular form of resistance can be encountered early in a group, which is the opposite of the conflict just mentioned. The group agrees that they feel equally warm and accepting toward all other members of the group when in fact, they don't. This can present silence problems later in the development of the group, because no group member will share themselves under these circumstances.

Another behind the scenes contributor of silence is due to one or several of the members feeling anxious and afraid to openly discuss their personal feelings and secrets (Flores, 1988). Much of this anxiety centers on what Rosenthal (1987) refers to as *superego resistance.* Here the client resists disclosure because of the shame, guilt and embarrassment of past drug and alcohol-related behaviors. Shame and guilt, play an important role at this juncture. What can be misinterpreted as resistance of silence, when it isn't, is the manner in which the discloser feels he/she will be judged after a secret is out (Flores, 1988). If they think the response will be a pejorative one, silence may be the response. When faced with this situation, I made sure the group members found out what the group really did think of them. For example, following a powerful disclosure, I have often seen a person cup their face in their hands, shake, weep, and wait. They often waiting for a "look of acceptance" from the other members. Then, I would move toward the crying client and whisper in his/her ear, "Look each group member in the eye, and ask each one of them what they think of you." No one has ever refused that request. As they raise their head from their hands, sobbing, they ask each group member by name, "What do you think of me?" Not once in the nearly twenty years of doing groups has someone disapproved of someone else. On the contrary, they have exhibited such an out pouring of acceptance and love that is overwhelming. This often sets the foundation for the highest quality recovery process I have been blessed to witness.

Excessive Talking

At the other end of this spectrum, is the group member who talks too much or monopolizes. Vannicelli (1992) classifies this, and similar types of group behaviors, as *disruptive defenses.* This can often take the form of endless recitals of grief and grievances. This will occupy much of a group's time without moving toward any resolution. I have experienced many such recitals and thought how the person who just vented would now behave. I assumed the vented would add to the recovery process. Often I was wrong, because excessive talkers come to group after group, and repeat the same story.

This is not to say that venting is not a good therapeutic process, but repeated ventilations with no recovery movement should be viewed with suspicion. In such situations, other group members will begin to "turn off," and roll their eyes because they

130

have heard this story many times before. These monopolizers seem to have no regard for the other group members, and creates a lot of resentment from the other members.

A thoughtful therapist will, in the above case, begin to speculate about what is really driving this "broken record." A good question to ask yourself, is what the client gains by this action? Each answer will have it's own specifics, but often the gain may entail a sense of attention seeking because some people are that needy. Such people may require new adaptive methods and contexts by which to gratify those needs. A group process can be helpful in coming up with new and alternative ideas for the excessive talker once a level of trust has been established.

Flight

Meissner (1988), Rosenthal (1987), and Bion (1959) discuss the group problem of flight, as a basic group motivational element. Yalom (1985) asks the question, "Flight from what?" This can have a variety of reasons including anxiety and fear. Yalom thinks flight can also be generated from a lack of clarity about a group's primary task, or it could be due to the lack of procedural norms. Often, the therapist does not spell out the manner of intended group interaction. In addition, the issues of confidentially or the role to be played by the group leader may not be clearly defined. The result is group confusion.

Yalom (ibid) notes a few additional antitherapeutic norms that can also result from the lack of clarity. One centers on the group members who take turns talking about themselves in a sequential, almost robotic like manner. This destroys any spontaneity, and certainly generate useless anxiety from the members as they wait their turn to talk. Another norm is of the "can you top this" variety. I have been in a number of groups in which I felt I was in a contest to see which member would out shine the others with their rendition of "the worst story that happened to me during my drinking" tale. These stories are often generated by talk that is meant to impress (glorify), and never get to the heart of recovery.

This flight behavior can also take the form of hostility and antagonism, or may take the form of joking, intellectualizing, disrupting a group session or actual attempts to escape from the group. The bottom line in all these cases is avoiding, or fleeing, from matters of substance. The avoidance may be the result of a fear of disclosure, of coming to terms with oneself and, or the fear of intimacy (Flores, 1988). Edelwich and Brodsky (1992) call these universal features of groups, because they always take the focus off the group process at hand. Once that happens, communication breaks down and the "flighers" get want they want--avoidance of their issues.

Other ways into flight and avoidance include blaming, gossip and the ever popular "playing therapist". This last issue is often found in a AOD groups. For example, this often starts with clients who have had been through several treatment programs, and have accumulated some group experience. They arrive in new group and begin to "run it," or criticize the way therapy is being conducted. If a group member succeeds in this role, the flight and avoidance of their own issues is a forgone conclusion. Interestingly, these clients then put the responsibility of "opening up" on the other members. They may also begin to diagnosis what seems to be ailing certain group members, if not the whole group or program.

Flight may also have a behavioral aspect to it. It could be one of being chronically late for the group, not showing up, or of leaving a group early. Vannicelli (1992) refers to these types of behaviors as deviations from contact. However, an interesting piece of research conducted by Gaskin and Little (1992) noted of 57 people who left treatment, did so because they claimed to have found other treatment options, or external events came about that prohibited their continued attendance. This study challenges the view that clients who dropped out of treatment were not motivated. One the other hand, Yalom (1985) states, "Resist the conclusion" that tardiness is due to transportation or other such excuses. According to him, such behaviors are manifestations of resistance, and need to be addressed.

These are two different points of view. The counselor's job is to find out what might be driving the tardy behavior and address it. It may be genuine tardiness, or it may be resistance. An AOD group counselor's best bet is to find out for themselves what's going on and address that.

Manipulation

Group manipulation can come in several forms including intimidation, seduction and scapegoating. The manipulation can be overt or covert. In the intimidation form, the manipulator is trying to get the focus off themselves, and is threatening you and the group to stay clear of certain subjects. Essentially they are saying, "don't push me" (Yalmon, 1985). They often claim that if you, or anybody in the group begins to "dig" into certain aspects of their past, they will leave the group. As a result, many groups stay away from this sulking individual. Rosenthal (1987) refers to these situations as limit setting, and are meant to protect the client's ego.

Seduction can serve the same purpose of getting the focus off the self and onto something else. It may be manifested through verbal flirtatious exhibitionism and body language' or out and out sexual invitations. The gains for the seducer are many (Edelwich & Brodsky, 1992). For instance, one goal may be to establish a power alliance, in which attention is drawn away from themselves, while another aim is to gain a status and strength through pseudo "bonding" with the group leader. This seduction may also happen with another member of the group. I have sometimes seen this seduction come about as a result of confusion with intimacy, and a strong need to be loved. After many years of chemical abuse, the dependent may be looking for some level of affection. However, because of the effects of an addiction, they never developed the skills to get beyond the physical level of affection, and only know a limited form of trying to get the love they want.

In the matter of scapegoating, group members will begin to hold another member responsible if the group doesn't go well. Not only can members of group scapegoat a particular member, the group leader can easily fall into this trap. Scapegoating, regardless where it originates, side-steps any kind of genuine group work.

Akin to this manipulation style, is what Yalom (1985) refers to as the *help-rejecting complainer*. This individual has the distinctive pattern of always complaining about the many problems they have, requesting some type of group help, and upon receiving that help, promptly reject it. The rejection is usually based on some quibble of, "I tried that and it didn't work," or, "That (suggested solution) isn't for me." It is as if they take pride in having the worst possible problems in the group. They often seek some type of medication which is usually taboo in a program. In group, they establish that they are the most needy. They are self-centered and can only address their own issues. This wears thin in an AOD group, and soon the other members become irritated, frustrated, and begin to tune them out. If not addressed, this individual can create many resistances problems.

The last in this series of manipulation types is the *self-righteous moralist* as described by Yalom (ibid). These individuals have the irritating characteristic of trying to be right all the time. They make sure any others are proven wrong. There is an issue of control in all manipulation types, but this last type centers on being morally right, and imposing that view on all other people. They refuse to concede points. This type of person challenges any group member who seeks a superior position, and may even challenge the counselor. What they end up doing to a group is generating a lot of resentment. That, as you can probably have guessed, leads to resistance.

Pairing or Alliances

In this type of resistance, a group member will begin to make side remarks to another group member in order to win a sense of approval or agreement for themselves (Meissner, 1988). These group members are saying to other members that they will support them, but, in turn, they require support. The alliance is built on the assumption that one party will come to the rescue of the other should it get too uncomfortable for either (Edelwich & Brodsky, 1992).

If the rescue does not occur within the group proper, then it can certainly occur outside the group where the alliance members can rally their cause. In this situation, the discussion tends to be one that complains about the group process, other group members, or the group leader. This type of alliance has the potential to undermine a group from working on recovery issues.

Acting Out

This is a behavioral expression of a group member's conflicts and fantasies in or outside the group (Meissner, 1988). It can range from out and out violence, running away from a topic perceived as uncomfortable, to verbal intimidation following a group, in person, or over the phone. Certainly any type of violence by one group member to another, in or out of the group, cannot be tolerated. Should this occur a post-mortem is in order to determine how and why this behavior took place. Such a review is essential if for no other reason than to prevent it again. Any kind of acting out, by one member, will have disruptive and resistive effects on the other members.

A similar attitude holds true for removing a group member. When this happens the group usually has definite reactions. As a group leader you want the group to integrate and learn from the experience, although many won't. When I have had to do this distasteful task, some of the group members became distrustful of me, the program I represented, and recovery in general. Even if I spend hours explaining the reasons, new waves of resistance often followed the episode. It seemed to touch some deep sense of anxiety, abandonment, or rejection for many of the group members. There would often be wild accusations leveled at me that, "I didn't care," and, "Was in it just for the money." In these situations, most all trust was fractured. Some group members who were, one day, quite active and involved, packed their bags and headed down the road. Others were visibly stunned and confused. Yet it seemed that following a short period of mourning, some group members started to pull together and reaffirm that their lives and recovery were still important.

Breaches of Confidentiality

If a group leader tries to do anything in a chemical dependency group, it is to instill a sense of trust. The belief comes from the core idea, that trust is central to the recovery process. Trust is tenuous to maintain if some of the members are not abiding by the confidentially rule. That is, "what is said in the group stays in the group." Somehow any breach eventually works it's way back into the group, and very often all hell breaks lose. Accusations go flying every which way. Clients become upset and defensive, and whatever level of trust a group created, quickly evaporates.

It takes time, patience, and hard work to regain any level of trust following a breach. Sometimes, it never comes back. In the situations where I've seen trust return, there seemed to be more of it after the process was worked through than existed before the breech. I noted in those times, forgiveness played a big part in the healing process and recovery.

Power in the Group

Power issues of many varieties can play into the creation of group resistance. For example, the group may go about it's business not based on the foundation of trust, but on a series of imposed "shoulds" and "oughts." In this case, the group turns into a factory of rules where members must abide by the established rules or be ostracized. It is a time of *peer-court* as Bach (1954) termed it. Group members are not making suggestions to one another out of acceptance and understanding, but out of power and the jockeying for position. The therapist may get caught up in power struggles, especially if the group members are not recovering according to their timetable or method of recovery. I refer you back to the power discussions sections in Chapter Two, and counselor power tactics discussed in Chapter Three, to see how such issues can generate resistance in a group setting.

Use of Chemicals by a Group Member While Still in Group

Vannicelli (1992) makes note of a resistance type in which a group member is actively using chemicals while in a recovery oriented group. The situation always presents a problem for the other group members, particularly if the group is relatively new. A big problem is the welfare of the other group members who might be effected, and in turn relapse themselves. Issues that revolve around the lack of faith in the group need to be addressed, as well addressing the member's anxieties and fears of relapsing. Another problem is of the client who has been using, and what to do about him/her. Some, in the field, have begun not to blame the client for the relapsing, but suspect a technique by the counselor that is not working. The idea is to not judge the individual, but try to correct his/her behavior with a new twist in strategy application. Framing a relapse as a mistake and not a failure is helpful for both the group and the member who relapsed (Taleff, 1992). For an extensive review of relapse prevention theory and strategies, I recommend the reader review Chiauzzi (1991); Gorski and Miller (1986); and Marlatt and Gordon (1985).

THE CONTEXT ORIENTED APPROACH TO GROUP RESISTANCE

Nicholas (1984) approaches group resistance as a matter of view or context. If a group member is not doing well, it is assumed that the treatment intervention needs adjustment, and it is not always some kind of resistance emanating from the client. Nichols also notes that some of our prime ideas on change have an effect on our the frame of reference and, in turn, reflect on the whole group. For instance, she notes that change is always happening, and it is the task of the group leader to determine what is changing in a group situation and to use more of it. This is vastly different from the assumption that denial, and a host of other resistances exist in every group member. It encourages the idea that change is taking place, and is occurring in the group. Nichols encourages the group leader to use "no resistance techniques" (see Chapter Six for examples). This approach encourages the idea that any change will beget even more change.

GENERAL GROUP TREATMENT RECOMMENDATIONS

Egan (1994), Corey (1990) and Flores, (1988) have outlined a few broad treatment recommendations for addressing resistance. They are directed at group approaches and the qualities of a good group leader. I have adjusted them for the AOD counselor.
- Strive for positive involvement from the group members. This can be fostered through empathy, respect, and authentic behavior. Always keep an eye out for your own hostility and impatience toward the client.
- Maintain a reasonably open therapeutic style, not one driven by dogma or the need to be right. Expectations of what a group can achieve, plus what the self is capable of are empowering.
- Encourage the group members to emulate positive role models for themselves.
- Teach the group the fine art of feedback and support. Many of these skills have been lost through the long use of chemicals.
- Avoid harsh confrontation methods but, at the same time, work for client empowerment, and encourage the group members to challenge themselves.
- Assist group members to develop specific and attainable goals.
- Constantly work for group trust that, hopefully, will be generalized beyond the group room.

- If it is in your method of operation, encourage a sense of spirituality in the recovery process.
- Avoid the use of techniques that aim at conquering resistance. Resistance may be considered normal or "nothing at all."

SECTION SUMMARY

We have reviewed group resistance and found that it can be sub-divided into two major categories. First, the content perspective sees resistance as real and describes manifestations of resistant behavior in terms of group silence, manipulation, and acting out. Second, the context perspective is one in which there is more emphasis on not accusing the group of being in resistance, and more on adjusting the treatment method to fit the client. The section ended with a short review of general treatment strategies that focused on developing and maintaining trust, while striving for empowerment and focusing energy on attainable goals.

CHAPTER 6

TECHNIQUES AND STRATEGIES

> Regard no practice as immutable. Change
> and be ready to change again. Accept no
> eternal verity. Experiment.
> B.F. Skinner

If we are to treat resistance in chemical dependency, we first need to take a look at what we mean by treatment. A treatment definition for the AOD client developed by the Institute of Medicine (1990) reads as, "...any activity that is directed toward changing a person's drinking behavior and reducing their alcohol consumption." Lindstrom (1992) adds that treatment can involve activities that alleviate the physical, psychological and social complications that maintain hazardous drinking. In addition, treatment has traditionally meant not only a restoration of one's physical and psychological health, but the return of a stable family, job, and certainly a renewed sense of spirit. These definitions apply as well to the host of other drugs of abuse.

Therefore, the general aim and goal of substance use treatment has been to start, and or maintain some kind of a recovery process. That process entails moving through presumed "stuck points," or resistances.

Before we travel any further we need to mention at least one caveat. It deals with what happens when we place too much importance on this thing called treatment. Just a few years ago, many in the field believed therapy was the most critical thing in the world. Many made outrageous and sweeping generalizations about the need for the whole world to be involved with some form of treatment. They assumed that if a client didn't finish treatment he/she was doomed to fail or worse--die. Of course, many of those things never come true. In fact, many times that client did better without our "life saving treatment."

The field has grown from a narrow perspective. Some have even begun to consider that treatment may not be all that necessary to a quality recovery process. For example, many individuals who never entered a treatment program got sober just by going to AA meetings, or beginning recovery process on their own. Edwards (1989) did a ten year review of AOD treatment and was able to state that it was absurd to assume that treatment was paramount to a client's life to the exclusion of other outside influences. Lindstrom (1992) noted that it may not be that treatment changed lives in and of itself, yet treatment supports a sober lifestyle, which in turn allows the influx of more positive psychological and social influences into the client's life. Bear in mind that this does not infer treatment does not work. The available data indicates otherwise. Those who state that one cannot develop a quality recovery without treatment may have over stepped their bounds, and that once this happens, it forges the rudiments of rigidity and thereafter--resistance.

Research on what is effective treatment outcome has come to the conclusion that no one treatment is superior to another (Institute of Medicine, 1990; Goodwin, 1988; Seventh Annual Report to Congress, 1990). Yet, there are some treatments that have shown more evidence of success than others (Hester, 1994).   Despite this documentation, many counselors remain adamant about their rightness of their positions. In addition, these rigid positions infer that other forms of treatment are ineffective, if not out and out harmful. Pattison (1982) refers to this kind of thinking as *competitive monolithic* or just plain *monopolistic.*

Despite the research findings, we practitioners are always looking for the best therapy to effectively treat the AOD client. With such a mind-set, we can easily fall prey to any number of authors who put forth the latest intervention and, in turn, fall for that infernal itch to be RIGHT.

Let us try to by pass all that and reframe the treatment question to: What is best for this client, given my assessment and the person's individual nature?   Perhaps the most important question is, "How do I minimize and or eliminate the resistance factors in my treatment?" When we ask that question, we generally have only two ways to consider an answer. The first is through the content mode we noted throughout this book. In this manner, we seek to institute some type of treatment strategy that reduces the assumed resistance factor. We can also drop the whole resistance idea and get on with a solution. I discuss both of these options.

A Possible Resistance Avoidance Template

People usually don't arrive at a destination without a map of some type. The same applies to chemical dependency treatment. However, what are those key elements of treatment?

Many in the AOD field might argue that developing some kind of insight leads to an understanding or acceptance of the problem. The traditional thought is that something is blocking that insight and acceptance. Many substance-use professionals are convinced that this block is denial and or some form of resistance.   The corollary, behind denial belief, is that the client has an intrinsic ability to really understand his/her predicament, and then do something about it.   They have the ability to comprehend, but the denial and other resistances get in the way. We have come up with a host of explanations of how this process starts, continues and is maintained. But all that theorizing comes back to the idea that denial blocks insight. If the client could get this insight, the problem would be on it's way to being resolved.

This is how most AOD treatment is conceptualized.   It has its attributes. A lot of people developed a long term recovery following this format. But the trouble is HOW to reduce the denial and resistance? How does one go about decreasing the resistance and increasing the insight? There are two ideas I wish to review that might help with this HOW...?

The first addresses how to make a difference. Usually somewhere along the AOD treatment continuum, an individual said something to a client, and it made a difference. AH! Made a difference. How does that work? I suggest we take a page from Bugental (1987) in order to find out.

According to Bugental (ibid), we need to communicate more fully with another person in order to make a difference.   He notes that what we often call communication is a preoccupation with content, symptoms, and dynamics. When we focus on the symptoms, we miss the "present-whole" individual right before us. We easily slide into reducing treatment to a transmission of fragmented information (watching videos, reading informational material, etc.), or we get involved in a speculative debate (You're an alcoholic ... No, I'm not!).

To avoid this predicament, Bugental suggests creating a presence with the client. That is, develop a relationship in which one communicates at a deep level, as fully as one is able. The process is different from being a critic, judge, observer, or commentator. It is a concern with the immediate, but also the distant. It is concerned with what goes on inside. Presence moves away from the old material of a AOD lifestyle, to self-discovery. It is emotional concern, from all parties involved, not a detached history of abuse. Presence also requires a sense of vulnerability, and is essential for deep human contact (Walkinstein, 1975).

At this level of communication, therapy makes a difference. How does one get there? Bugental indicates that we need to pass through several levels before we get to the one that counts. The first is what he calls *formal occasions*. Here communication is transmitted according to cultural folkways. For example, at this level we shake hands, bow, and use titles (Ms., Mr., Dr.). There is strong emphasis on maintaining a front or an image. Talk at this level is generally objective and impersonal. The effort at this level is to be correct. Spontaneity is at a minimum and the talk is rather sterile. The stage, according to our culture, may be one in which we must necessarily pass. However, I have seen seasoned AOD counselors mistake this as resistance on the part of the newly arrived client. The perception is as if the client was not allowed to first pass through this level to get to the next. Instead, they were expected to immediately work on their problems, and anything short of that was considered to be a reflection of resistance.

The second stage of communication is called *contact maintenance*. At this level, people generally respond to each other with factual information (age, type of work, address, etc.). In therapy, this is where needed information is gathered, but the counselor also needs to be aware of any signals that might indicate that the client is ready to move to deeper levels of relating. At this second level, the client may still be suspicious, on guard, and aloof. This should not be interpreted as resistance, but as a careful analysis on the part of the clients before they commit to change.

The third level of communication is called *standard conservation*. It is at this level that most of us carry on the usual everyday office-type talk. We maintain a balance between projecting our "image" and truly expressing our inner feelings. At this time there may be some slang intermixed at this point little resistance, and some true contact conversation.

The fourth level of communication is entitled *critical occasions*. Critical, in this case, means just that they make a difference. Here conversations go on for a time, of there own accord, and are more focused on inner experiences rather than images. Talk is varied in tempo, form, and emotional tone. There are more adjectives and adverbs used in order to convey the color and experience of the whatever is being discussed. Body posture is more relaxed and open. At this level, individuals are caught up and express and extend themselves. The listener will also be caught up in accessing every little drop of this experience so that it is making a profound impression on them. Conversations at this level will result in genuine changes in the client as well as the therapist. There is no need for resistance at this stage. This is the beginning of therapy.

The last level of communication as outlined by Bugental is that of *intimacy*. When two or more people relate at this level there is a maximum of expressiveness and accessibility. The client is not concerned about image and the counselor is receiving in a total manner. This expression and accessing may even begin to shift the other way around. Boundaries may become blurred, but they are not pathological. In such moments, the therapist will feel one client's dread, joy and even fall silent in appreciation of the human being before you. Individuals here are vitally and intimately involved. The state is considered true therapy!

These last two levels are not considered to be change agents in and of themselves. These levels do however provide the client with increased vision, and increased opportunities so that change can occur. They make a difference.

This is not a technique you pick up in a workshop and use with only half a thought to it. It requires a big step for many people. The process requires that you step out from behind you protected fortress of theories, and ready made answers, and RISK. That's right, risk being yourself. Get in there with that client who is really a human being, not a resistance label. Then watch what happens to resistance at these levels of communication.

A Second Possible Avoidance Resistance Template

If Bugental speculates where in the course of therapy the possibility of change will occur, then Prochaska and DiClemente (1982, 1986; Porchaska, DiClemente & Norcross, 1992; Di Clemente, 1993) denote six stages that account for how the change process might occur. For our purposes, it is critical to know where the client might be in this in this scheme. That knowledge may suggest treatment that is matched to the client's stage of change and avoid a mismatch, which create a resistance.

For instance, the first stage in this process is called *precontemplation*. Here the client is not even a client yet because they do not see the necessity of change. Some would say this type just is not ready. To attempt to cajole this individual into treatment will result in resistance. How does one get this individual into the treatment that they need? One possibility is to raise doubt in the mind of the client, so they will reexamine their need for change. In this case, Prochaska (1995) suggests that therapeutic orientations that are more insight-oriented such as the analytic, Adlerian, Sullivanian, and the Strategic therapies. These schools of therapy are designed to raise consciousness. A second possibility is to view such individuals as "hidden customers" and sell them something they already want as the solution-orientation asks. Do not repeat treatment interventions that have been tried and failed with this of person. Repeating failed interventions will surely create more resistance.

The second stage in this change process is called the *contemplation* stage. Individuals, at this stage, consider change and then reject it. Clients may go back and forth between reasons for and against change. They may say things like, "I don't have a problem with coke. But, I do spend a lot of money on the stuff." The idea here is not to assault them and demand they make up their mind, but to swing the balance toward change. How to do that? Consider a better rapport or attempt to move to a deeper level of communication as outlined above. Prochaska (ibid) suggests the cognitive, rational-emotive, or even existential approach may be appropriate at this level. In addition, institute some of the strategies listed below (metaphor, reframe, solution-based approaches).

The next stage of change is one of *preparation*. When the balance does tip toward change, then the client may become very determined about his/her efforts. They may be heard to say things like: "This is crazy! I can't go on like this. What do I have to do to change?" Many would say that this is the end point of treatment. They are now willing to do what ever it takes. Right? Wrong! There is always the possibility that they change their mind again and slip back to the contemplation level. So the counselor needs to help the determined client develop a set of treatment strategies that will be acceptable, appropriate and effective. Otherwise the client is liable to give up and regress. Strategies to initiate at this point may revolve around Gestalt methods, challenging the client, setting attainable goals, and using skill-development techniques (e.g., refusal, stress reduction and coping skills).

The fourth stage of change is called *action*. This is what most people think therapy is, coming to some kind of thinking and behavioral alteration. Here the client finally institutes a plan and a change results. Treatment interventions would include the behavioral methods. But is that enough? Is treatment now over because they did what they said they would do? As many of us know first hand, the answer to that question is a resounding--no.

Contemplation, determination and even action is not enough. Change, if it is to occur in the recovery process, needs *maintenance*. In this case, the treatment needs to shift from insight to rehearsed and sustained skill development to avoid relapse. The client may know they cannot safely use chemicals, but haven't the skills to sustain this new lifestyle. Interventions at this level need to center on relapse prevention and proficiency development. Such skills would include identifying triggers and cues that would contribute to a relapse like handling stress and anger, Techniques to address these issues include refining and refusing behaviors, and developing contingency plans to offset this issues. If a counselor were to go back to the beginning of this cycle, because they thought the client never really came to accept themselves as an addict would be redundant and resistance producing.

The last stage of change is entitled *relapse*. Relapse, some might claim, is not a stage of change. It's relapse pure and simple. Perhaps, but it is rather normal in a field such as ours, and it requires a special mode of treatment. That mode of treatment needs to center on avoiding discouragement and demoralization on the part of the client. Here treatment strategies need to focus on recontemplating change, resuming action, and refining maintenance efforts. They do not require another round of inventories and needless confrontations.

In this model, the helping relationship cuts across all these stages of change. This client centered approach is critical. It is a shared identity of mutual trust, and one in which the client is as influenced as much as is the therapist. If the client does not believe you can identify and understand his/her situation, resistance may develop.

The intervention ideas presented here as well as those of Bugental are rough "treatment maps," which can be used as a guide to resolving resistance, especially if it is conceptualized in the insight and content mode of assessment and AOD treatment. To make these maps really work, professionals have to be specific in their strategy selection, given the client's strengths and liabilities. It is here the therapist needs to match those assessed client characteristics to a treatment that will form fit the assessment.

Patient Matching - Content Style

The patient matching idea is not very new. In 1804, Thomas Trotter a British physician, suggested very different remedies for alcohol abusers (Lindstrom, 1992). Even Jellnick supported this idea (Lindstrom, ibid). In fact, this patient-matching approach in AOD treatment has been seen as the vision that promises to improve outcome (Institute of Medicine, 1990).

How does one define this patient-matching thing? Glaser and Skinner (1981) define it as, "...the deliberate and consistent attempt to select a specific candidate for a specific method of intervention in order to achieve specific goals" We are differentiating treatment here, and not using a standard approach for interaction with the client which is actually an impediment to treatment (Lazarous, 1981). In this view, treatment needs to based on what is assessed from client specifics, and not based on a diagnostic obligation or categorization. Even Carl Rogers (1971) noted that what is proper for one person is not proper for another.

It is true that many facilities today offer a screening process to ascertain who and what they can effectively treat. This is progress, and is to be commended. Yet it falls short of what is really meant by patient-matching. Matching involves varying the principle treatment approach from one individual to another, according to the assessed need and specifics of the client.

What are some of the larger decision making processes behind this matching process? Anderson and Carter (1982) indicate that three variables should be considered in the patient matching process. These include the factors of gender, social class, and culture. Marlett (1988) and L'Abate (1992) also espouse a specific treatment approach, and not a uniform one. This is in contrast to the formula approach that considers all addictive individuals to be the same, and in need of the same treatment. This sameness idea will generalize the client, and that as we have seen can lead to significant resistance according to Marlett, Baer, Donavan and Kivalhan,(1988). These authors ask the therapist to consider the following questions, when they face that new admission
1. Which theory should be used to match an addiction with a specific type of treatment?
2. According to what assessment have I matched the treatment?
3. If the same type of treatment is administered indiscriminately with any kind of addiction, what will be the results?
4. How is the effectiveness of the treatment to be assessed? Can and should we use just one type of therapy for all forms of addiction?

It is interesting that the Project MATCH results indicate that if different treatments are delivered well, they all seem to be equally effective (Leary, 1996)

These questions are designed to make you think, and actually consider the possibility of doing additional research on this subject. For example, Beutler, Machado, Engle, and Mohr (1993) noted that if a therapist used authoritarian interventions with a "highly-resistant" client, the client would resist even more. Yet, if the therapist used the more directive and authoritarian strategies with "less resistant" clients, those individuals would respond more favorably. Thus, it makes sense to match the treatment intervention to the client.

Should you decide to follow this line of thinking, then you need to step back and take a look at how you do your evaluation. The following assessment guide is not meant to solve that problem, but only to give the reader an opportunity to review their own assessment skills.

Recall that the overriding question in this approach is how to go about reducing the resistance factors in each particular case?

Assessment Guide - Content Patient Matching

This assessment guide is based on the Sir William Osler's statement, "Ask not what kind of a disease a person has, ask what kind of person has the disease."

- What are the predominant personality traits/styles of the person sitting in front of me? For example, are they, according to Jung (1968), a thinking, feeling, intuitive or sensation type. Is the treatment strategy I am about to engage one that dovetails with the client's personality or collides with it?
- What is the mental status of this individual? Does the treatment I propose compliment it or oppose it?
- What is the principal pathology in this case; how will the therapeutic strategy I institute assist or resist it? Are there complications in the pathology; how does that effect my treatment plans?
- What is the developmental level of the client? Can they readily understand the meanings of the treatment I propose to use, or will they become frustrated by material I present as being "beyond them" or too abstract?
- Can they comprehend the material that will be presented to them, or will they consider "too hard", too difficult or lack the skills to use it? McCrady (1987) refers to this as the client's individual learning rate. Have I accounted for this, or do I assume the client to have the sufficient skills to do any assignment I give them?
- What is the access style of the client? How do they learn best? How do they take in information that will make a difference?
- What are the meanings, the message, overt and covert, the client is attempting to relay? What is their choice of words? What are they not saying?
- How might my own biases get in the way of this client's recovery? What do I need to do to minimize the impact of me?
- How might the facility in which I conduct treatment create resistance?
- Perhaps the most important assessment procedure according to Erickson is to really look at your client. Really see them. Observe! (Otani, 1989).

The idea to see how unique the person is, and what you need to do to make "contact" not resistance with such a creation.

Lindstrom (1992) would agree with this patient matching approach, but feels it doesn't go far enough. He suggests that, in addition to patient matching, a systems approach be added to this selective treatment pairing. The systems idea applies the matching approach to whole program networks. In this scheme of things, programs would clearly define the specific populations to which they work best. Cooperation with agencies, so clients are directed to the program that could best serve their needs would be important. In this systems approach, individual programs could retain their uniqueness, but work toward this broad goal of recovery, and decrease the possibility of resistance.

Patient Matching - Context Type

Remember those folks who would do away with the entire concept of resistance? Well, they would have a difficult time with the content style of patient matching. Case in point is the argument presented by deShazer (1985; 1988) in which he notes that content-matching can lead to much complexity, which will inevitably lead to confusion, chaos and resistance. Patient matching, according to the this line of reasoning, is a focus on the lock versus a focus on the key to the lock. The key analogy is then considered to be a fit, not a match. The focus is on change (the key) not pathology (the lock). The fit is considered to be more flexible, and involves a high degree of trust between the client and counselor. In the concept of fit, each person in the treatment situation is paying very close attention to one another. Perhaps most importantly, both parties in this approach "accept each other's world as valid, valuable, and meaningful."

Duncan, et al. (1992) echo this match position. They point out that to match a treatment to a client implies that the therapist is an expert who is armed with objective facts. According to the match position, the therapist is the authority and dispenser of "the truth." in our case the recovery truth. This cannot but be an interaction in which the therapist is always in a one up (superior) position, which sets the stage for opposition and eventual resistance.

The concept of fit is encouraged for the counselor and client to co-create treatment goals by virtue of the counselor's training and the experience and the resources and strengths that the client brings to the treatment. Cooperation is believed to be enhanced by assuming this position. Collaboration is the basic delivery style.

How, you ask, is this accomplished? Hold on, we will get to it in a few pages. First, let's swing back to a few more issues in that content resistance reducing realm.

MORE IDEAS TO REDUCE RESISTANCE

Despite any favored school of therapy, there are some very broad based interventions that all quality counselors do (Carkhuff & Berenson; 1967; Bandler & Grindler; 1979; Pietrofesa, Hoffman & Spete, 1984). These center on four major counseling components, and are a part of Carkhuff's concept of human nourishment: regard/respect - empathy - authenticity - concreteness.

Well, so what, some might wonder. This is nothing new. [Indeed it isn't, but just to make sure, I checked six traditional, late published, chemical dependency books, and could not find any significant discussions on these topics.] Some didn't even mention these items. With that in mind I do want to review the attributes, and apply these features to AOD treatment. We then need to ask some very simple but profound questions about the use or need of these cornerstones of treatment.

These concepts are the fertile ground of effective treatment. There seems to be a need for the set-up of treatment even before the true work of therapy begins. Some in the field have the tendency to barge into therapy without preparing the ground work. The following items can be of immense help in creating that fertile framework of effective AOD counseling.

REGARD/RESPECT

Regard

Pietrofesa, et al. (1984) denotes regard as an attitude the counselor holds toward the client or to anyone, for that matter. If the regard for that client is not there, sooner or later subtle little factors of resistance could emerge.

This regard is akin to Carl Roger's unconditional positive regard concept (1942). There is a sense of prizing and esteem in regarding. That is a difficult attitude to consistently achieve, let alone with a "belligerent" alcoholic. Many would just tag the client with a label alcoholic. That is not regarding. Consider what some basic genuine regard might do to any budding resistance?

Respect

If regard is the attitude one takes toward another human, then the way it is manifested or acted out is through respect. Egan (1994) listed the main attributes of this concept which include the following.
1. Actively attend and listen, and wait for the client to finish talking before you reply with a response. Not waiting and interfering does not induce respect, it causes resistance. I have had many clients thank me for not interrupting while they told me their issues. I believe that it develops a stronger rapport and less resistance when you are attentively listening to the client's story.
2. Suspend judgment. As we have noted, to throw out a premature label or judgment call does not create a sense of relationship. It creates resistance. Duncan et al. (1992) state that respect for the client is to place the value and worth of the client above any theoretical perspective and accept their meaning system. That requires a suspension of judgment.
3. Help identify or encourage the client to cultivate his/her internal resources. Traditionally, resources are considered to be bankrupt from the chemical dependent. In place of the internal resources, the traditionalists insist that some outside force like a self-help meetings or a higher power will restore them to normal. There is nothing wrong with that as long as one does not insist. To insist is not to respect which subtly creates resistance. After the chemicals left their system, many recovering individuals I

have worked with let me know that it felt good to know that some old strengths they once had where returning, or new ones were emerging.

4. Warmth and a good dose of understanding will go a long way in to diminishing resistance and fostering a solid working relationship. Despite what the hard-nosed AOD counselors say about this approach ("You'll get conned and used."), it keeps you in touch with another human being, not with a label or case number.

This is not emotional mush that the AOD client could see as a weakness and use against you to "get over." When used at it's best, these concepts are firm and disciplined. In fact, it requires a lot of work on the part of the counselor to maintain this positive attitude in any relationship. Emotional mush, on the other hand, is just that--mush. The attitude is a not caring one and tends to be intermixed with laziness and lack of commitment to the other. When the AOD counselor conceives of regard and respect as mush, they will generate needless resistance.

Milton Erikson (O'Hanlon & Martin, 1992) was reported to have always worked in this sensitive range. He is also reported to go to any lengths to help his client. That requires great regard and respect. deShazer (1988) also emphases respect for the client's ability to have the potential to solve their problems. It is the counselor's job is to facilitate the client's ability to "know that they know." Once established, a "fit" of mutual process and regard and respect is achieved, which will diminish resistance.

EMPATHY

Simply put, empathy is that dimension of human interaction which is the ability to understand the feelings and attitudes if not thinking of others (Pietrofesa, et.al., ibid). Empathy is a core condition of change (Otani, 1989). Take a minute and consider what we are talking about here. Savor the concept if you will. We are talking about touching the "living parts" of another human being.

What is often seen in the AOD field is a superficial glance at the concept. Worse is that many counselors will have had one or two preconceived notions of empathy that destroy its very essence. One notion is to believe that you know what the other has experienced. A good example is stating something like, "I know what it's like, I've been there." That is only partly correct. How can anyone truly know the feelings of another? If you think you can, you set yourself up to close off the unique character of the other. When you think you "know" how the other feels, what you are really saying is that, "I know how it was for me, and I assume it was the same way for you." It is your own strong feeling that you understand. That feeling, however, distorts true empathy. Miller and Rollnick (1991) refer to true empathy as the demanding task by which the therapist can understand the other's meaning whether or not you have had similar experiences.

The other notion is referred to as "patient deluge." After you see and interview a few thousand clients, a blending of sorts may occur, and all clients could begin to look alike. When that happens, empathy disappears.

A good test to see if you are really empathizing with your client is to use a four step process outlined by Keefe (1976). First, you listen carefully to what the client says. Second, generate a feeling about the other person's world without stereotyping and detach that feeling from your own perspective. Third, do the Rogerian step of restating back to the client what he/she just said. Be careful not to parrot back to them the words syllable by syllable. You want to send back the important essence of what has been said. The fourth item, perhaps the most important, is to carefully determine whether the client agrees with what you just said. If they do, in language and manner, then you have probably been empathizing.

Additional guidelines of not empathizing include using the interpretative mode, i.e., "That sounds like some old trauma bothering you," or, "That is a symptom of addiction if I ever heard one." If you are doing this, then your not empathizing. More often than not, people who interpret are evoking a pet theory, not empathy. As Duncan et al. (1992) notes, empathy is placing the client's perception and experience above your favorite theory of addictive behavior.

A system to measure empathy was developed by Carkhuff (1969) and outlined by Patterson (1974). It is meant to help locate at what empathic level the counselor might operate. You will notice that at the lower levels of this scale the counselor interaction does not contribute the rapport of the therapeutic situation. In fact, an argument could be made that at these lower levels the counselor may be aiding the resistance process.

LEVEL 1: The lowest level of interpersonal functioning. Here the counselor's responses do not attend to and significantly detract from the expressions of the client. At this level, the return of expression from the counselor has less communication in it than was received in the first place. If a client declares a certain feeling state, and the counselor expresses something different in return one can bet the counselor is not listening. If this continues, resistance will emerge because clients will not feel understood and they will begin to distrust the counselor and become defensive in order to protect themselves. The germs of resistance are forming in such a scenario.

LEVEL 2: At this level, the counselor does respond to the expressed feelings of the client, but does so in a manner which still subtracts from what the client is trying to express. Perhaps, the result is not so much resistance, but there is a feeling on the part of the client that he/she is not understood. The defensiveness we mentioned may not develop quite as quickly as it did at level one, but it will develop.

LEVEL 3: At this level and above, the counselors responses add to the professional relationship. Specifically, the expressions of feelings and behavior are interchangeable with those of the client. What the client has been attempting to state will be essentially what the counselor will feed back to the client. There is less chance of resistance under these circumstances.

LEVEL 4: Here the responses of the counselor to the client's expression add noticeably to what was initially disclosed. In fact, the counselor's response may help the client to more deeply understand what they were trying to say than they could express themselves. Consider what a series of responses like this could do to any budding resistance.

LEVEL 5: At these rarefied levels, the response of the counselor is such that it will significantly add to the feeling and meaning state of the client. It can do this by helping the client understand what emotions are just below the surface, what the person him/herself was trying to express, and that one human is as about as close as they can get to another. At this level, there is little in the way of resistance.

So what is to be gained by being empathic? Perhaps, most of you thought, "It builds trust." Yes, but what else does it do? Advanced levels of empathy can also help the client:

- Develop deeper levels of communication
- increase the desire to explore intrapsychic dynamic and foster more self-examination
- Stay focused to the task at hand -- recovery
- Foster an increased level of intelligence, according to Madanes (1992).

Empathy leads to intelligent treatment. Outcome studies (Institute of Medicine, 1990; Miller & Rollnick, 1991) indicate that empathy has been shown to be a positive variable in effective chemical dependency treatment.

AUTHENTICITY

This is that therapeutic dimension that involves being real and genuine. A solid therapeutic relationship is always based on this concept. Without it you can have the beginnings of resistance-like behavior. Becoming authentic involves risk and anxiety, not for the client, but for the counselor as well. Most of us relate to one another in terms of the roles or facades we have built up over the years. In fact, many of us deliberately hide by playing these roles in order to protect ourselves from a variety of imagined and real concerns. Adhering to a pet theory is a perfect way to conceal oneself.

Key elements of authenticity include:

- Being natural, or as many have termed it, spontaneous, i.e., acting freely within the presence of another human.
- Being real and honest
- Being somewhat transparent and self-disclosive when the need arises (Jourard, 1968). AOD counselors have to be careful in that they do not disclose all the time and not allow the client a chance to talk. In addition, if therapists do too much disclosing there is a chance that they will lose their potency as a professional by telling the client too much of their own problems. The client may begin wonder who has the problem?
- Duncan et al., (1992) would add, that genuineness is gained by avoiding both phoniness and an overemphasis of authority.

CONCRETENESS

The last but not least of the four major behaviors successful counselors employ, centers on using everyday language. The language is very different from the theoretical and ambiguous terminology used in the field. In the counseling session the language has to be specific all right, but it also needs to match the developmental level of the client as well as their representational system. The developmental match is one in which the counselor is talking at the same level as the client is functioning. Essentially, the counselor talks less in abstract terms and more in concrete terms if necessary. Listening clients explain their plight will allow most AOD counselors to ascertain at what level the client is communicating and to reciprocate in kind.

What is to be gained by being so concrete? Concreteness helps to keep the client stay focused on, and attentive to, the problem at hand. In addition, concreteness can improve the level of understanding in the therapeutic relationship.

THE FINE ART OF FEEDBACK (CRITICISM) Technically, feedback is simply sharing information. Yet, almost any feedback you ever give a client is going to be viewed in terms of intrusion and danger. Most people do not react to criticism well. The reactions will manifest themselves in any number of ways, which includes defending, denying, counterattack and withdraw.

There are some implicit negative assumptions to the criticism process which are difficult to avoid (Bright, 1988). For example, it is believed that the giver of the feedback is right and the receiver is wrong. The one who criticizes disapproves of the recipient's behavior. It is assumed that the feedback will somehow improve the behavior of the receiver as a result of the criticism. The point remains that criticism does not feel good. In order to soften the blow of feedback, Bright (ibid) and Headman (1988) cite a few suggestions.

First, it is important to plan any proposed feedback session and to be clear about your motives. The plan needs to revolve around what is said and as importantly, around how that feedback is delivered. Tones to avoid include those that are sarcasm, or imply an accusation and blame. In addition, certain words and phrases can elicit resistance such as *you should have, must, disappointment, stupid, irresponsible, bad attitude,* or *must*. Consider your feedback to be of an advisory and teaching nature, and not of an authoritative one.

In line with the delivery tone, is the inflection that you can put on a single word. For example, "You did a good job on this fourth step, *but...*" It is the inflection often given at conjunctions which have overtones of you did not quite measure up. This can begin to seed the roots of subtle resistance on the part of the client.

Second, time the action. Through timing you have to examine a few essential questions. Such queries center on whether the client is ready to hear the feedback. In addition, you have to assess whether they have the ego strength to take the feedback. Many traditional AOD professionals disagree with this because they believe the client is NEVER ready. Therefore, the blunt approach is considered the best approach. However, as we have seen this blunt tactic can get the client to turn off and tune out all feedback, which can lead to additional resistance.

Perhaps, the most important of these precautions is that of establishing a rapport with the client first before "telling them the truth." There is a general tendency of people, including clients, to be more receptive to feedback if it comes from someone who is felt to be trustworthy and elicits some kind of regard and respect.

Another important point is to concentrate framing the feedback in terms of how the person can improve. Giving dead-end remarks like, "You'll never make it," prove nothing. Instead of using those dead-end remarks, utilize some of those presuppositional question that the solution-based theorists provide (Miller & Berg, 1995; Berg & Miller, 1992). For example, questions like, "How will you begin to know that things will get better for you?"

"In what small way will you be different by the time I see you next week?" are types of questions challenge and place the responsibility of change on the shoulders of the client. They encourage clients to think and consider recovery possibilities, and do not focus on character defects.

When you give feedback you need to protect a person's self-esteem in the process. To attack the essence of another human by calling him/her names or to make disparaging remarks about his/her character serves no purpose. It only alienates and creates resistance.

The next thing to remember when you give feedback is to allow the person a chance to respond. The art of the feedback is to get an honest opinion of what you just had to say. Just to ask a client how he/she felt about an item of feedback, is to invite dialogue.

Feedback, when it occurs, needs to be framed in a helping spirit, rather than a manner suggesting, "I'm out to get you and demean you." Any criticism is easier to accept if recipients believes it shows concern for their welfare, and is not the type that is out to discredit them. Often solid feedback can and will motivate certain individuals to begin to look more closely at themselves. Further, when you do give feedback, frame it in terms of specific directions and recommendations for the improvement of the recipient. Criticize the behavior, not the person. Heldmann (ibid) put together rough list of motives of the criticizer. It has been modified for our purposes. The focus is on the intent of the critic (counselor) as to whether they will be positive or negative when considering a feedback session.

(Counselor) NEGATIVE INTENT	(Counselor) POSITIVE INTENT
to dominate and control	to motivate
to manipulate	to improve the relationship
to put the client down	to show concern
to show the client who's boss	to show compassion
to abuse/undermine	to improve behavior
to punish/get even	to care and nurture

It is critical that if one of these negatives should begin to show itself, abort the exchange! In addition, abort the exchange if one of the following are present.

1. You're really angry, stressed or irritable.
2. The client cannot or will not take any action from the criticism.
3. You have not molded the feedback to the preferred representational style of the client.
4. The criticism is of the nature which can't be backed up with solid data and information.
5. You know that the client is in such a mood that they will not be open to it, and end up resenting it and you.
6. You have not considered gender and cultural ramifications.

LISTENING - REALLY LISTENING

What we have delineated so far are a series of processes that can effectively diminish resistance in the treatment of chemical dependency process. Listening ranks high on that list of things to do to reduce resistance. Rogers (1980) captures the essence of real listening when he states, "Almost always when a person realizes he has been deeply heard, his eyes moisten. I think in some real sense he is weeping for joy. It is as though he were saying, "Thank God, somebody heard me. Someone knows what it's like to be me." Listening, re al listening, cannot help but reduce resistance.

The Poor Listening Behaviors

Strean (1993) might say that all that follows are manifestations of the counselors resistance to listening.

Interrupting. When there is a steady stream of interruptions by the counselor, that process will create resistance by virtue of defocusing the client's attention and stream of thought. Some would say, "But not to interrupt would be to give covert credence to someone's excuses." Perhaps, but just because you think it is excuse-making that doesn't mean that it is from the client's perspective. Remember look for what is useful. Listen for the positive behaviors, and then use them in your treatment process.

Overidentifying. It is not the job of the therapist to identify with the client or visa versa. It is the job of the client to identity with their own recovery process. Stating to a client "The very same thing happened to me," and then proceeding to tell your story in the name of rapport development is not listening to the client. A good argument could be made that by overidentifying with the client, you do not really want to hear the client. You only want to hear yourself talk.

Ordering/Directing. Hopefully, it is clear by now that any kind of direct order to AOD clients is usually a waste of time. They have probability have had a million orders screamed at them, all to no avail. Recall that you do not want to repeat the mistakes of those who came before you. Those failures often included orders from counselors, spouses, and bosses. If that approach had worked, you would never have met the client.

Warnings. Here's another close cousin of the ordering and directing problem. Threatening and throwing out dire warnings isn't treatment, and rarely increases the client's level of understanding. It's a power play pure and simple.

Advice/Suggestions. These items are always peppered with an ample supply of "shoulds", "musts" and "oughts." This spells danger for the client because they very often have been ingrained with a steady supply of these inflexibles. In addition, there is a paternalistic feel, a talking down to the client overtone to them. All that does is make that client feel demeaned and disparaged. That has happened enough to them through out their chemical use careers. Advising and suggesting are not listening.

Lecturing. This is a close relative of the advise/suggestion category. However, in this case, there is more of that patronizing/parental overtone to it. It is your job, as a AOD professional, to help clients determine what is best for them. Lecturing will foster more resistance than recovery.

There's an old saying in the field that goes something like, "Get the cotton out of your ears an put it in your mouth." That's suppose to mean that the client should not do so much talking but more listening. I purpose the same thing for the counselor. All that we have reviewed, will review in this section, is based on the counselor being judgmental and imposing. That is not listening.

Interpreting. Being presumptuous enough to say to a client, "What you really mean by this is..." borders on telling the client what you think, not what they, really mean. A good interpretation takes what a client says and compares it to some standard. Many interpretations. however, border on telling the other person what and how to feel. Presumptuous interpretations are not listening. A good interpretation which is timed and thought through may have an impact.

Gordon (1970) summarizes a list that typifies the non-listening stance. They include:

1. Ordering or commanding
2. Warning or threatening
3. Advise giving and providing solutions
4. Arguing and lecturing
5. Moralizing, preaching
6. Blaming and judging
7. Approving and praising
8. Shaming and labeling
9. Interpreting or analyzing
10. Sympathizing consoling
11. Questioning and probing
12. Distracting or changing the subject

Positive Listening Behaviors

We looked at negative listening skills, let us turn to a list of the positive listening skills one can do to reduce resistance. Keep in mind that we are not listening for something from the client, we are just listening. That's the secret. Genuine listening according to Benjamin (1974) and Piaget (1972) is hard work and should not to be taken as just some thoughtless mechanical procedure.

Silence

Heldmann (1988) states that one cannot talk and listen at the same time, which applies equally well to the AOD field. The very a posture of attentive listening relays respect to the one who is doing the sharing. As we noted, this respectful attitude is a prime element in reducing resistance. Boy and Pine (1982) refer to this type of listening as sensitive listening. It is nonevaluative in nature and enables the counselor to feel the client's emotions, not just listen with one ear and think about something else.

A technique to facilitate this type of listening is to hold your response for a second or two, after the other has finished talking. An immediate response often signals that you were not really listening. As one truly listens, one's mind will wonder less and will hear more. "Hearing more" is the main idea behind that type of listening, which demonstrates respect and reduces resistance.

Acknowledgment

It is important to confirm the client, on a regular basis through good eye contact. Using body posture is also important way to acknowledge the client. Keep an open posture, not with one's arms folded high on the chest, or sitting in a turned away. A few nods or "uh-huhs" will certainly let the client know you are listening to them. According to Benjanim (1974), "We hear with our ears, but we listen with our eyes, and mind and heart and skin and guts as well."

Probes

This a way in which the counselor can entice clients to talk more about their past or explore more of how they came into the treatment process. These came in a variety of statements like:

"Is there something on your mind?"
"You seem distant today. Want to talk about it?"
"You don't seem yourself. What's up?"

Benjanim (1974) offers a few suggestions on developing listening with understanding. They are adapted to AOD treatment.

1. Listen to how clients think and feel about themselves, especially the active chemical using self and the consequences of that use.
2. Listen to how clients describes those who are important to them. Do they describe significant others as distant, close, caring, loving?
3. Listen to how clients perceive the interaction and the relationship between themselves and significant others. Do they describe these others as supportive or as barrier to recovery?

4. Listen to how clients perceives the issues that brought them into treatment. Are they hostile? Was the admission against their will?

5. Listen to the goals, aspirations--the preferred style of interaction and defensive style if present.

6. Listen to the dreams, values, and philosophy of life. Spending a little time on these issues will give you much useful information.

What is the treatment goal of all this listening? Strean (1993) would say, "...that several wonderful things inevitably do begin to happen when clients are the recipients of patient, warm, quiet listening. Clients begin to feel they are people of value, and this feeling of self-worth strengthens them to use their (healthy) coping mechanisms more effectively." Is this not a definition of a quality recovery process?

THE BIGGIE - CONFRONTATION

It goes without saying that a confrontational or an oppositional style of intervention has typified treatment in this field. This confrontation has come in forms that range from the mild to the down right noxious. How and why did that state of affairs come about? How effective is it? Why is AOD treatment inexorably tied in with confrontation? Miller and Rollnick (1991) provide a respectable account of that origin, but I wish to add some additional questions and perspectives.

First, why resort to confrontation in order to begin a recovery process? Talk to any traditional AOD counselor today on the need to confront and you will hear the following snippets. It is believed the client has some insight, some acceptance of their problem, which is blocked by their denial. Every client is assumed to be in this denial state especially in the early stages of recovery. As long as the denial remains in place, the client's problems and use of chemicals will persist. Confrontation is considered an attack upon the wall of defenses of the addict not upon the addict personally (DiCicco, Unterberger, & Mack, 1978; DuWors, 1992; Johnson, 1986). It is the job and duty of the AOD therapist or program to provide insight. In order for the insight to come through, the denial needs to confronted. No other form of treatment is considered to be effective in cracking denial. It is repeatedly referred to as breaking down the denial, (Bishop, 1991; Cox & Price, 1990; Forrest, 1982; Klein, 1988; Lawson & Lawson, 1989; Siegal & Moore, 1985).

How did this belief come about? Miller and Rollnick (1991) and Deitch and Zweben (1984) indicate that it may have has its origin with the very early treatment centers such as Synanon. Here "treatment" terms such as "attack therapy" and "the hot seat" were born. These methods were difficult to distinguish from tactics of coercion. I recall this method years ago in which the community of patients would all sit on the floor of an auditorium. The staff would ruthlessly attack anything and anybody in that room. The attack was always rationalized to be therapeutic and necessary. The thinking twenty years ago was that these hard drug addicts would not respond to any other form of treatment. Hard core addicts could and would, "Pull the wool over the eyes of the psychiatrists, who didn't know how to treat addicts." In addition, mental health professionals where failed to produce effective outcomes.

There was some truth to the idea. The mental health professionals were truly frustrated with the recidivism rate and non-responsiveness AOD dependents. The theories and strategies of the time certainly could not account for the seemingly bizarre addictive behavior.

Drug and alcohol treatment in those days was desperately looking for it's own unique identity, not one that was borrowed from psychology. It found part of that identity in the attack therapy of Synanon, and part through the 12-Step program of Alcoholics Anonymous. AA stated in order to recovery one had to accept their alcoholism (develop the insight), and the methodology was to confront, via the attack mode provided by Synanon.

About the same time came Johnson's (1973) idea of using confrontation to defeat and oppose this denial process, as well as any other defense the alcoholic had to offer. He offered the following as the rationale to confront the client. "The patient uses the first session to discover what defenses will be most useful (to ward off the counselor's treatment attempts). The patient sees the counselor as the enemy who is out to destroy him." Enemy! That was some pretty strong language to describe clients. It provided a powerful mind-set about AOD clients. Being perceived as the enemy would certainly sanction a confrontational approach. The word enemy suggests that one is in battle not treatment, and confrontation is the main weapon.

In addition, Hatcher and Brooks (1977) advocated the use of confrontation when a clients denied their problem or de-emphasized the nature of the problem. In addition, Milam and Ketcham (1981) indicated that clients would always reject (deny) any idea that they should stop drinking. These authors also noted that most alcoholics fight the need for treatment and resent anyone who helps them into treatment. All this parallels Johnson's views of confrontation. This mind-set does not leave one with many options other to oppose the client.

This approach was often utilized in what has been called the "Minnesota Model". Treatment program after treatment program adopted this idea in the early days. The predominate sense at the time was that it was something we developed from our own experience and pain. At last, we were gaining some sense of "legitimacy." Just enough people were developing a new found sense of recovery and reporting back to the treatment centers that "Your confrontation saved my life. Thanks for being so tough. I needed that." Here was the justification. All you needed thereafter was a dash of generalized thinking, sprinkled with some simplistic ideas about treatment, and you had the beginnings of a methodology that suggested the confrontation of all addicts.

The advancement of this confrontational treatment method developed mostly in the inpatient treatment centers of that day. It did not begin in AA as some believe. In those old inpatient days, clients could have their emotional guts ripped out in the treatment program proper, but that never happened in an AA meeting. In fact, Bill Wilson (Alcoholics Anonymous, 1976) wrote, "Let him steer the conversation in any direction he wants. You will be most successful with alcoholics if you do not exhibit any passion or crusade or reform. Never talk down to the alcoholic. He must decide for himself whether he wants to go on." It goes without question the Bill Wilson did not condone the confrontational style so often used in AOD treatment.

For sure, the harsh treatment methods of the past have abated. Even the programs which have espoused the Minnesota Model have encouraged a moderation of confrontational methods (Hazelden Foundation, 1985; Johnson Institute, 1987). But this general confrontational methodology still continues today, despite the lack of evidence to support its use (Guy, 1988).

There are mixed messages that come from the self-help community on this matter. Attend any open AA meeting, and you will hear the characteristics of the alcoholic described as "Self-will run riot" and "Alcoholics are stubbornly self-willed and trying to dominate and control others". If that is the perception, then those with the more assertive treatment style will point to these characteristics and decry the need of confrontation to crack this "self-will run riot."

They will often parade their confrontational methods in staff meetings with statement like, "You should have seen me blast the son-of-a-bitch today," referring to a client. And, "I really put that jerk in his place during group." This perception creates a immensely strong power base from which to operate. You can still see it in the boot camp approaches we try with criminals today. To these professionals nothing else works.

The point of all of this had been to note how many in the field have no other treatment strategy save the one of confrontation. In fact, recent research (Miller, Benefield & Tonigen, 1993) indicated that a therapeutic style of directive-confrontation yielded significantly more resistant clients and predicted poorer outcomes at follow-ups of one year. Additional evidence for the ineffectiveness of confrontation is reported in Sobell and Sobell (1993), Annis and Chan, (1983), Miller, (1983), and Miller and Sovereign (1988). Addition evidence indicates that confrontation is especially contraindicated with women (Davis, 1990). A recent research indicated that confrontation was not warranted with women due to the fact that it can intensify shame in women who already experience too much of it (O'Conner, Berry, Inaba, Weiss, & Morrison, 1994). If all I see are "nails" in front of me and I consider myself to be a hammer--guess what?

CONFRONTATION PROPER

Some say confrontation cannot be avoided, nor should it be (Mann, 1973; Thoreson, 1983). However, these same authors note, the aim of confrontation is to teach something to the receiver through confrontation. Another purpose according to Weisman (1973) is to, "... separate what a man is from what he seems to be, states himself to be, or would have us believe us to believe he is." A pretty good description of how confrontation is defined in AOD treatment circles today.

Interestingly enough, this AOD confrontation has many of its origins with the psychoanalytic movement (Adler & Myerson, 1973). That view may have contributed to the present day denial-confrontation cycle in which many AOD practitioners find themselves sealed (Miller & Rollnick, 1991). For instance, Greenson (1967), notes that if patients are unaware of their resistance, then it is essential to confront them with the fact that the resistance is present before one attempts anything further. Again a pretty good description of how AOD treatment would view the confrontation. However, Weisman (1973) notes that although confrontation is supposed to be the effort to penetrate a screen of denial, aversion, or description; it takes the direction that most forms of communication do not. That direction is toward significant vulnerability and heightened defensiveness.

Closer to the chemical dependency field is the position on confrontation as espoused by Lawson, Ellis and Rivers, (1984). They state that, "Confrontation is an essential skill of the chemical dependency counselor because of the clients' adeptness at concealing, avoiding, and distorting the truth in order to protect their addiction." Concurrent with this view is that of Maynard (1993) who notes that "There seems to be no doubt among practitioners in the addictions field that confrontation is a necessary part of our work." Forman (1988) denotes some five steps that he feels are necessary for dealing with denial, and of those five steps he considers confrontation to be the first. Even Wright and Wright (1990) took this confrontational method and applied it to the family of practicing addicts. They titled their book *Dare to Confront*. It is essentially advocates the confrontational position of Johnson, i.e., they make it clear that due to the character of addiction (intrinsic denial) confrontation is needed, hence the title of the book.

With all this talk about confrontation, Christner (1993) states that the method of confrontation as presented by Johnson has been a useful tool for the AOD field, but the abusive type was never the intent of confrontation. Along those same lines, Tatarsky and Washton (1992), Flores (1988), Bratter and Forrest, (1985), and Wallace (1978) indicated that to attack the client will only serve to raise the defenses of the client. They note that to attack is to adopt a moralistic, punitive, and superior attitude. This can be evidenced by the counselor who is personally frustrated with a client and who vents their own hostility at the client (Perez, 1986). Anger without care is a killer (Walkinstein, 1973). Prematurely confronting the client's defenses will increase the probability of further drinking. Derby (1992) argues that the harsh confrontation will push the client into a self-protective mode, if not a superficial compliance with treatment.

This implies a constructive nature of confrontation as noted by Augsburger (1973), Trice and Beyer (1981), and Thoreson (1983). This constructive confrontation is meant to confront the individual with the facts of their situation but in a non-judgmental manner. In fact, Thoreson (ibid) indicates that empathy and confrontation are not mutually exclusive, but, "... empathy demands confrontation." In addition, he notes that true confrontation is an intense, direct, deep encounter, with the objective of helping the client reconcile the conflicting aspects of themselves. Bates and Johnson (1972) state that, "Confrontation offered with empathy is an act of grace. Confrontation offered with animosity is a graceless act."

Twerski (1983) points out that the goal of confrontation is to get the patient to recognize that they need treatment before they hit bottom. In addition, confrontation will give the client time to mull over problems and perhaps decrease some of their denial. So there you have it. Not a definitive or all encompassing opinion of the necessity of confrontation, but one that indeed represents much of the AOD treatment thinking.

If You Feel You Have Use Confrontation, Try This

For those who think that confrontation is a must and who determined not to abandon the principle, let us review the more appropriate ways to utilize it. First, Walkinstein (1973) makes it very clear that to force the moment to a crises as confrontation often does requires that the therapist care enough to do it. She notes, care = dare = anxiety = conflict = struggle = change. Consider framing the confrontation in terms of challenging clients to examine, if not modify, their behavior (Gladding, 1992; Hutchins & Cole, 1992). In order to accomplish that, Berenson and Mitchell (1974) outline five different types of confrontation that may be useful to the practitioner.

1. *Experimental.* This is the type of confrontation that focuses on discrepancies between reality, and the perception the client supposedly has of reality. Many a traditional AOD counselor will state that this is supposed to be the very essence of confrontation (Maynard, 1993). The client is in denial, which is very different from what is considered to be the true reality. The counselors job therefore is to continuously confront the client's perception, so they will end up seeing true reality, and begin to remedy the situation (Lawson, et al, 1984).

2. *Didactic.* Confrontation that is used to correct misinformation or remedy the lack of information. This might not be considered confrontation by some (Maynard, 1993), but interjecting more correct information in the treatment situation. This done because the client is espousing some inaccurate facts that could qualify for some level of confrontation.

3. *Confrontation of Strength.* This type centers on the positive side of confrontation. For example, if your client has a relapse after a period of time and is feeling disappointed in themselves, and just about ready to give up, this type of confrontation might be just the ticket. That is, asking them to recall things they did in the past that kept them sober. Once they recall those things, then encouraging them to repeat what was working for them.

4. *Confrontation of Weakness.* As I have reviewed and challenged the concept of confrontation, I believe this to this type that I have directed most of my opposition. To confront anyone on their failings, flaws and short-comings can hardly be called treatment. This is more like a put-down than therapy. The vast majority of our clients have been in that position for most of their lives. What purpose does that type of confrontation serve?

To say to a client "That this is your fourth rehab. We think you are a loser." Or, "You haven't done shit while you've been in this program. So pack your bags and get the hell out of here," borders on sin. This type of confrontation usually attacks, and is usually is born out of the therapist's frustration. Its target is the very essence of the client, not their behaviors and actions. Name-calling is also a part of this method. This type of confrontation passes judgment and useless opinions. I tell all my clients if faced with this type of a situation, they should get up and walk out of the door.

5. *Confrontation which encourages the client to take action.* This is the type that is akin to what good coaches use to get that extra second or foot out of a good athlete. It has a ring of challenge to it, purpose, and direction. Accomplishment is the confrontational goal here.

Berengson and Mitchell (1974) also note that research indicates that the high functioning counselors tend not to use confrontation. When they do resort to it, the confrontation tends to be of the experiential, strength, and action types.

Should you still feel the need to confront consider following suggestions which are drawn from Hutchins and Cole, (1992); Edelwich and Brodsky, (1992); Lawson et al. (1984), Thoreson, (1983); Washton (1989), and Vriend and Dyer (1973).

1. Develop a solid rapport with the client before and confrontation takes place. Acceptance and expressed concern toward the client is critical before one launches into a confrontation. Determine whether the client is ready for it.
2. The confrontation is never to be stated as a demand, rather it should be delivered as a suggestion or perhaps an invitation. Consider the tone in which you will deliver this confrontation. Can it be empathic and accomplished with concern?
3. The confrontation proper is to be descriptive and directed toward the concrete behavior of the client rather than at the person. It includes examples, and does not include judgments, interpretations and opinions.
4. If you feel you just have to confront off in order to get honest with your client, reconsider your motives. "There is brutality and there is honesty. There is no such thing as brutal honesty" (Anthony, 1985).
5. The confrontation needs to be prompt and direct, not long and drawn out, and it should be positive, not negative.
6. The confrontation needs to address facts, not opinions or hearsay.
7. Timing is critical. Consider where the client is in the treatment process.
8. The feedback will be helpful only if the client can do something about the problem.

Certainly all the above are important factors before one engages in a confrontation. Review your own motives and consider the client before you proceed with a confrontation.

As Twerski (1983) notes, there are certainly risks involved with any confrontation. It is traditionally supposed to bring on a crises, which somehow will shock clients into accepting help or coming to their senses. But, there have been many times in which the confrontation has backfired.

Although many AOD counselors might think otherwise, confrontation is not the only technique necessary to work with addicted persons (Lewis, Dana, & Blevins, 1988). But if you think you must use this method, remember the Hill Street Blues sergeants adage ..."Hey, HEY! Let's be careful out there."

CONTEXTUAL RESISTANCE INTERVENTIONS

What we have focused on so far has been the development of insight to help solve the client's problem. These have been the traditional approaches that allow the client to take in information by way of the "front door" so as to say. With this method, the client is to mull over the treatment action, and come to some kind of a realization that their past conduct has been inappropriate, and the resulting insight will be the path out of their present troubles.

The material below doesn't necessarily do that. It focuses more on the changing the meaning of the problem, and strives more on changing the solution to the problem more than trying to change the problem itself.

METAPHORS

Parables and fables are some of the oldest methods of communication and art forms known to man. With a simple story or in a few selected words, they can touch the coldest heart. A good tale can transfix a single person, an audience, an entire nation or civilization. It can state with ease what reams of books, lectures, and testimonials attempt to say without success.

Case in point: (deMello, 1982)

> On a street I saw a naked child, shivering in the cold.
> I became angry and said to God, "Why don't you do
> something?"
> For a while God said nothing. That night He replied,
> quite suddenly, "I certainly did something, I made you."

A parable on the meanings of life? Perhaps, but it does make one pause and reflect. Metaphors do that. They make you reflect! There's little or no resistance, you just ponder.

Using a metaphor requires that we pretend that something is the case when, symbolically it is not (Weiner, 1991). It is a comparison, suggesting likeness, and is a useful method to tell a story about the client without raising resistance (Cromier & Cormier, 1991). Metaphors act as a lens in which the self and the world is viewed in a new light. They can illuminate what has previously been impenetrable and uncover new meanings. For our purposes, the metaphor is a powerful strategy because it defuses resistance in a story that is "once removed" because it offers new possibilities and intriguing suggestions rather than commands (Wallas, 1985). When we use metaphors we insure that the messages that will be accessed in many different dimensions (Combs & Freedman, 1990).

Friedman (1990) believes that people can only hear one another when they are moving toward each other. They seem less likely to hear the words one speaks, let alone content, when the words are pursuing them. "Even the choicest words lose their power when they are used to overpower." This has lead to a colossal misunderstanding according to Friedman. It has been believed that insight will not work with people who are unmotivated to change. What, then, are you left with? The answer, according to Friedman is the emotional context--the metaphor.

The problem as we have noted is that very often that AOD counselor tries so damn hard to drill into the clients what we think is good for them. In this mode, we easily drift into overpowering the them with the recovery rhetoric. All the while, we believe that insight will somehow take place. When it doesn't, we become frustrated and try essentially the same strategy again, but this time with a little more force, which only creates a little more resistance. The problem all along was that we were pursuing someone who didn't want to hear our message.

Friedman also indicates that the initial problem of attempting to communicate with another is to get past the "...interference of the resistance demons who inhabit the other." What makes the task of communication even more difficult is that the nature of the resistance is to stiffen when engaging it straight on, although these very resistances will diminish when the demons no longer feel threatened or assaulted. In this case, one engages their own imaginative capacity and only gives the enough information to prick their curiosity. Metaphors, when delivered correctly, do just that.

A case in point was a situation some years ago in which a young man I was working with had this righteous feeling of resentment toward some long past injustice that was perpetrated against him. In group session after group session, he would labor on and on about how he had been wronged and would one day get his revenge. I listened to this story a couple of times, and following each rendition I would tell how that resentment would be the ruin of his recovery, if not his life. Needless to say, not one word got through. Then it struck me, I was going about therapy in the wrong way. I considered the use of a metaphor. I searched and found what I was looking for and waited for the right moment to use it. That moment arrived one day and rather than go onto my lame "It's no good for you." routine I told him the following story. (Paraphrased version of deMello, 1982.)

There were these two monks walking through an ancient Chinese forest. Their vows included the usual fasting, prayer, silence, and avoidance of women.

They soon came to a small river and at the bank stood a very beautiful woman who, as they, wished to cross. The river was high and without a word, one of the monks lifted her up and carried her across.

He gently placed her on the far side of the river and the two monks continued in their way. About a mile down the road the other monk could take it no more. He blurted out "Brother have you forgotten your vows? We are not to talk to women let alone touch them or carry them on our backs. What will people say?" And so on and so on.

The other monk listened patiently to this lecture and finally said, "Brother I left that women at the river bank. Why are you still carrying her?"

Well, you could have heard a pin drop. The resentful client just sat there sort of transfixed and deep in thought. He mumbled something about, "I see what you're trying to say. I'm still carrying my resentment." The next day no whining, no poor me, no resentful stories. He never brought up the issue again and I never questioned why. We were able to get on with the business of focusing more on maintaining a quality recovery.

Metaphor Construction

This is not to say that this strategy works every time. It doesn't. Authors just like to bring up little tales like the above is to point out their successes and highlight a point they are trying to make. But, if you use some simple planning you might be more successful than not, For example, not all metaphors need to be complex. They can be one-liners, or you can make complex and elaborate stories (Romig & Gruenke, 1991). These stories will be useful only if they fit the frame of reference of the client. This framework needs to be identified by the therapist's assessment process to determine occupation, personal history, specific likes, and dislikes among other things, in which the metaphor might fit. If you can construct a metaphor around something that captures the client's attention, the metaphor will more than likely make some kind of impact. (See Wallas, (1985); Combs & Freedman, (1990); Friedman (1990) for the specifics of metaphor construction.)

Just reading these things can get you to think about them more, and then you can use them when a certain situation arises. Whatever you do, do not randomly throw these things out and expect results. Many counselors I have supervised tried this metaphor thing once or twice, found that it didn't work so well, and went back to their old style of treatment, which didn't work well either. However, they made sure to let me know that "that crap" didn't work, and more often than not, they could then justify their old confrontational approach. What a waste.

Let us consider some examples that will show how to choose a specific metaphor for your client. Forman (1985) put together a few metaphors for alcoholism. In one story, (I've paraphrased) he describes a corporation that is falling apart through wear and tear plus neglect. It is in need of repair. The workers are in a state of discontent and are ready to walk out. So this organization has called on a business consultant to help with a renovation. If this doesn't happen the corporation will continue to decline.

It doesn't take a Ph.D. to see who is the corporation, who is the family of the corporation, who is the therapist, and what needs to be done to save the corporation. This is a basic trouble-theme metaphor, and the symbols can be easily changed to fit most other individuals who have trouble in their lives. For example, say the client your are working with is a car enthusiast. Guess who could be the car? Who do you suppose could be considered the passengers? And, who would be the car mechanic? If you are in the mood, take a few minutes and try creating a metaphor around these figures. How about a building a metaphor for a client who is a college professor, or a coal miner, or a bank teller. Consider using other forms in the metaphor like sporting events, music, cooking and recipes, and government. Generally, if you can construct a metaphor for one individual you can do it for many others.

Cromier and Cromier (1985) offer a few other metahpor hints to match the client's problem. Above, we only addressed a problem theme. What about issues such as intimacy, self-image, and family concerns. How would you go about developing a metaphor around an AOD client who is having problems with one of these?

Select a central character in the story (person, animal or object) around which the story will revolve. Don't get too descriptive, the images the client can create can be more powerful than yours. Anyway, a little ambiguity will force clients to use their minds. As you know, that is difficult to do while in an active addiction. Attempt to construct the metaphor or have the client construct the metaphor using all the senses: smell, sight, hearing, taste, touch, hot-cold and even balance (Wallas, 1985). If you are introducing the metaphor, use the client's strengths in the metaphor so they will begin to see those strengths, and then use them. Focus on the central character's behavior. It is the behavior in the metaphor that is to change. It is the message of action that needs to get across to the client, as well as placing the change in a solution frame.

Remember the indirectness of the metaphor allows the client to try out a new perceptual framework. By virtue of this indirectness the client does not have to consciously decide whether to accept it or reject it (Combs & Freedman, 1990). Metaphors do not necessarily offer new facts to the client, but do offer a new meaning to what they already know. The beauty of a good metaphor is that it rarely meets with any resistance. Allow the person or family time to process the metaphor, and if it makes sense to the person or family, then it may be time to openly discuss the problem and or new ideas to solve it.

It is now my turn to share a few metaphors with the reader, and the AOD field in general. The first is courtesy of Anthony (1983) and the second by deMello (1984).

(For the reader)

"If you require someone to change,
you require that person to lie to you."

(For the field)

THE FORMULA
The mystic was back from the desert.
"Tell us," they said, "what God is like,"

But how could he ever tell them what he had
experienced in his heart?
Can God be put into words?

He finally gave them a formula--so inaccurate,
so inadequate--in the hope that some of them
might be tempted to experience it for themselves.

They seized upon the formula.
They made it a sacred text.
They imposed it upon others as a holy belief.
They went to great pains to spread it in foreign lands.
Some even gave their lives for it.

The mystic was sad.
It might have been better if he had said
nothing.

Reframing

"The meaning that any event has depends upon the "frame" in which we perceive it" (Bandler & Grinder, 1982). Change the frame and you change the meaning. In essence, reframing is the changing of meaning for the individual, so that the original meaning no longer feels the same for the client (Kingsbury, 1992). When there is a reframe, the person's way of seeing things is changed. Watzlawick, Weakland, and Fisch (1974) refer to this process as changing the conception, emotion sitting or viewpoint of a situation of a person and then to place those "facts" into another frame that fits just as well or even better. This shift of frame changes the whole meaning and the consequence for the person in question. Tennen, Eron, and Rohrbaugh (1991) describe reframing as, "... redefining the meaning of a behavior in a way that makes change possible."

A reframe is different from an interpretation. By interpretation the therapist believes that the feedback she has dispensed carries some kernel of truth. In the reframe, that which works is considered to be true, not some therapist's view of reality. The reframe attempts to construct a view of reality that is conducive to change. "Although reframing is an essential part of therapy, it is usually not sufficient to bring about change by itself" (Weeks, 1991). Cade and O'Hanlon (1993) talk about helping the client "jump out" of a frame that limits their ability to see other alternatives to their problems. If that can be created then the client may begin to experiment with new behaviors that fit the new frame.

What does all this have to do with chemical dependency? Well, consider the possible ways in which it might work. How about reframing a client's sense of failure, in which he/she claims he/she can't seem to maintain long periods of abstinence, to something more appropriate. In the failure frame, he/she sounds doomed. Practically every therapist who has ever worked with one of these people knows how difficult they can be, and seemingly resistant to any treatment. They never change because they frame all their endeavors in failure.

For example, a few years age I was working with such a client. She was forever relapsing in an outpatient program in which I was working. However, she always came back to the groups to inform us of her failure. She seemed unwilling to give up. Persistent, I thought. She belabored her plight, and was often heard to say she was a hopeless case. After the traditional methods were not helping, we stumbled onto a reframe which turned her failure into persistence. In this frame, the focus was directed toward the effort she put into recovery not the outcome. So we changed the frame from defeat and failure to commitment. That reframe in and of itself was not sufficient to change things, but it did give the her a new way to look at her behavior. That may have created some possibilities or new alternatives to her old doomed behavior, in that she was able to put together longer periods of abstinence. The reframe may have given her options she had never seen before. That is what you want the client to do, consider alternatives they have never considered. Allow them to see things in a new context (Otani, 1989). Watzlawick, et al. (1974) also notes that in order for the reframe to be successful it must lift the problem out of the "symptom" frame into a frame that doesn't carry the implication of unchangeability.

What is essential in the use of the reframe, if it is to be effective, is that it is congenial to the client's way of thinking and conceptualizing of their reality (Seltzer, 1986). In the case above, the client did not like to consider herself a quitter. We changed the focus from problem to process. This did not come easy in the above case. I stumbled through a variety of other interventions without much success. It started to dawn on me that unless she changed her mind-set of failure then the therapy was not going to go far. After the reframe, we seemed to be on the right track.

Watzlawick, et al. (ibid), and Wexler (1991) note that there are three assumptions that contribute to all reframes. First, all people arrange and pigeonhole things according to their own classification system. Second, once they do that, the classification system becomes rigid and difficult to change. Third, the reframe can alter that rigid mind-set and, once changed, it is difficult to return to the original inflexible and limited view. Thus, at the core of the reframe is the belief that one can find a less painful and more adaptive means of viewing the world (LaClave & Brack, 1989). The reframe teaches a different option to the client. It is this new option which might allow the client to try new behavior.

SOLUTION/BRIEF APPROACHES TO TREATING RESISTANCE

The point of this chapter was to outline those therapeutic practices that could decrease the resistance factor. Then why not engage a theoretical model that does away with the resistance idea completely, and get right to the changing of meaning and behavior from the onset? If that is your choice, then solution/brief therapy will be to your liking.

This position epitomizes this broad contextual realm. It takes a bit of work on the part of the AOD therapist to integrate this way of seeing things. This is true, especially if all you have been used to is the traditional way of perceiving things. So with that in mind, a little background is required to get a good framework of how this strategy works. Once that is established watch what happens to the way you see you clients, and the creative ways you will do treatment.

Some Basics

What you are about to read, for those of you who have not experienced this form of therapy before, runs counter to the cherished beliefs of the AOD field. A few of those challenges include (Miller & Berg, 1995; Berg & Miller, 1992; O'Hanlon & Weiner-Davis, 1989):

1. There may not be any deep underlying cause of behaviors and symptoms. We believe behaviors have underlying symptoms because it was taught to us, or we read it in a book, and it made sense to us. Those beliefs, in turn, became a reality.

2. Awareness and insight are not necessary for change to occur. Change more easily can occur without it. Certainly, resistance will be reduced if one can avoid painful insight.

3. Just removing symptoms has never been considered to be enough, because that is considered to be shallow and the symptom will come back in another fashion. Many people, however, make significant and lasting change by starting out with small behavioral steps that remove symptoms.

4. Symptoms serve a function and there is a reason for them. Not necessarily true.

Another equally rational explanation is that the symptom has gained the status of an autonomous function, i.e., a habit. No function involved here, just habit.

5. Real change takes time. Brief interventions are shallow and do not last. There has been some growing evidence that even a single visit to a professional has profound change to the client (IOM, 1990).

6. The correct way to do treatment is to focus on the client's pathology, identify it, and correct it. That, as we have seen, will often just create a lot of resistance.

The terminology by which to call these theories ranges from paradoxical to strategic to brief to solution. They all seem to have many of the same basic postulates associated with them.

With the basics in mind, let us proceed. Berg and Miller (1992) appear to have been the first to write a book using solution-focused material with the emphasis on chemical dependency. O'Hanlen and Weiner-Davis's (1989) book is a solid and easily understood introduction to this method. Both works use many of the same principles to explain this solution/brief perspective and will be used as a foundation of this discussion, unless noted by the inserts of other authors.

A first perspective outlined by those authors addresses the focus on the clients successes, rather than on what went wrong with them. One can immediately see how this is not in line with the traditional method of AOD treatment. This therapy repeatedly focuses on the clients problems. This includes listing inventories which are designed to seek out these problems and determine as clearly as possible the extent of destruction the dependency caused the individual. Brief therapy says, 'don't do that." It feels such a focus only creates needless obstructions in the overall therapy. They advocate looking for successes. That is, look for what went right in the client's life and use that in therapy. This shift in perspective bypasses the possible resistance factors implicit in the traditional strategies. Remember the traditional approach expects denial and resistance. This viewpoint does not.

This leads to a major principle, called *utilization* (an Ericksonian term). This approach is especially effective with resistant clients (Miller, 1991). Here the therapist attempts to work within the client's frame of reference, and elicit from the client their strengths so that these strengths can be used in the recovery process. The traditional view of addiction holds that the client frame of reference is distorted by the very nature of their "disease," and further, these individuals have no strengths because of their years of dependency. Traditionally, the client is considered to start in a deficit position, which implies some kind of resistance is operating. Utilization, on the other hand, focuses on the client's frame of things and resources. This perspective believes the client comes to treatment with such items. The therapist's task is to find those frames and strengths and use them, not dwell on the deficits. Not only is this more positive and less resistive-producing, it is empowering. Taking a treatment position that the client possesses the necessary skills and resources to resolve their problems cannot help but to empower the client (Duncan, et al., 1992). This empowerment can lead to a greater sense of responsibility and make for less resistance. For instance, Taleff (1994) notes that most clients are forced into AOD treatment by their spouse, boss, and, or probation officer. As a result, they walk into a counselor's office very angry, defensive. In the traditional way of seeing things, this behavior could easily be construed as denial. According to this utilization principle, the therapist needs to see things according to the client's perspective. At this juncture a possible answer to avoiding resistance may be found. Rather than confront this angry client with the usual, "You're an alcoholic in denial," why not look for the "hidden customer" in the client. Sell him/her something he/she already values and wants. Utilize and appeal to the hidden customer who would like to get their spouse, boss and Probation Officer out of their hair. The treatment goal is to formulate a plan with that in mind. Let the client begin to develop that plan by giving him/her the task of coming up with a series of ideas in which those "in my hair" people would begin to notice a change in him/her. This new behavior could then start the process of easing the pressure, and the whole presumed resistance phenomena would ease. The client is sold something he/she wants, and those around him/her want. In many instances, that plan includes the decrease and or cessation of chemicals. But in this scenario, it is the client who comes up with the plan. It is empowering to the client and it helps save face. Plus, there is no resistance.

No assumptions are made about what is the truth of the disease or problem. No one theory is considered to be encompassing enough to include all the variables of the individual. There is no absolute truth. Truthful labels are seen as concepts that limit treatment alternatives. The idea is to avoid such labels, especially if they are associated with a poor prognosis (Duncan, et al., 1992). In this way, no one is confronted and forced to admit they have a disease, or a cognitive, irrational thinking pattern, or any such label that might create resistance.

Parsimony is the next solution/brief principle. It indicates that the most direct and simple approaches be utilized in treatment. So one might say that the traditional phrase of "Keep it simple" might apply here. In one sense this is accurate, and in another sense it is not. To use only what works is favored by both approaches, but the traditional approach is steeped in the content (insight) mode of thinking, while the solution/brief approach is directed toward the context (shift the meaning) mode. The insight mode, as we have seen, is littered with inherent resistance ideas that are assumed to block insight, while the context view discounts the very idea of resistance.

The next principle is that change is always assumed to be taking place. This is not true in the traditional view. In fact, there are formulations that a person's development slows down during the active addiction, so one can be assumed to be in a developmental lag after years of drinking and drugging (Fusillo & Shoch, 1981). However, there is no data available to confirm such a theory (Taleff, 1987).

The next postulate is a strong orientation toward the present and future. Again, traditional treatment is geared toward the focus of one's past via personal histories that are designed to uncover that addictive past. This view has spawned numerous workbooks that focus on the past whether they are family problems or any number of traumas that must be uncovered and re-felt.

The next principle is *cooperation*. This approach does not consider the client as the "enemy." We, in the helping profession, are supposed to be with our clients and not against them. Being with them does not create much resistance, however, considering them the enemy and in a high state of denial does create resistance.

The final principle is trying to find out what works. Once that is discovered, the job of the therapies is to amplify, and do more of what works. If a selected intervention doesn't work, one does not do it again. You do something else. Whereas, in the tradition mode, the essential method of treatment is to come to some insight and then surrender. This traditional view is predicated on the belief that clients have done something wrong. They did not "get it," and need to go back and do it again till they do get it. The clients are considered at fault. The treatment strategy is not thought to be inappropriate, the client is just did not do it well. One can see how resistance may be created by letting the client know they are wrong, and then to use the same treatment again that didn't work in the first place.

So how do these solution/brief theorists go about treating AOD clients but not get resistance? First, they keep the goal small, concrete, and easily achieved, then make sure that the goal is important to the client. In order to insure that importance, they let the client define the goals. That, of course, is blasphemy in the traditional treatment methods. To allow the client to define their own goals, the solutionists believe that clients will not longer feel that someone pushes a treatment goal on them, which saves a lot of resistance.

In addition, the goals are stated in terms of a beginning, something to be done first rather than as an end-product. There are no negatives used in treatment planning, e.g., "I won't visit the neighborhood bar this week-end," and "You won't drink at my nephews wedding." Goals are stated in proactive terms of what the client will do. For example, "I will look for those situations in which I didn't drink on weekends, and at weddings, and repeat that particular behavior(s). This type of goal looks for positive exceptions to the usual behavior, which is considered an untapped resource. Such behavior is amplified and encouraged.

Solution goals need to be stated in terms of hard work. The frame of hard work has the tendency to save the dignity of the client, just in case the client doesn't complete the agreed upon goal.

The actual treatment methods require empathy and respect, as we noted above. In this case, the counselor is encouraged to match the client's language and manner. These are the pacing methods we summarized in the neurolinguistic programming section. Further, it is important to move away from psychological language and to keep the session language in everyday terms. This includes staying away from the pathological mind-set talk, and the sarcasm, which can accompany this one-up-manship mentality (Tennen, Eron & Rohrbaugh, 1991).

A last issue for the actual treatment session includes restructuring the traditional approach of questioning to a solution-oriented approach. Compared to other types of interrogatives, presuppositional questions have an air of expectation to them. They don't ask if change will occur, they assume it will and ask when the change will happen. They ask how the client will be different at some future time. What will be a sign that things are going in the right direction? In these examples, the client is thrown into a solution mode of thinking. They don't completer workbooks in order to dig up old trauma, rather they are placed in a solution process. It is difficult to create resistance when you encourage solutions, rather than seek pathology. This frame has the client look for solutions and places the total responsibility on the client to find and use new behaviors.

This approach does not encourage starting the session with, "What's the problem?" or "Did you finish the assignment as I asked?" Instead, the therapist starts with, "What was happening that you would like to see continue?" Again the shift is to possible solutions rather than pathology, and away from possible resistance.

These solution-oriented questions generally fall into four separate categories. The first highlights what change many have happened prior to the first meeting. Many individuals begin to show improvement before they meet the counselor. If that is indicated, the client is on to a positive solution, and that behavior should be investigated in order to build on what is working. The next type of solution-oriented question looks for periods of time in which there was no AOD use. If such episodes are found, the counselor amplifies them and asks the client to repeat the behaviors that have shown to be effective. The third is the scaling question. For example, I often start a group by asking the members, "On a scale of one to ten, ten being the best you ever felt, and one the worse. What number would you give yourself to right now." Once that is established, I ask what small thing could the client do today to increase that number by a half or full point. The last type of solution-oriented question is called the coping question. Many times AOD clients express negative feelings of hopelessness and depression. Rather than try to cheer them up, the coping question asks them how they managed to make it through life with all such problems. Clients often see this an invitation to tell you how they managed to survive their addiction. Once you hear how they did it, amplify and ask them to repeat the surviving tactic.

Perhaps some readers have said, what if my client doesn't have any past successes from which to establish their resources? The solution/brief approach suggests you ask the client to use the *miracle question*. The miracle question asks clients how they think they might be different they woke up tomorrow and a miracle occurred and the problem they had would be gone. What small behavior would be different? This shifts the focus to possible solutions not   pathology.

All these questions are aimed at getting the client into a customer relationship of treatment. This relationship is defined or occurs when the therapist and client together identify an issue, and the client is then able to see themselves as part of the solution and is willing to do something about it. This is certainly the ideal relationship, but the solution approach recognizes two other relationships. The second is called the *complainant type.* Here the client can see the problem and can envision a goal, but do not know how to go about achieving the goal. The third relationship is called the *visitor type.* In this case, the client does not see the problem and therefore cannot see the need of a goal. Often this type will believe others are to blame for their present predicament.

The variety of solution-oriented questions outlined above are designed to get an individual from the visitor or complainant relationship to a customer one. Remember, the hidden customer and wanting to get people off his back or out of his hair.

Paths That Lead to Resistance

The solution/brief approach believes that there are several paths that are literally guaranteed to result in problems or, in our terms, resistance. This occurs when you do not know where the treatment is going, perhaps you start with an unclear goal, or you lose sight of the original treatment goals. This is evident when the therapist is asked, as he is on his way to group, what he intends to do today. The response is often, "Let's see what happens."

Other ways of creating resistance is to repeat a past therapist's ineffective methods. This sounds almost simplistic, but clients will often tell you what didn't work in their past treatment(s). That is a sure sign not to repeat what did not work them the first time.

The next in the series of what not to do is to fail to notice what did work for the client in the past but, then, not amplify or use it. Further, resistance will continue to be perpetuated by the client's sometimes incessant unhelpful or self-defeating statements. The therapist needs to interrupt those statements and reframe or interject some presuppositional questions to shift the client's direction from seeking problems to one of seeking solutions.

The last thing the AOD counselor should NOT do may be the most important. That is to look for resistance. As we have stated time and again, if you look for the resistance you will probably find it.

deShazer (1988) indicates that many therapists often assume that a complicated problem (such as AOD) needs a complicated description, which then calls for a complicated solution. That is not the case with the brief therapy approach. In this view of things, a simple change can often lead to unpredictable growth.

Haley (1994) notes that this type of an approach is similar to Zen. The focus of therapy is on action to resolve issues, not insight, learning, or cognitions. The approach needs to be unique to each individual who comes into your office. The client, as well as the counselor, may need to give up his/her cherished theories in order to attain enlightenment.

There exists a host of paradoxical approaches that the AOD therapist can use, but as with anything, that requires that you read and study and, especially, that you tailor these methods to the AOD field. That is where it gets creative and fascinating. If interested, it is suggested one get a start at these interventions by reading the references I've cited and keep a close watch for workshops in this topic area.

CHAPTER SUMMARY

The crux of the chapter has centered on how a drug an AOD counselor creates the appropriate atmosphere for change. The chapter attempted to shy away from formulas. As Bandler and Grinder (1982) indicate, they generally don't work for all the individuals one may meet in the course of their work. The mistake, as these two authors note, is that somebody tried a particular strategy and it worked, then the person thought, "We'll use it with everything." Of course it doesn't work that way. In addiction treatment, formulas tend to become reified over time.

The way to start and maintain movement in the counseling field is to observe. What does the client give you that can be utilized in the service of change? We noted some broad templates and made suggestions as developed by others, but you, the counselor, should never apply a thoughtless treatment onto a client. You need to carefully tailor and deliver well, a treatment program for each and every unique client

POSTSCRIPT

We have traveled through a complex array of ideas on the subject of resistance, and found a few broad themes. First, resistance is simply not a matter of client resistance alone. Resistance can also apply to those who treat the client, the field in general and to families and groups. Second, resistance is a matter of perspective. Many authors have developed different opinions on the subject. This rich complexity has serious implications for the AOD counselors who do assessments. The one I adopt will, in some manner, bias my view of an individual. In addition, drug and alcohol counselors cannot be content to simplify a client's behavior into a favored viewpoint, just because it feels good. Such actions get dangerously close to unethical behavior, because of the generalizing and subsequent injustice it does to the those we serve and to ourselves.

Compound the influences of the counselor's potential resistance, plus those of a group, system, or the field, and we run head-long into a quagmire of ideas, opinions, and conjecture on the subject. Without some sort of guide, the quagmire can be overwhelming to the novice as well as to the experienced counselor.

This book has attempted to provide some guidance, and hopefully give the reader a better perspective on the subject. With attitudes, hopefully resistance will lose some of its mystery and frustration. Theapist and clients, then, can benefit from the clarity.

REFERENCES

Abel, E.L. & Sokol, R.J. (1990). Is occasional light drinking during pregnancy harmful? In Ruth C. Engs (ed.). Controversies in the addictions field. Vol. I. (p: 158-165). Dubuque, Iowa: Kendall/Hunt.

Adler, A.. (1927/1954). Understanding nature. Greenwich, CN: Fawcett.

Adler, G. & Myerson, P.G. (1973). Confrontation in Psychotherapy. New York: Science House.

Alcoholics Anonymous. (1976). New York: AA World Services. Inc.

Allan, C. (1991). Acknowledging alcohol problems: The use of a visual analogue scale to measure denial. The Journal of Nervous and Mental Disease. 179, 620-25.

Allport, G. W. (1954). Nature of prejudice . New York: Doubleday Anchor.

Amodeo, M. & Liftik, J. (Mar. 1990). Working through denial in alcoholism: Families in society. Journal of Contemporary Human Services, 131-135.

Anderson, D. (1981). The psychopathology of denial. Center City, MN: Hazelden.

Anderson, L. & Carter, J.H. (1982). Psychotherapy: Patient-Therapist matching reconsidered. Journal of the National Medical Association, 74, 461-464.

Anderson, C.M. & Stewart, S. (1983). Mastering resistance: A practical guide to family therapy. New York: Guilford.

Annis, H.M. & Chan, D. (1983). The differential treatment model: empirical evidence from a personality typology of adult offenders. Criminal Justice and Behavior, 10, 159-173.

Anthony, R. (1983). Think. New York: Berkeley.

Apthorp, S.P. (1985). Alcohol and substance abuse: A clergy handbook. Wilton, Conn: Morehouse-Barlow.

Augsburger, D. (1973). Caring enough to confront. Ventura, CA: Regal.

Bach, G. (1954). Intensive group psychotherapy. New York: Ronald Press.

Baekland, F. & Lundwall, L.K. (1977). Engaging the alcoholic in treatment and keeping him there. In B. Kissin & H. Begleiter (Eds.). Treatment and rehabilitation of the chronic alcoholic. New York: Plenum.

Bandler, R. & Grinder, J. (1982). Reframing: Neuro-linguisitc programming and the transformation of meaning. Moab, Utah: Real People Press.

Bandler, R. & Grinder, J. (1979). Frogs into princes: Neuro-linguistic programming. Moab, Utah: Real People Press.

Baptiste, D.A. (1983). Family therapy with reconstituted families: A crisis-induction approach. The American Journal of Family Therapy, 11, 5-15.

Bates, M. & Johnson, C. (1972). Group Leadership: A manual for group counseling leaders. Denver, CO: Love.

Baumeister, R.F. (1993). Lying to yourself: The enigma of self-deception. In M. Lewis & C. Saarni (Eds.). Lying and deception in everyday life. New York: Guilford.

Bean-Bagog, M. Alcoholism as a cause of psychopathology. Hospital and Community Psychiatry, 39, 352-354.

Bean, M.H. (1981). Denial and the psychological complications of alcoholism. In M.H. Bean & N.E.

Beattie, M. (1986). Denial. Center City, MN: Hazelden.

Beck, A.T. & Emerg, G.E. (1977). Cognitive therapy of substance abuse. Philadelphia, PA: Center for Cognitive Therapy.

Beck, A.T. , Wright, F.D., Newman, C.F., & Liese, B.S. (1993). Cognitive therapy of substance abuse. New York, NY: Guilford.

Beitman, B.D. , Goldfried, M.R., & Norcross, J.C. (1989). The movement toward integrating the psychotherapies: An overview. American Journal of Psychotherapy, 146, 138-146.

Benjamin, A. (1974). The helping interview. (2nd. ed.). Boston, MA: Houghton-Mifflin.

Berenson, B. G. & Mitchell, K.B. (1974). Confrontation for better or worse. Amherst, MA: Human Development Press.

Berenson, D. & Woodside-Schrier,E. (1991). Addressing denial in the therapy of alcohol problems. Family Dynamics and Addiction Quarterly, 1, 21-30.

Bepko, C. & Krestan, J. (1985). The responsibility trap: A blue print for treating the alcoholic family. New York, NY: Free Press.

Berg, I.K. & Miller, S. (1992). Working with the problem drinker: A solution-focused approach. New York, NY: Norton.

Berglas, S. (1987). Self-handicapping model. In H.T. Blane & K.E. Leonard (Eds.). Psychological theories of drinking and alcoholism. New York, NY: Guilford.

Berger, L. (1974). From instinct to identity: The development of personality. Englewood Cliffs, NJ: Prentice-Hall.

Bion, W.R. (1959). Experience in groups and other papers. New York, NY: Basic.

Bishop, D.R. (1991). Clinical aspects of denial in chemical dependency. Individual Psychology, 47, 199-209.

Black, C. (Fall, 1979). Children of alcoholics. Alcohol Health and Research World, 23-27.

Black, C. (1981). It will never happen to me. Denver, CO: M.A.C.

Blane, H.T. (1968). The personality of the alcoholic. New York, NY: Harper & Row.

Blatt, S.J. & Erlich, S. (1982). Levels of resistance in the psychotherapy process. In P.L. Wachtel (Ed.). Resistance: Psychodynamic and behavioral approaches. New York, NY: Plenum.

Blau, T. (1988). Psychotherapy tradecraft: The technique and style of doing therapy. New York, NY: Brunner/Mazel.

Blum, K. & Payne, J.E. (1991). Alcohol and the addictive brain. New York: Free Press.

Book, H.E. (1991). Is empathy cost efficient? American Journal of Psychotherapy, 45, 21-30.

Boszormenyi-Nogy, I. & Ulich, D.N. (1981). Contextual family therapy. In A.S. Gurman & D.P. Kniskern (Eds.). Handbook of family therapy, Vol.1. New York, NY: Brunner/Mazel.

Boszormenyinogy, I. & Krosner, B.R. (1986). Between give and take: A clinical guide to contextual therapy. New York, NY: Brunner/Mazel.

Boy, A.U. & Pine, G.J. (1982). Client-centered counseling: A renewal. Boston, MA: Allyn & Bacon.

Brandon, N. (1969). The psychology of self-esteem. New York, NY: Bantam.

Bratter, T.E. & Forrest, G.G. (1985). Alcoholism and substance abuse: Strategies for clinical intervention. New York, NY: Free Press.

Brehm, J.W. (1966). A theory of psychological reactance. New York, NY: Academic Press.

Breshgold, E. (1989). Resistance in Gestalt therapy: An historical theoretical perspective. The Gestalt Journal, 12, 73-102.

Breuer, J. & Freud, S. (1893-1899). Standard edition. Volume II. New York, NY: Basic.

Bright, D. (1988). Criticism in your life: How to give it, how to take it, how to make it work for you. New York, NY: Master Media.

Brower, K.J., Blow, F.C., & Beresford, T.P. (1989). Treatment implications of chemical dependency models: An integrative approach. Journal of Substance Abuse Treatment, 6,147-157.

Boesky, D. (1985). Resistance and character theory: A reconsideration of the concept of character resistance. In H.D. Blum (Ed.), Defense and Resistance. Hillside, NJ: Lawrence Erlbaum.

Bok, S. (1978). Lying: Moral choice in public and private life. New York, NY: Vintage.

Brown, S. (1985). Treating the alcoholic: A developmental model of recovery. New York, NY: Wiley.

Bugental, J.F.T. (1987). The art of the psychotherapist. New York, NY: Norton.
Cade, B. & O'Hanlon, W.H. (1993). A brief guide to brief therapy. New York, NY. Norton.

Caprio, D. (1974). Personality theories. Philadelphia: W. B. Saunders.

Caton, C.L.M., Gralnick, A., Bender, S. & Simon, R. (1989). Young chronic patients and substance abuse. Hospital and Community Psychiatry, 40, 1037-1049.

Carkhuff, R.C. & Berenson, B.G. (1967). Beyond counseling and therapy. New York, NY: Holt, Rinehart, and Winston.

Cermak, T. (1986). Diagnosing and treating co-dependence. Minneapolis, MN: Johnson Institute Books.

Chan, A.W. (1993). Recent development on detection and biological indicators of alcoholism. In G.J.Conners (ed.), Innovations in alcoholism treatment: State of the art reviews an their implications for clinical practice. (pp: 31-67). New York: Haworth.

Chaney, E. (1989). Social skills training. In R.K. Haster & W.R. Miller (Eds.). Handbook of alcoholism treatment approaches: Effective alternatives. New York, NY: Pergamon.

Chessick, R.D. (1974). Technique and practice of intensive psychotherapy. New York, NY: Jason Aronson.

Chiauzzi, E.J. (1992). Preventing relapse in the addictions: A biopsychosocial approach. New York, NY: Pergamon.

Christner, A.M. (Ed.). (1993). Reference guide to addiction counseling. Providence, R.I.: Manisses Communication Group.

Christian, J.L. (1977). Philosophy: An introduction to the art of wondering: New York, NY: Holt, Rinehart, and Winston.

Clark, W. (1991). Alcoholism: Blocks to diagnosis and treatment. American Journal of Medicine, 71, 275-285.

Clark, J.C., & Saunders, J.B. (1988). Alcoholism and problem drinking: Theories and Treatment. New York.

Cohen, S. (1985). The substance abuse problems: Volume II. New York, NY: Haworth.

Coleman, S. (Ed.), (1985). Failure in family therapy. New York, NY: Guilford.

Coles, R. (1989). The call of stories: Teaching and moral imagination. Boston, MA: Houghton Mifflin.

Combs, G. & Freedman, J. (1990). Symbol story and ceremony: Using metaphor in individual and family therapy. New York, NY: Norton.

Constantine, J.A., Fish, L.S., & Pierce, F. P. (1984). A systemic procedure teaching positive connotation. Journal of Marital and Family Therapy, 10, 313-15.

Corey, G. (1990). Theory and practice of group counseling. (3rd ed.). Pacific Grove, CA: Brooks/Cole.

Cormier, W. H. , & Cormier, L. S. (1991). Interviewing strategies for helpers: fundamental skills and cognitive behavioral interventions. (3rd. ed.). Pacific Grove, CA: Brooks/Cole.

Cox, K. L. & Price, K. (1990). Breaking through: Incident drawings with adolescent substance abusers. Arts in Psychotherapy, 17, 333-37.

Crisman, W. (1991). The opposite of everything is there: Reflections on denial in alcoholic families. New York, NY: William Morrison.

Csikszentmihalyi, M. (1990). Flow: The psychology of optimal experience. New York, NY: Harper and Row.

Cummings, N. & Sayama, M. (1995). Focused psychotherapy: A casebook of brief intermittent psychotherapy throughout the life cycle. New York: Brunner/Mazal.

Daniels, V. & Horowitz, L. J. (1976). Being and caring. San Francisco, CA: San Francisco Book Company.

Davanloo, H. (1986). Intensive short-term psychotherapy with highly resistant patients. I. Handling resistance. International Journal of Short-term Psychotherapy, 1, 107-33.

Davis, D.J. (1990). Prevention issues in developing programs. In R.C. Engs (Ed.), Women: Alcohol and drugs. New York: Kendall/Hunt.

Dawes, R.M. (1994). House of cards: Psychology and psychotherapy built on myth. New York: Free Press.

Dean, J. C. & Poremba, G. A. (1983). The alcoholic stigma and the disease concept. The International Journal of the Addictions, 18, 739-751.

Deitch, D. A. & Zweben, J. E. (1984). Coercion in the therapeutic community. Journal of Psychoactive Drugs, 16 35-41.

DeMello, A. (1982). Song of the bird. New York, NY: Image.

Derby, K. (1992). Some difficulties in the treatment of character-disordered addicts. In B. Wallace (Ed.). The chemically dependent: Phases of treatment and recovery. New York, NY: Brunner/ Mazel.

Dershowitz, A.M. (1994). The abuse excuse. Boston: Little, Brown.

DeShazer, S. (1984). The death of resistance. Family Process, 23, 11-17.

DeShazer, S. (1985). Keys to solution in brief therapy. New York, NY: Norton.

DeShazer, S. (1988). Once you have your doctors, what have you got? A brief therapy approach to "difficult cases". In E. W. Nunnally, C. S. Chilman, & F. M. Cox (Eds). Mental illness, delinquency, addictions, and neglect: Families in trouble series, Vol. 4, Newburg Park, CA: Sage.

DeShazer, S. (1988). Clues: Investigating solutions in brief therapy. New York, NY: Norton.

Dewald, P. A. (1982). Psychoanalytic perspectives on resistance. In P.L. Wachtel (Ed.). Resistance: Psychodynamic and behavioral approaches. New York, NY: Plenum.

Dealing with denial. (1975). Center City, MN: Hazelden.

Diagnostic and statistical manual of mental disorders. (1994). (4th. ed.). Washington, DC: American Psychiatric Association.

DiCicco, L. Unterberger, H. & Mack, J. E. (1978). Confronting denial: An alcoholism intervention strategy. Psychiatric Annals, 8, 596-606.

DiClemente, C. C. (1993). Changing addictive behaviors: A process perspective. Current Directions in Psychological Science, 2, 101-106.

DiClemente, C. C. (1991). Motivational interviewing and the stages of change. In W. R. Miller & S. Rollnick (Eds.). Motivational interviewing: Preparing people to change addictive behavior. New York, NY: Guilford.

Doctoroff, J. (1988). Bill Moyers' world of ideas: Noam Chomsky-Part II. [Television]. New York, NY: Public Affairs Television, Inc.

Donovan, D.M, & Marlatt, G. P. (1988). Assessment of addictive behaviors. New York: Guilford.

Donovan, D.M. Walker, R.D. & Kivlahan, D. R. (1987). Recovery and remediations of neuropsychological functions: Implications for alcoholism rehabilitation process and outcome. In O.A. Parsons, N. Butters, & P.E. Nathan (Eds) Neuropsychology of alcoholism: Implications for diagnosis and treatment. (pp. 339-60). New York: Guilford.

Dorpat, T. L. (1985). Denial and defense in the therapeutic situation. New York, NY: Jason Aronson.

Dowd, E. T. & Seibel, C. A. (1990). A cognitive theory of resistance and reactance: Implication for treatment. Journal of Mental Health Counseling, 12, 458-469.

Dowd, E. T. Milne, C. R., & Wise, S. C. (1991). The therapeutic reactance scale: A measure of psychological reactance. Journal of Counseling and Development, 69, 541-545.

Doweiko, H. F. (1993). Concepts of chemical dependency. Pacific Grove, CA: Brooks/Cole.

Duncan, B. L., Solovey, A. D., and Rusk, G. S. (1992). Changing the rules: A client-centered approach to therapy. New York, NY: Guilford.

Dunst, C., Triuette, C., & Deal, A. (1988). Enabling and empowering families: Principles and guidelines for practice. Cambridge, MA: Brookline.

Dyer, W. & Vriend, J. (1988). Counseling techniques that work. American Association for Counseling and Development.

Edelwich, J. & Brodsky, A. (1992). Group counseling for the resistant client: A practical guide to group process. New York, NY: Lexington.

Edelstein, E. L., Nathanson, D. L., & Stone, A. M. (Eds.). Denial: A clarification of concepts and research. New York, NY: Plenum.

Edwards, G. (1985). As the years go rolling by: Drinking problems in the time dimension. British Journal of Psychiatry, 154, 18-26.

Egan, G. (1994). The skilled helper. (5th. ed.) Pacific Grove, CA: Brooks/ Cole.

Ehrenberg, O. & Ehrenberg, M. (1977). The psychotherapy maze. New York, NY: Winston.

Elkind, S. N. (1992). Resolving impasses in therapeutic relationships. New York, NY: Guilford.

Ellis, A., McInerney, J. F., DiGiusepper, R., & Yeayer, R. J. (1988). Rational-emotive therapy with alcoholics and substance abusers. New York, NY: Pergamon.

Ellis, A. (1985). Overcoming resistance: Rational-emotive therapy with difficult clients. New York, NY: Springer.

Ellis, A. (1973). Humanistic psychology: The rational-emotive approach. New York, NY: Julian.

Ellis, A. (1967). Rational-emotive psychotherapy. In D. Azbuckle, (Ed.), Counseling and psychotherapy. New York, NY: McGraw-Hill.

Emrick, C. D. & Aarons, G. A. (1990). Cognitive-behavioral treatment of problem drinking. In H. B. Milkman & L. I. Sederer (Eds.). Treatment choices for alcoholism and substance abuse. New York, NY: Lexington.

Estes , N. J. & Heinemann, M. E. (1977). Alcoholism: Development, consequences, and interventions. St. Louis, MO: C. U. Mosby.

Fearside, W. & Holther, W. (1959). Fallacy: The counterfeit of argument. Englewood Cliffs, NJ: Prentice-Hall.

Festinger, L . (1957). A theory of cognitive dissonance. Stanford, CA: Stanford University Press.

Fine, R. (1973). The development of Freud's thought. New York: Jason Aronson.

Fingarette, H. (1988). Heavy drinking: the myth of alcoholism as a disease. Berkeley, CA: University of California Press.

Fischer, B. (1983). Working with the resistant client. Focus on the Family, 32, 39-40.

Flores, P. J. (1988). Group psychotherapy with addicted populations. New York, NY: Haworth.

Fong, M. (1995). Assessment and DSM-IV diagnosis of personality disorders: A primer for counselors. Journal of Counseling & Development , 73, 635-639.

Forest, G. G. (1982). Confrontation: In psychotherapy with the alcoholic. Holmes Beach, FL: Learning Publications.

Forman, R. F. (1985). The use of metaphors in substance abuse counseling. Addictionary, 1, 1-3.

Forman, R. (1988). A technique for overcoming substance abuse denial. In P. A. Keller & S. R. Heyman (Eds.). Innovations in clinical practice: A source book. Sarasota, FL: Professional Resource Center.

Fox, R. (1967). A multi-disciplinary approach to the treatment of alcoholism. American Journal of Psychotherapy, 123, 769-778.

Fox, V. (1993). Addiction change and choice: The new view of alcoholism. Tuscon, AZ: Sharp.

Fremont, S.K. & Anderson, W. (1988). Investigation of factors involved in therapists' annoyance of clients. Professional Psychology Research and Practice, 19, 330-35.

Freud, S. (1920/1965). A general introduction to psychoanalysis. New York, NY: Washington Square.

Freud, A. (1966). The ego and the mechanisms of defense: The writings of Anna Freud, Vol. II. Madison, CT: International Universities Press.

Freud, A. (1946). The ego and mechanisms of defense. New York, NY: International Universities Press.

Freud, S. (1910/1957). The future prospects of psychoanalytic therapy. In J. Strachy (Ed.). The standard edition of the complete psychological works of Sigmund Freud. London, England: Hogarth Press.

Freud, S. (1926/1959). Inhibitions, symptoms, and anxiety. London, England: Hogarth Press.

Friedman, E. H. (1990). Friedman's fables. New York, NY: Guilford.

Fusillo, M. & Skoch, E. M. (1981). The psychiatric hospital treatment of alcoholism: The multidisiplinary approach. National Association of Psychiatric Hospitals Journal, 12, 97-101.

Gaylin, W. (1979). Feelings: our vital signs. New York: Harper & Row.

Gashin, J. E. & Little, H. J. (1992). Why and when substance abusers drop out of treatment: Some surprising findings. Substance Abuse, 13, 53-62.

George, R. L. (1990). Counseling the chemically dependent: Theory and practice. Englewood Cliff, NJ: Prentice Hall.

Gladding, S. (1992). Counseling: A comprehensive profession. New York, NY: Macmillan.

Glaser, F. B.. & Skinner, H. A. (1981). Matching in the real world: A practical approach. In E. Gottril, & K. A. Druly (Eds.). Matching patient needs and treatment methods in alcoholism and drug abuse. Springfield, IL: Charles C. Thomas.

Goldmsith, R.J. & Green, B.L. (1988). A rating scale for alcohol denial. The Journal of Nervous and Mental Disease, 176, 614-20.

Goleman, D. (1985). Vital lies, simple truths: The psychology of self-deception. New York, NY: Simon & Shuster.

Goleman, D. (1995). Emotional intelligence. New York: Bantam.

Goodwin, D. (1988). Alcohol and the writer. New York, NY: Penguin.

Goodwin, D. W. (1988). Is alcoholism hereditary? New York, NY: Ballantine.

Goodwin, F. K. (1991). Report to Congress on what works in drug treatment. Rockville, MD: Alcohol, Drug Abuse, and Mental Health Administration.

Gordon, K. B. (1993). The treatment of addictive disorders in a private clinical setting. In S. L. A. Straussner (Ed.). Clinical work with substance-abusing clients. New York, NY: Guilford.

Gordon, M. A., Kennedy, B. P., & McPeske, J. D. (1988). Neuropsychologically impaired alcoholics Assessment, treatment considerations, and rehabilitation. Journal of Substance Abuse, 5, 99-104.

Gordon, T. (1970). Parent effectiveness training. New York, NY: Wyden.

Gorski, T. T. & Miller, M. (1986). Stay sober: A guide for relapse prevention. Independence, MO: Independence.

Gray, J. L. & Starke, F. A. (1977). Organizational behavior: Concepts and applications. Columbus, Ohio: Charles E. Merrill.

Greenson, R. (1967). The technique and practice of psychoanalysis. New York, NY: International Universities Press.

Griffin, R. E. (1991). Assessing the drug involved client. Families in society. Journal of Contemporary Human Service, 72, 87-94.

Groves, J. (1978). Taking care of the hopeful patient. The New England Journal of Medicine, 16, 883-887.

Gurman, A. S. (1984). Transference and Resistance in marital therapy. The American Journal of Family Therapy, 12, 70-73.

Guy, E. (1988). Synanon. New York, NY: Doubleday.

Halberstan, J. (1993). Everyday ethics: Solutions to real life dilemmas. New York, NY: Viking.

Haley, J. (1987). Problem solving therapy. San Francisco, CA: Jossey-Boss.

Haley, J. (1994). Zen and the art of therapy. The Family Networker, 18, 55-60.

Halpern, D. F. (1989). Thought and knowledge: An introduction to critical thinking. Hillside, NJ: Lawarence Erlbaum.

Hamachek, D. E. (1968). What research tells us about the characteristics of "good" and "bad" therapies. In D. E. Hamachek (Ed.). Human dynamics in psychology and education. Boston, MA: Allyn and Bacon.

Hatcher, C. & Brooks, B. (1977). Innovations in counseling psychology. Washington, D. C.: Jossey-Bass.

Hazelden Foundation (1985). You don't have to tear 'em down to build 'em up. Hazelden Professional Update. 4(2), 2.

Heldmann, M.L. (1988). When words meet: How to keep criticism from undermining your self-esteem. New York, NY: Ballantine.

Hester, R.K. (1994). Outcome research. In M.Galanter & H.D. Kleber (Eds.). Textbook of substance abuse treatment (2nd ed., pp. 35-43). Washington, DC: American Psychiatric Press.

Hill, A. (1974). The alcoholic on alcoholism. Canadian Literature, 62, 33-48.

Hinsie, L. & Campbell, R. (1970). Psychiatric dictionary. New York, NY: Oxford.

Hoff, E. C. (1977). Alcoholism: The hidden addiction. New York, NY Seabury.

Hoffer, E. (1951). The true believer. New York, NY: Perennial Library.

Hoffer, E. (1967). The order of change. New York, NY: Perennial Library.

Hutchins, D. E., & Cole, C. G. (1992). Helping relationships and strategies. Pacific Grove, CA: Brooks Cole.

Ihilevich, D., & Glesser, G. C. (1993). Defense mechanisms: Their classification, correlates, and measurement with the defense mechanisms inventory. Odessa, FL: Psychological Assessment Resources.

Imhof, J. Hirsch, R., & Terenz, R. (1983). Countertranferential and attitudinal considerations in the treatment of drug abuse and addiction. The International Journal of the Addictions, 18, 491-510.

Institute of Medicine. (1990). Broadening the base of alcohol problems. Washington, DC: National Academy Press.

Isaacson, E. B. (1991). Chemical Dependency: Theoretical approaches and strategies. Journal of Chemical Dependency Treatment, 4, 7-27.

Jackson, D. D. (1957). The question of family homeostasis. Psychiatric Quarterly Supplement, 31, 79-90.

Jacobson, G. R. (1989). Identification of problem drinkers and alcoholics. In R. R. Watson (Ed), Diagnosis of alcohol abuse. Boca Raton, FL: CRE Press.

Jacobson, M. S. (1981). Behavioral marital therapy. In A. S. German & D. P. Kniskern (Eds). Handbook of family therapy. New York, NY: Brennen/Mazel.

Jahn, D. L. & Lichstein, K.L. (1980). The resistive client: a neglected phenomenon in behavior therapy. Behavior Modification, 4, 302-20.

Janis, I. L. (1983). Groupthink: Psychological studies of policy decisions and fiascoes. Boston, MA: Houghton-Mifflin.

Jellineck, E. B. (1960). The disease concept of alcoholism. New Haven, CT: College and University Press.

Johnson Institute (1987). How to use intervention in your professional practice. Minneapolis, MN: Johnson Institute Books.

Johnson, V. (1986). Intervention. Minnesota, MN: Johnson Institute Books.

Jones, R., Weinrott, M. R., & Howard, J. R. (1981). National Institute of Mental Health evaluation. In J. Q. Wilson (1983) Atlantic Monthly, 252, 45-51.

Jourard, S. M. (1968). Disclosing man to himself. Princeton, NJ: D. Van Nostand.

Jung, C. G. (1968). Analytical Psychology: Its theory and practice. New York, NY: Vintage.

Kasl, C. D. (1992). Many roads, one journey: Moving beyond the twelve steps. New York: Harper Perennial.

Kaufman, E. (1992). Family therapy: A treatment approach with substance abuse. In J. H. Lowinson, P. Ruiz, R. D. Millman, & J. G. Langrod (Eds.). Substance Abuse: A comprehensive textbook. Baltimore, MD: Williams & Wilkins.

Kaufman, E. (1994). Family therapy: Other drugs. In M. Golanter & H. D. Kleber (Eds.). The American psychiatric press textbook of substance abuse. Washington, D.C.: American Psychiatric Press.

Kaufman, E. (1994). Paychotherapy of addicted persons. New York: Guilford.

Kearney, R.J. (1996). Within the wall of denial: Conquering addictive behaviors. New York: Norton.

Keefe, T. (1976). Empathy: The critical skill. Social Work, 21, 10-14.

Kellerman, J. L. (1980). Alcoholism: A merry-go-round named denial. Center City, MN: Hazelden.

Kelly, G. (1963). A theory of personality: The psychology of personal constructs. New York, NY: Norton.

Kernberg, O. (1975). Borderline conditions and pathological narcissism. New York: Jason Aronson.

Kirmayer, L. J. (1990). Resistance, reactance, and reluctance to change: A cognitive attributional approach to strategic interventions. Journal of Cognitive Psychotherapy: An International Quarterly, 4, 83-104.

Klein, J. M. (1988). Abstinence-oriented inpatient treatment of the substance abuser. Occupational Therapy in Mental Health, 8, 47-59.

Kemp, C. G. (1962). Influence of dogmatism in the training of counselors. Journal of Counseling Psychology, 9, 155-157.

Kempler, W. (1981). Experiential psychotherapy within families. New York, NY: Brunner/Mazel.

Kernberg, O. (1975). Borderline conditions and pathological narcissism. New York, NY: Jason Aronson.

Kingsburg, S. J. (1992). Ericksonian therapy. Harvard Mental Health Letter, 9, 4-5.

Korb, M. P., Gorrell, J., Riet, V. (1989). Gestalt therapy practice and theory. New York, NY: Pergamon.

Kottler, J. A. (1992). Compassionate therapy: Working with difficult clients. San Francisco, CA: Jossey-Bass.

Kramier, W. (1992). I'm dysfunctional, you're dysfunctional. Reading, MA: Addison-Wesley.

Kubler-Ross, E. (1971). The five stages of dying. Encyclopedia Science Supplement. (pp: 92-7). NewYork: Groler.

Kurtz, E. (1979). Not-God: A history of Alcoholics Anonymous. Center City, MI: Hazelden Educational Materials.

L'Abote, L. (1992). Major therapeutic issues. In L. L'Abote, J. E. Farrar, & D.A. Serritella (Eds). Handbook of differential treatments for addictions. Boston, MA: Allyn & Bacon.

Laclave L. J. & Brack, G. (1989). Reframing to deal with patient resistance: Practical application. American Journal of Psychotherapy, 43, 68-75.
Langs, R. (1981). Resistances and interventions. New York, NY: Jason Aronson.

Langer, E. (1989). Mindfulness. Reading, MA: Addison-Wesley.

Laplanche, J. & Pontalis, J. The language of psychoanalysis. (D. Nicholson-Smith, Trans.) New York, NY: Norton.

Lawson, G. W., Ellis, D. C., & Rivers, P.C. (1984). Essentials of chemical dependency counseling. Rockville, MD: Aspen.

Lawson, G. W., & Lawson, A. W. (1989). Alcoholism and substance abuse in special populations. Rockville, MD: Aspen.

Lawson, A. W. & Lawson, G. W. (1991). Classic articles in the field of family dynamics of addiction: The early years, 1953-1980. Family Dynamics Addictions Quarterly, 1, 59-70.

Lawson, G., Peterson, J. S., & Lawson, A. (1983). Alcoholism and the family: A guide to treatment and prevention. Rockville, MD: Aspen.

Lazarus, A. (1981). The practice of multimodal therapy: Systemic, comprehensive, and effective psychotherapy. New York, NY: McGraw-Hill.

188

Lazarus, A. A., & Fay, A. (1982). Resistance or rationalization? A cognitive-behavioral perspective. In P.L. Wachtel (Ed.). Resistance: Psychodynamic and behavioral approaches. New York, NY: Plenum.

Lazarus, R. S. (1983). Psychological stress. New York, NY: McGraw-Hill.

Leary, W.E. (1996, December 18). Responses of alcoholics to therapies seem similar. New York Times, p. A17

Lehman, A. F., Myers, C. P., & Corty, E. (1989). Assessment and classification of patients with psychiatric and substance abuse syndromes. Hospital and Community Psychiatry, 40, 1019-1030.

Lenord Schierse, L. (1990). Witness to the fire: Creativity and the veil of addiction. Boston, MA: Shambala.

Levin, J. D. (1991). Recovery from alcoholism: Beyond your wildest dreams. Northvale, NJ: Aronson, Inc.

Lewis, J., Dona, R., & Blevins, G. (1988). Substance abuse counseling: An individualized approach. Pacific Grove, CA: Brooks/ Cole.

Lewis, J. P. (1992). Treating the alcohol-effected family. In L.L'Abote, J. E. Farrar, & D.A. Serritella (Eds.). Handbook of differential treatments for addictions. Boston, MA: Allyn & Bacon.

Lewis, M. (1993). The development of deception. In M. Lewis & C. Saarni (Eds). Lying and deception in everyday life. New York, NY: Guilford.

Lieberman, M.A., Yalom, I. D., & Miles, M. B. (1973). Encounter groups: First facts. New York, NY: Basic.

Lindstrom, L. (1992). Managing alcoholism: Matching clients to treatments. New York, NY: Oxford.

The little red book: An orthodox interpretation of the steps of the Alcoholics Anonymous program. (1957). Center City, MN: Hazelden.

Loevinger, J. (1977). Ego development. San Francisco, CA: Jossey-Bass.

Lovern, J. (1991). Pathways to reality: Erickson-inspired treatment approaches to chemical dependency. New York, NY: Brunner/Mazel.

McAuliffe, R. M. & McAuliffe, M. B. (1975). Essentials for the diagnosis of chemical dependency, alcoholism, and other dependencies. Minneapolis, MN: An Essentials book.

McCown, G. & Johnson, J. (1993). Therapy with treatment resistant families: A consultation-crisis-intervention model. New York, NY: Haworth.

McGrady, B. (1987). Implications of neuropsychological research findings for the treatment and rehabilitation of alcoholics. In O. Parsons, N. Butters, P. Nathan (Eds.. Neuropsychology of alcoholism: Implications for diagnosis and treatment. New York, NY: Guilford.

McIntyre, J. R. (1993). Family treatment of substance abuse. In S. L. A. Straussner (Ed). Clinical work with substance-abusing clients. New York, NY: Guilford.

McKay, M. & Fanning, P. (1991). Prisoners of belief: Exposing and changing beliefs that control your life. Oakland, CA: New Harbinger.

McLachlan, J. F. C. (1972). Benefit from group therapy as a function of patient-therapist match on conceptual levels. Psychotherapy: Theory, Research, and Practice, 9, 317-323.

McLachlan, J. F. C. (1974). Therapy strategies, personality orientation, and recovery from alcoholism. Canadian Psychiatric Association Journal, 19, 25-30.

McMahon, J. and Jones, B. T. (1992). The change process in alcoholics: Client motivation and denial in the treatment of alcoholism within the context of nursing. Journal of Advanced Nursing, 17, 173-186.

McWhirter, E. H. (1991). Empowerment in counseling. Journal of Counseling and Development, 69, 222-227.

Mack, J. E. (1981). Alcoholism, AA, and the governance of the self. In M. H. Bean & N. E. Zinberg, (Eds.). Dynamic approaches to understanding and treatment of alcoholism. New York, NY: Free Press.

Mackinnon, R. A. & Michels, R. (1971). The psychiatric interview in clinical practice. Philadelphia, PA: W. B. Saunders.

Madanes, C., Dukes, J., & Harbin, H. (1980). Family ties of heroin addicts. Archives of General Psychiatry, 37, 889-894.

Maedler, T. (1989). Wounded healers. Atlantic Monthly, 37-47.

Mahalik, J. R. (1994). Development of the client resistance scale. Journal of Counseling Psychology, 41, 58-68.

Mahoney, M.J. (1991). Human change process. New York: Basic Books.

Mahrer, A.R., Murphy, L., Gagnon, R., & Gingras, N. (1994). The counselor as cause and cure of client resistance. Canadian Journal of Counseling, 28, 125-34.

Mann, J. (1973). Confrontation as a mode of teaching. In G. Adler & P.G. Myerson (Eds.). Confrontation in psychotherapy. New York, NY: Science House.

Marlett, G. A. (1985). Cognitive assessment as intervention procedures. In G. A. Marlett & J. Gordon (Eds.). Relapse Prevention. New York, NY: Guilford.

Marlatt, G. A. & Gordon, J. R. (1985). Relapse prevention. New York, NY: Guilford.

Marlatt, G. A., Baer, J. S., Donovan, D. M., & Kivlhan, D. R. (1988). Addictive behaviors: Etiology and treatment. Annual Review of Psychology, 39, 223-252.

Marlatt, G. A. (1988). Matching clients to treatment: Treatment models and stages of change. In D. M. Donovan & G. A. Marlatt (Eds.). Assessment of addictive behaviors. New York, NY: Guilford.

Marlatt, G. A. & Barrett, K. (1994). Relapse prevention. In M. Galanter & H. D. Kleber (Eds.). The American psychiatric press textbook of substance abuse treatment. Washington,
D. C. : American Psychiatric Press.

Marshall, R. J. (1972). The treatment of resistances in psychotherapy children and adolescents. Psychotherapy: theory, research and practice., 9, 143-48.

May, G. (1988). Addictions and grace. New York; Harper.

May, R. (1989). The art of counseling. New York: Gridner press.

Maynard, J. A. (1993). Confrontation: Necessary but often misunderstood. In A. M. Christner (Ed.). Reference guide to addiction counseling. Providence, RI: Manisses Communication Group.

Meichenbaum, D. & Gilmore, J. B. (1982). Resistance from a cognitive behavior perspective. In P. L. Wachtel (Ed.). Resistance: Psychodynamic and behavioral approaches. New York, NY: Plenum.

Meissner, W. W. (1988). The psychotherapies: Individual, family, and group. In A. M. Nichol (Ed.). The new Harvard guide to psychiatry. Cambridge, MA: Harvard University Press.

Menninger, K. (1988). Theory of psychiatric technique. New York, NY: Basic Books.

Metzgar, L. (1988). From denial to recovery. San Francisco, CA: Jossey-Bass.

Milam, J. R. & Ketcham, K. (1981). Under the influence. New York, NY: Bantam.

Milhorn, H. T. (1991). Relapse: The mind-body connection. The Counselor, 9, 16-18.

Miller, S.D. & Berg, I.S. (1995). The Miracle Method. New York: Norton.

Miller, N.S. (1995). Addiction psychiatry: Current diagnosis and treatment. New York: Wiley-Liss.

Miller, W. A. (1991). Using hypnotherapy in communicating with the recovering addicted patient. Alcoholism Treatment Quarterly, 8, 1-18.

Miller, W.R., Benefield, R.G. & Tonigan, J.S. (1993). Motivation for change in problem drinking: A controlled comparison of two therapist styles. Journal of Consulting and Clinical Psychology, 61, 455-61.

Miller, W. R. (1985). Motivation for treatment: A review with special emphasis on alcoholism. Psychological Bulletin, 98, 84-107.

Miller, W. R. (1989). Increasing motivation for change. In R. K. Hester & W. R. Miller (Eds.). Handbook of alcoholism treatment: Effective alternatives. New York, NY: Pergamon.

Miller, W. R. & Sovereign, R. G. (1988). A comparison of two styles of therapeutic confrontation. Unpublished manuscript, University of New Mexico.

Miller, W. R. (1983). Motivational interviewing with problem drinkers. Behavioral psychotherapy, 11, 147-172.

Miller, W. R. & Rollnick, S. (1991). Motivational interviewing: Preparing people to change addictive behavior. New York, NY: Guilford.

Mischel, W. (1986). Introduction to personality. New York: Holt, Rinehart and Winston.

Minkoff, K. (1989). An integrated model for dual diagnosis of psychosis and addiction. Hospital and Community Psychiatry, 40, 1031-1036.

Minuchin, S. (1974). Families and family therapy. Cambridge, MA: Harvard University Press.

Moore, B. & Fine, F. (1968). A glossary of psychoanalytic terms and concepts. New York, NY: The American Psychiatric Association.

Moore, R. A. & Murphy, T. C. (1961). Denial of alcoholism as an obstacle to recovery. Quarterly Journal of Studies on Alcohol, 22, 597-609.

Morse, R. & Flavin, D. (1992). The definition of alcoholism. The Journal of the American Medical Association, 268, 1012-1014.

Morrison, J. (1995). The first interview. New York: Guilford.

Morgenstern, J. & McGrady, B. S. (1992). Curative factors in alcohol and drug treatment: Behavioral and disease model perspectives. British Journal of Addiction, 87, 901-912.

Mueller, L. A. & Ketcham, K. (1987). Recovering: How to get and stay sober. New York, NY: Bantam.

Munjack, D. J. & Oziel, R. J. (1978). Resistance in the behavioral treatment of sexual dysfunction. Journal of Sex and Marital Therapy, 4, 122-128.

Nace, E. R. (1990). Substance abuse & personality disorder. In D. F. O'Connell (Ed.), Managing the dually diagnosed patient. New York, NY: Haworth.

Neikirk, J. (May/June 1984). Characteristics of the pedestal counselor. Focus on Family, 7, 26, 28, 31.

Neuhaus, C. (1993). The disease controversy revisited: An ontologic perspective. Journal of Drug Issues, 23, 463-78.

Newsome, R.D. & Ditzler, T. (1993). Assessing alcoholic denial: Further examination of the denial rating scale. The Journal of Nervous and Mental Disease, 181, 689-94.

Nicholas, M. W. (1984). Change in the context of group therapy. New York, NY: Brunner/Mazel.

Nicholi, Jr., A. (1988). The therapist-patient relationship. In Armand M. Nicholi, Jr. (Ed). The new Harvard guide to psychiatry. Cambridge, MA: Harvard University Press.

Notman, M. T., Khantzian, E. J., & Koumas, A. J. (1987). Psychotherapy with the substance dependent physician. American Journal of Psychotherapy, 41, 220-30.

Nowiski, J. (1990). Substance abuse in adolescents and young adults. New York, NY: Norton.

O'Brien, R. & Chafetz, M. (1982). The encyclopedia of alcoholism. New York, NY: Facts on File Publications.

O'Conner, L.E., Berry, J.W., Inaba, D., Weiss, J. & Morrison, A. (1994). Shame, guilt and depression in men and women from addiction. Journal of Substance Abuse Treatment, 11, 503-10.

O'Hanlon, W. & Weiner-Davis, M. (1989). In search of solutions: A new direction in therapy. NewYork, NY: Norton.

O'Hanlon, W.H. & Martin, M. (1992). Solution-orientated hypnosis: An Ericksonian approach. New York: Norton.

Ohlsen, M.M. (1970). Group counseling. New York: Holt, Rinehart and Winston. Orlin, L. & Davis, J. (1993). Assessment and intervention with drug and alcohol abusers in psychiatric settings. In S. L. A. Straussner (Ed.). Clinical work with substance-abusing clients. New York, NY: Guilford.

Otani, A. (1989). Client resistance in counseling: Its theoretical rationale and taxonomic classification. Journal of Counseling and Development, 67, 458-461.

Otani, A. (1989). Integrating Milton H. Erickson's hypnotheraputic techniques into general counseling and psychotherapy. Journal of Counseling and Development, 68, 203-207.

Otani, A. (1994). A cognitive contextual theory and classification of Milton H. Erickson's
hypnotherapeutic techniques. In S.R. Lankton & K.K. Erickson (Eds.). The essence of a single-session success. (p:36-53). New York: Brunner/Mazel.

Paredes, A. (1974). Denial, deceptive maneuvers, and consistency in the behavior of alcoholics. Annals of the New York Academy of Sciences, 233, 23-33.

Paul, R. (1993). Critical Thinking (3rd ed.). Santa Rosa, CA: Foundation for Critical Thinking.

Patterson, C. H. (1966). Theories of counseling and psychotherapy. New York, NY: Harper & Row.

Patterson, C. H. (1974). Relationship counseling and psychotherapy. New York, NY: Harper & Row.

Pattison, E. M. (1982). A multivariate-multimodal model of alcoholism. In E. M. Pattison (Ed.). Selection of treatment for alcoholics. New Brunswick, NJ: Publications division of Rutgers Center of Alcohol Studies.

Peele, S. (1989). Diseasing of America: Addiction treatment out of control. Lexington, MA: Lexington.

Perez, J. (1986). Counseling the alcoholic group. New York, NY: Gardner.

Perls, F., Heffrine, R. F., & Goodman, P. (1951/1977). Gestalt therapy: Excitement and growth in the human personality. New York, NY: Bantam.

Perls, F. (1947/1965). Ego, hunger, and aggression. New York, NY: Vintage.

Pietrofesa, J. J., Hoffman, A., & Splete, H. H. (1984). Counseling: An introduction. Boston, MA: Houghton Mifflin.

Piaget, G. W. (1972). Training patients to communicate. In A. A. Lazarus (Ed.), Clinical behavior therapy. New York, NY: Brunner/Mazel.

Polster, E., & Polster, M. (1973). Gestalt therapy integrated. New York, NY: Vintage.

Polster, E. & Polster, M. (1976). Therapy without resistance: Gestalt therapy. In A. Burton (Ed). What makes behavior change possible? New York, NY: Brunner/Mazel.

Prochaska, J.G. (1995). An eclectic and integrative approach: Transtheoritical therapy. In A.S. Gurman & S.B.Messer (Eds). Essential psychotherapies: Theory and practice. (p. 403-440). New York: Guilford.

Prochaska, J. G. & DiClemente, C. C. (1982). Transtheoretical therapy: Toward a more integrative model of change. Psychotherapy: Theory, Research, and Practice, 19, 276-288.

Prochaska, J. G. & DiClemente, C.C. (1986). Toward a comprehensive model of change. In W. R.Miller & N. Heather (Eds.). Treating addictive behaviors: Processes of change. New York, NY:Plenum.

Prochaska, J. G., DiClemente, C. C. & Norcross, J. C. (1992). In search of how people change: Applications to addictive behaviors. American Psychologist, 47, 1102-1114.

Ranew, L. F. & Serritello, D. A. (1992). Substance abuse and addiction. In L. L'Abate, J. E. Farrar, & D. A. Serritella (Eds.). Handbook of differential treatments for addictions. Boston, MA: Allyn and Bacon.

Reich, W. (1933/1976). Character analysis. (3rd ed.), New York, NY: Pocket.

Ritchie, M. H. (1986). Counseling the involuntary client. Journal of Counseling and Development, 64, 516-18.

Robertson, N. (1988). Getting better: Inside Alcoholics Anonymous. New York, NY: William Morrow and Company.

Rogers, C. R. (1942). Counseling and psychotherapy. New York, NY: Houghton-Mifflin.

Rogers, C. R. (1980). A way of being. Boston, MA: Houghton Mifflin.

Rogers, C. R. & Stevens, B. (1971). Person to person: The problem of being human - A new trend in psychology. New York, NY: Pocket.

Rogers, R. L., McMillin, C. S., & Hill, M. A. (1988). The twelve steps revisited. New York, NY: Bantam.

Rogers, R. L. & McMillin, C. S. (1989). The healing bond: Treating addictions in groups. New York, NY: Norton.

Romig, C. A. & Gruenke, C. (1991). The use of metaphor to overcome inmate resistance to mental health counseling. Journal of Counseling and Development, 69, 414-418.

Rosenthal, L. (1987). Resolving resistances in group psychotherapy. Northvale, NJ: Jason Aronson.

Rothenberg, A. (1988). The creative process of psychotherapy. New York, NY: Norton.

Rothschild, D. E. (1992). Treating the substance abuser: Psychotherapy thought out in the recovery process. In B. Wallace (Ed.). The chemically dependent: Phases of treatment and recovery. New York, NY: Brunner/ Mazel.

Sager, C. J. (1981). Couples therapy and marriage counseling. In A. S. Gurman & D. P. Kniskern (Eds.). Handbook of family therapy, Vol. 1. New York, NY: Brunner/Mazel.

Sapp, J. S. (1985). The family's reaction to an alcoholic: An application of Kubler-Ross's five stages. Alcoholism Treatment Quarterly, 2, 49-60.

Satir, V. (1972). Peoplemaking. Palo Alto, CA: Science of Behavior.

Satir, V. (1983). Conjoint family therapy (3rd ed.). Palo Alto, CA: Science of Behavior.

Saunders, B., Wilkinson, C. & Towers, T. (1996). Motivation and addictive behaviors: Theoretical perspectives. In F. Rotgers, D.S. Keller, & J. Morgenstern (Eds.). Treating substance abuse: Theory and practice. (pp. 241-65). New York: Guilford.

Schlesinger, H. J. (1982). Resistance as process. In P.L. Wachtel (Ed). Resistance: Psychodynamic and behavioral approaches. New York, NY: Plenum.

Schierse Leonard, L. (1990). Witness to the fire: Creativity and veil of addiction. Boston: Shambhala.

Schuckit, M. A. (1973). Alcoholism and sociopathy: Diagnostic confusion. Quarterly Journal of Studies on Alcohol, 34, 157-164.

Sederer, L. I. (1990). Mental disorders and substance abuse. In H. B. Milkman & L.I. Sederer (Eds.). Treatment choices for alcoholism and substance abuse. New York, NY: Lexington.

Seligman, L. & Gaaserud, L. (1994). Difficult clients: Who's are they and how do we help them? Canadian Journal of Counseling, 28, 25-42.

Seligman, M. (1974). Depression and learned helplessness. In R. J. Friedman & M.M. Katz (Eds). The psychology of depression: Contemporary theory and research. Washington, D. C.: Winston.

Seligman, M. (1991). Learned optimism. New York, NY: Alfred A. Knopf.

Selzer, M. L. (1967). The personality of the alcoholic as an impediment to psychotherapy. Psychiatric Quarterly, 41, 38-45.

Seventh special report to the U. S. Congress on alcohol and health. (1990). Rockville, MD: U. S. Department of Health and Human Services.

Szasz, T. (1992). Our right to drugs: the case for a free market. New York: Praeger.

Shaffer, H. J. & Gambino, B. (1990). Epilogue: Integrating treatment choices. In H.B. Milkman & L.I. Sederer (Eds.). Treatment choices for alcoholism and substance abuse. New York, NY: Lexington.

Shaffer, H.J. & Robbins, M. (1995). Paychotherapy for addictive behavior: A stage-change approach to meaning making. In A. Washton (Ed). Psychotherapy and substance abuse: A practitioner's handbook. (pp. 103-123). NewYork: Guilford.

Shelton, J. L. & Levy, R. L. (1981). Behavioral assignments and treatment compliance. Champaign, IL: Research Press.

Shibahara, S. (1989). Prejudices and fallacies in psychology. Japan: Tottori Press.

Siegal, H. A. & Moore, D. C. (1985). The weekend intervention program at Wright State University School of Medicine. Journal of Substance Abuse, 2, 233-237.

Sigmon, S. T. & Snyder, C. R. (1993). Looking at oneself in a rose colored mirror: The role of excuses in the negotiation of personal reality. In M. Lewis & C. Saarni (Eds.). Lying and deception in everyday life. New York, NY: Guilford.

Simkin, J. S. (Speaker) (!970). Individual Gestalt therapy (Cassette recording #1). Philadelphia, PA: American Academy of Psychotherapists.

Simon, R. (1992). One on one: Conversations with the shapers of family therapy. New York: Guilford.

Snyder, C. R. (1988). From defenses to self- protection: An evolutionary perspective. Journal of Social and Clinical Psychology, 6, 155-158.

Sobell, M. B. & Sobell, L. C. (1993). Problem drinkers: Guided self-change treatment. New York, NY: Guilford.

Solomon, R. C. (1993). What a tangled web: Deception and self-deception in philosophy. In M. Lewis and C. Saarni (Eds.). Lying and deception in everyday life. New York, NY: Guilford.

Spengler, P.M., Strohmer, D.C., & Prout, H.T. (1990). Testing the robustness of the overshadowing bias. American Journal on Mental Retardation, 95, 204-14.

Spengler, P.M., Strohmer, D.C., Dixon, D.N. & Shivy, V.A. (1995). A scientist-practitioner model of psychological assessment: Implications for training, practice, and research. The Counseling Psychologist, 23, 506-34.

Straussner, S. L. A. (1993). Assessment of treatment of clients with alcohol and other drug abuser problems. In S. L. A. Straussner (Ed.). Clinical work with substance-abusing clients. New York, NY: Guilford.

Strean, H. S. (1990). Resolving resistances in psychotherapy. New York, NY: Brunner/Mazel.

Strean, H. S. (1993). Resolving countertransferences in psychotherapy. New York, NY: Brunner/ Mazel.

Strong, S. R. & Matross, R. P. (1973). Change process in counseling and psychotherapy. Journal of Counseling Psychology, 20, 25-37.

Strupp, H. H. & Binder, J. L. (1984). Psychotherapy in a new key: A guide to the time-limited dynamic psychotherapy. New York, NY: Basic.

The Substance Abuse Subtle Screening Inventory Manual. (1985). Spencer, IN: Spencer Evening World.

Sullivan, H. S. (1953). The interpersonal theory of psychiatry. New York, NY: Norton.

Sullivan, H. S. (1956). Clinical studies in psychiatry. New York, NY: Norton.

Sutherland, S. (1994). Irrationality: Why we don't think straight. New Brunswick, NJ: Rutgers University Press.

Szasz, T. (1992). Our Right to Drugs: The Case for a Free Market. New York: Praeger.

Taleff, M.J. (1987). Ego development in adult male alcoholics. Unpublished doctoral dissertation, University of Pittsburgh.

Taleff, M.J. (Feb. 1992). A model of relapse prevention in an outpatient setting. Professional Counselor, 6, 52-4.

Taleff, M.J. (May/June, 1994). The well-deserved death of denial. Behavioral Health Management, 14, 51-52.

Tarter, R.E., Alterman, A.I. & Edwards, K.L. (1984). Alcoholic denial: A biopsycological interpretation. Journal of Studies on Alcohol, 45, 214-18
Tatarsky, A. & Washton, A.M. (1992). Intensive outpatient treatment: A psychological perspective. In B. Wallace (Ed.). The chemically dependent: Phases of treatment and recovery. NewYork, NY: Brunner/Mazel.

Taylor, S.E. (1989). Positive illusions: creative self-deception and the healthy mind. New York: Basic Books.

Tennen, H., Eron, J. B., & Rohrbaugh, M. (1991). Paradox in context. In G. R. Weeks (Ed.). Promoting change through paradoxical therapy. New York, NY: Brunner/ Mazel.

Thoreson, R. W. (July/August, 1983). Positive confrontation techniques for the rehabilitation counselor. Journal of Rehabilitation, 47-51.

Tiebout, H. M. (1953). The act of surrender in the therapeutic process. Quarterly Journal of Studies on Alcohol, 14, 58-68.

Todd, T. C. (1988). Treating families with a chemically dependent member. In E. W. Nunnally, C. S. Chilman, & F. M. Cox (Eds.). Mental illness, delinquency, addictions, and neglect: Families in trouble series, Vol. 4. Newbury Park, CA: Sage.

Travis, C. (1982). Anger : The misunderstood emotion. New York: Touchstone.

Trice, H. M. & Byer, J. M. (1981). A data based examination of selection bias in the evolution of a job based alcoholism program. Alcoholism: Clinical and experimental research, 5, 489-496.

Trimpey, J. (1989). The small book: A revolutionary alternative for overcoming alcohol and drug dependence. New York, NY: Bantam.

Trimpey, J. (1991). The small book. Lotus, CA: Lotus Press.

Troise, F.P. (1995). Conceptualization of co-dependency as personality disorder. Alcoholism Treatment Quarterly, 12, 1-15

Trunnell, E. E. & Holt, W. E. (1974). The concept of denial or disavowal. Journal of the American Psychoanalytic Association, 22, 769-784.

Turock, A. (1978). Effective challenging through additive empathy. Personal and Guidance Journal, 57, 144-49.

Twerski, A. (1981). Caution: Kindness can be dangerous to the alcoholic. New York, NY: Prentice Hall.

Twerski, A. (1982). Beware the labeling. Pennsylvania Medicine, 29-32.

Twerski, A. J. (1983). Early intervention in alcoholism: Confrontational techniques. Hospital and Community Psychiatry, 34, 1027-1030.

Twerski,. A. J. (1990). Addictive thinking: Why do we lie to ourselves? Why do others believe us? Center City, MN: Hazelden Educational Materials.

Valliant, G. E. & Milofsky, E. A. (1982). The etiology of alcoholism: A perspective viewpoint. American Psychologist, 37, 494-503.

Valliant, G. E. (1988). The alcohol-dependent and drug-dependent person. In A. M. Nicholi (Ed.). The new Harvard guide to psychiatry. Cambridge, MA: Harvard University Press.

Vancelli, M. (1992). Removing the road blocks: Group psychotherapy with substance abusers and family members. New York, NY: Guilford.

Vaughn, C. (1984). Addictive drinking: The road to recovery for problem drinkers and those who love them. New York, NY: Penguin.

Vos Savant, Marilyn. (1990). Brain building. New York, Bantam Books, Inc.

Vriend, J. & Dyer, W. (1973). Counseling the reluctant client. Journal of Counseling Psychology, 3, 240-246.

Walker, A. (Ed.). (1995). Thesaurus of psychological index terms. Washington, DC: American Psychological Association.

Wallace, J. (1971). Alcoholism from the inside out: A phenomenologic analysis. In N. J. Estes and M. E. Heinemann (Eds.). Alcoholism: Development, consequences, and interventions. St. Louis, MO: Mosby.

Wallace, J. (1978). Working with the preferred defense structure of the recovering alcoholic. In S. Zimberg, J. Wallace, S. Blume (Eds.). Practical approaches to alcoholism psychotherapy. New York, NY: Plenum.

Wallace, J. (1985). Alcoholism: New light on the disease. Newport, RI: Edgehill.

Wallace, J. (1996). Theory of 12-step orientated treatment. In F.Rotgers, D.S.Keller, and J.Morganstern (Eds.). Treating substance abuse. (pp. 13-36). New York: Guilford.

Wallas, L. (1985). Stories for the third ear. New York, NY: Norton.

Wallerstein, A. M. (1985). Defenses, defense mechanisms, and the struggle of the mind. In H. D. Blum (Ed.). Defense and resistance. Lawrence Erlbaum.

Walkenstein, E. (1975). Don't shrink to fit!. New York: Grove Press.

Walter, J.L. & Peller, J.E. (1992). Becoming solution-focused in brief therapy. New York: Brunner/Mazel.

Ward, D. (1983). Alcoholism: Introduction to theory and treatment. Dubuque, IA: Kendall/Hunt.

Washton, A. M. (1989). Cocaine addiction: Treatment, recovery, and relapse prevention. New York, NY: Norton.

Watson, C. (1991). A Delphi study of paradox in therapy. In G. R. Weeks (Ed.). Promoting change through paradoxical therapy. New York, NY: Brunner/Mazel.

Watzlawick, P., Weakland, J. H., & Fisch, Z. (1974). Change: Principles of problem formation and problem resolution. New York, NY: Norton.

Watzlawick, P. (1976). How real is real? Confusion, disinformation, and communication. New York, NY: Vintage.

Watzlawick, P. (1990). Munchhausen's pigtail or psychotherapy and "reality" essays and lectures. New York, NY: Norton.

Weeks, G. R. (1991). Metatheory of paradox. In G. R. Weeks (Ed.). Promoting change through paradoxical therapy. New York, NY: Brunner/Mazel.

Wegner, D. M. (1989). White bears and other unwanted thoughts: Suppression, obsession, and the psychology of mental control. New York, NY: Viking.

Wegscheider, S. (1981). From the family trap to family freedom. Alcoholism, 36-39.

Weinberg, G. (1984). The heart of psychotherapy. New York, NY: St. Martin's Press.

Weiner, B. (1991). Metaphors in motivation and attribution. American Psychologist, 46, 921-930.

Weisman, A. D. (1973). Confrontation, countertransference, and context. In G. Adler & P. G. Myerson (Eds.). Confrontation in psychotherapy. New York, NY: International Universities Press.

Wexler, D. B. (1991). The adolescent self: Strategies for self-management, self-soothing, and self-esteem in adolescents. New York, NY: Norton.

Whalen, F. L. (1978). Investigation of the use of denial as a defense mechanism in alcoholic and non-alcoholic persons. Unpublished master's thesis. California State University, Long Beach, CA.

Whalen-Fitzgerald, K. (1988). Alcoholism: The genetic inheritance. New York, NY: Doubleday.

Wheeler, G. (1991). Gestalt reconsidered: A new approach to contact and resistance. New York, NY: Gardner.

Whitaker, C. A. & Keith, D. V. (1981). Symbolic-experiential family therapy. In A. S. Gurman & D. P. Kniskern (Eds.). Handbook of family therapy, Vol. 1. New York, NY: Brunner/ Mazel.

Whyte, W. H. (1957). The organization man. New York, NY: Doubleday Anchor.

Willick, M. S. (1985). On the concept of primitive defenses. In H. P. Blum (Ed.). Defense and resistance: Historical perspectives and cultural concepts. New York, NY: International Universities Press.

Worden, M. (1987). Denial: The defense that disables. Phonenia, AZ: D. I. N.

Wright, B. & Wright, D. G. (1990). Dare to confront! How to intervene when someone you care about has a drinking problem. New York, NY: Master media Limited.

Wurmser, L. (1978). The hidden dimension: Psychodynamics in compulsive drug use. New York, NY: Jason Aronson.

Wuss, D. (1973). Psychoanalytic Schools from the Beginning to the Present. New York: Jason Aronson, Inc.

Yalisove, D. L. (1992). Survey of contemporary psychoanalytically oriented clinicians on the treatment of addictions: A synthesis. In B. Wallace (Ed.). The chemically dependent phases of treatment and recovery. New York, NY: Brunner/Mazel.

Yalom, I. D. (1985). The theory and practice of group psychotherapy. (3rd edition). New York, NY: Basic.

Yalom, I. (1989). Loves executioner and other roles of psychotherapy. New York, NY: Perrennial.

Yankofsky, L., Wilson, G. T., Adler, W. H., & Vrana, S. (1986). The effect of alcohol on self-evaluation and perception of negative interpersonal feedback. Journal of Studies on Alcohol, 47, 26-33.

Zimmerman, J. L. & Dickerson, V. C. (1993). Bringing forth the restraining influence of pattern in couples therapy. In S. Gilligan & R. Price (Eds.). Therapeutic conversations. New York, NY: Norton.

Zinker, J. (1977). Creative process in Gestalt therapy. New York, NY: Vintage.

Zuckerman, E. L. (1991). <u>The clinician's thesaurus: A guidebook for working psychological reports and other publications</u>. Pittsburgh, PA: Three Wishes Press.

Zweben, J. E. (1989). Recovery-oriented psychotherapy: Patient resistances and therapist dilemmas. <u>Journal of Substance Abuse Treatment, 6</u>, 123-132.

—C—

change, levels of, 140–42
  action, 141
  contemplation, 140
  maintenance, 141
  precontemplation, 140
  preparation, 141
  relapse, 141
communication levels, 138–40
  contact maintenance, 139
  critical occasions, 139
  formal occasions, 139
  intimacy, 140
  standard conversation, 139
confrontation, 154–59
  didactic approach, 158
  experimental approach, 158
  history of, 154
  purpose & need, 156
  ratrional for, 154
  strenght approach, 158
  suggestions, 159
  take action, 159
  weakness approach, 158
conscious element of denial, 27–31
  deception, 27
  excuses, 27
  self-deception, 27
counselor resistance, 3, 83–85
  attribute to failure of client, 84
  being right, 84
counselors, pedestal types, 96
  all-knowing, 96
  assumptive manner, 97
  too busy, 97
countertransference, 85–87
  defined, 85
  manifestations of, 86
  Psychiatric Dictionary, 86

—D—

defences, ten major (AOD dependency), 50
defensive styles, Freudian, 45–47
  epinosic gain, 46
  offset guilt, 47
  repetition compulsion, 46
  repression, 45
  transference, 46
denial, 3, 11
denial decision tree, 11–40
  introduction of, 11
  summary, 38
denial look alikes
  ambivalence, 34
  confusion, 33
  disinclined/reluctant to change, 36
  personality disorders, 37
  psychologically naive, 35
  reactance, 37
  systems/environmental, 35
denial lookalikes, 31–38
  physiological, 31

—E—

enabling, 120
  joiner, 120
  messiah, 120
  silent sufferer, 120
exclusive dependence on one theory, 3

—F—

family barriers, 121–23
  inital, 121
family barriers, inital
  avoid decisions, 122
  cancel appointment, 123
  denial, 121
  dictate treatment, 121
  disagree with problem, 123
  dismiss treatment, 121
  entrenched beliefs, 121
  good offence vs poor defence, 122
  no complience, 122
  no talking, 122
  superficial cooperation, 123
  treatment recommendations, 121
family treatment recommendations, 124–26
  not suggested, 125
  suggested, 125

feedback, 149–50
   delivery tone, 149
   framing, 149
   motives of criticizer, 150
   planning, 149
   timing, 149
field resistance, 3

—G—

general forms of denial, 12–13
   complexity of, 12
   Diagnostic and Statistical Manual, 13
   in Big Book, 13
   in other fields, 13
   mislabeling, 12
   national survey, 13
Gestalt "resistances", 53–54
   confluence, 54
   deflection, 54
   introjection, 53
   projection, 53
   retroflection, 54

—L—

listening, 151–52
   advice, 151
   interperting, 152
   interrupting, 151
   lecturing, 152
   ordering, 151
   overidentifying, 151
   warnings, 151
listening, positive, 152–54
   acknowledge, 153
   probe, 153
   silence, 153

—M—

metaphor, 160–63
   construction of, 162
mind idols, 115–16
   market, 115
   the cave, 115
   theater, 115

motivations of deception, 28–30
motivations of deception
   conflict between euphora and
     consequences, 30
   failure, 30
   fear, 30
   guilt, shame, remorse, 29
   labeling, moral degeneracy, 29
   love of chemicals, 30
   pride, 28
   private logic, 29
   ranking, 29
   stigma, 30

—N—

non-traditional views of denial, 20–23
   "alcoholic in denial" theory, 21
   chronic intoxicating effects, 21
   faulty perception, 20
   find solutions (vs.confrontation), 22
   healthy, 21
   normal, 21
   not good predictor of treatment outcome,
     20
   over labeling, 20
   solution approach, 22
   white middle class males, 20

—P—

patient-matching, content orientation, 142–44
   assessment guide, 143
patient-matching,, context orientation, 144
personal issues, 3
poor thinking, 91–93
   entrapment, 92
   hasty generalization, 91
   inclusive generalizing, 92
   retrospective distortion, 92
   steps to offset, 93
   unrepresentative, 92
preferred defense structure, 64–65
   all or nothing, 64
   conflict minimization & avoidance, 64
   obsessional focusing, 65
   preference for nonanalytic thinking &
     perceiving, 65

self-centered attention, 64
problems with unconscious approach, 25–26
   conscious lying, 26
   definitional problems, 25
   not thinking, 25
professionals in denial, 19

—R—

reactance, 3
reframing, 164
Reich, 47
relapse and denial, 19
resistance - a matter of perspective, 4
resistance - content, 41
resistance in relapse, 65–66
   alternative explanations, 66
   not failure, 65
   problem-solving skills, 66
resistance, a cognitive style, 57–60
   automatic thinking, 58
   distortions, 58
   dysfunctional beliefs, 57
resistance, analytic, 44
resistance, attribution, 60–63
   dissonance, 62
   emotional exacerbation, 62
   felt loss of control, 63
   inerventions, 63
   primary control, 61
   reactance, 62
   secondary control, 61
resistance, boat-rockers, 79
resistance, category A, 72
resistance, category B
   emotional display, 73
   future/past preoccupation, 74
   intellectual talk, 73
   rhetorical questions, 75
   symptom preoccupation, 74
resistance, category C, 75–78
   counselor stroking, 76
   discounting, 75
   externalization, 76
   forgetting/not understanding, 77
   limit setting, 76
   second guessing, 76
   seductiveness, 77

resistance, category D, 78
   delay or refuse payment, 78
   poor appointment keeping, 78
resistance, cognitive perspective, 55–60
resistance, context view, 66–69
   death of, 67
   treatment strategies, 68
resistance, counselor generated, 87–96
   "one-way" to recovery, 89
   "personal experience", 93
   acting from a single perspective, 91
   developmental impediments, 88
   frustration, 87
   lack of preperation, 96
   mindlessness, 90
   novice anxiety, 94
   poor thinking, 91
   poor training, 89
   power, 97
   premature cognitive commitment, 90
   technical terms/labeling, 95
resistance, counselor traits that diminish, 98
resistance, developmental, 80
resistance, education induced, 110
resistance, everyday, 70
resistance, family oriented, 117–20
   boundaries, 119
   context, 123
   family roles, 119
   homeostasis, 119
   lack of insight, 117
   loyalty, 119
   pride, 119
   process, 118
resistance, generated by, 70–72
   anxiety, 70
   negative social influence, 72
   noncompliance, 70
resistance, generated by literature, 109
resistance, Gestalt
   Perls, 52
resistance, Gestalt view, 52–54
resistance, group, 127–34
   acting out, 132
   alliances, 132
   ambivalance, 128
   confidentially breach, 133
   content type, 127

context type, 134
excessive talk, 129
flight, 130
manipulation, 131
personal recovery issue, 107
power issues, 133
silence, 128
treatment, 134
use of chemicals, 133
resistance, misconception of treatment, 79
resistance, neo-Freudian, 47
resistance, Otani perspective, 70
resistance, program, 108–15
"arrived" mass movements, 109
coercion, 113
countertransference, 109
facility rules, 113
money, 114
reward for conformity, 114
staff enabler, 108
subordinate position of client, 112
resistance, program/field, 103–14
act/think according to expectations, 105
anti-groupthink remedies, 107
demean renegade, 105
developmental differences of staff, 111
diagnose certain pathology, 106
groupthink, 105
loyalty/norms, 106
nature of facililty, 112
pressure to conform, 105
pressure to produce, 112
ritual, 106
thinking by field, 103
thinking style, 111
resistance, protective function, 78
resistance, proverbial view, 4
resistance, Rational-Emotive-Behavioral
Therapy
treatment recommendations, 56
resistance, Rational-Emotive-Behavioral
Therapy, 55–56
types of addictive thinking, 55
resistance-content
definitions of, 41

—S—

Surrender, Acceptance, Avowal, 23

—T—

tales of being stuck, 7
traditional approach to, 13–19
Dealing with Denial, 15
Defence Mechanisms Inventory, 14
Encyolpedia of Alcoholism, 14
Jellinek, 14
National Council on Alcoholism, 18
Psychiatric Dictionary, 14
Substance Abuse Subtle Screening
Inventory, 14
various definations, 14
treatment, 137–70
authenticity, 148
caveat, 137
concreteness, 148
empathy, 146
outcome research, 137
regard, 145
repect, 145
solution/brief, challenges of, 165
solution/brief, paths to avoid, 169
solution/brief, questions, 168
solution/brief, strategies, 168
solutoin/brief, principles of, 166
true denial, 23–31

—U—

unconscious factor in denial, 24–25
morality issue, 24
no blame nor responsibility for onset, 24
not willful lying, 24
protect from pain, 24
reshape reality, 24
splitting the ego, 24
truly pathological, 24
willful dishonesty, 24
unconscious factors in denial
self-destruction, 24

—V—

Vaillant, 48
  hierarchy of defences, 49